1st Workshop on Language Models for Underserved Communities (LM4UC 2025)

Albuquerque, New Mexico, USA
4 May 2025

ISBN: 979-8-3313-1922-9

Printed from e-media with permission by:

Curran Associates, Inc.
57 Morehouse Lane
Red Hook, NY 12571

CURRAN ASSOCIATES INC. proceedings.com

Some format issues inherent in the e-media version may also appear in this print version.

Association for Computational Linguistics
209 N. Eighth Street
Stroudsburg, Pennsylvania 18360

Phone: 1-570-476-8006
Fax: 1-570-476-0860

acl@aclweb.org

Additional copies of this publication are available from:

Curran Associates, Inc.
57 Morehouse Lane
Red Hook, NY 12571 USA
Phone: 845-758-0400
Fax: 845-758-2633
Email: curran@proceedings.com
Web: www.proceedings.com

LM4UC 2025

The 1st Workshop on Language Models for Underserved Communities

Proceedings of the Workshop

May 4, 2025

Order copies of this and other ACL proceedings from:

Association for Computational Linguistics (ACL)
317 Sidney Baker St. S
Suite 400 - 134
Kerrville, TX 78028
USA
Tel: +1-855-225-1962
acl@aclweb.org

Introduction

We are delighted to welcome you to the NAACL 2025 Workshop on Language Models for Underserved Communities (LM4UC), held in Albuquerque, New Mexico, on May 4, 2025. This workshop aims to address the persistent gaps in natural language processing (NLP) technologies for underserved communities, ensuring equitable and culturally sensitive advancements in artificial intelligence (AI).

The rapid advancement of natural language processing technologies has unlocked transformative opportunities across numerous domains, from communication to knowledge preservation. However, these benefits are not equitably distributed, leaving many underserved communities—speakers of Indigenous languages, regional dialects, and minority languages spoken by smaller populations—without adequate access to these innovations. This disparity stems from multiple factors, including limited linguistic data, insufficient computational resources, and a lack of commercial prioritization. Such languages, which include examples like Yoruba, Igbo, Native American languages, and dialects in multilingual nations such as India and Indonesia, are often both low-resource and underserved, compounded by challenges in AI governance and cultural representation. To address these inequities, the LM4UC initiative aims to foster rigorous research and dialogue centered on three critical pillars:

- **AI Governance**: Establishing robust legal and ethical frameworks to ensure fairness, transparency, and data sovereignty in the development and deployment of language models.
- **Cultural NLP**: Designing models that preserve linguistic diversity and accurately reflect cultural nuances, safeguarding unique heritage and values embedded in language.
- **Sustainable NLP**: Developing efficient, scalable models optimized for low-resource environments, aligning with environmental sustainability and accessibility goals.

This year, we received numerous high-quality submissions addressing a broad spectrum of topics, including democratizing AI access, preserving linguistic diversity, encoding cultural norms, and building efficient language models. We appreciate the dedication of the authors, reviewers, and program committee members in maintaining the scientific rigor and diversity of perspectives that enrich this workshop.

Invited Speakers

We are privileged to host an exceptional group of invited speakers, featuring Timothy Baldwin from MBZUAI, Timnit Gebru from Google, Pratyusha Ria Kalluri from Stanford, David Ifeoluwa Adelani from McGill, and Genta Indra Winata from Capital One. Their presentations will provide valuable insights into the pressing challenges and pioneering solutions within the field of natural language processing, with a particular focus on addressing the needs of underserved communities.

Acknowledgments

We extend our gratitude to the speakers and organizing committee for their unwavering commitment in making this workshop possible. Special thanks also go to our sponsors and supporters for their invaluable contributions. We hope this workshop serves as a platform for vibrant discussions, meaningful collaborations, and impactful research that advances the inclusivity of language technologies worldwide. Thank you for joining us at LM4UC 2025—we look forward to an engaging and productive event.

Sincerely,
The LM4UC Workshop Organizers

Organizing Committee

Workshop Chairs

Sang Truong, Stanford University, USA
Rifki Afina Putri, Korea Advanced Institute of Science & Technology, Korea
Duc Nguyen, HCM University of Technology - VNU-HCM, Vietnam
Angelina Wang, Stanford University, USA
Daniel Ho, Stanford University, USA
Alice Oh, Korea Advanced Institute of Science & Technology, Korea
Sanmi Koyejo, Stanford University, USA

Table of Contents

Program

Sunday, May 4, 2025

09:00 - 09:30 *(In-person) Opening Remarks: Alice Oh*

09:30 - 10:00 *(In-person) Keynote 1: David Ifeoluwa Adelani*

10:00 - 10:30 *(Virtual) Keynote 2: Timnit Gebru*

10:30 - 11:00 *(Hybrid) Structured Networking Event + Tea Break*

11:00 - 11:30 *(In-person) Keynote 3: Genta Indra Winata*

11:30 - 12:00 *(Virtual) Keynote 4: Timothy Baldwin*

12:00 - 12:30 *(Virtual) Keynote 5: Pratyusha Ria Kalluri*

12:30 - 13:00 *(Hybrid) Structured Networking Event + Lunch Break*

13:00 - 13:50 *(Hybrid) Panel Discussion by Angelina Wang*

13:50 - 15:30 *(Hybrid) Student Oral Presentation*

ABDUL: A New Approach to Build Language Models for Dialects Using Formal Language Corpora Only
Yassine Toughrai, Kamel Smaïli and David Langlois

Untangling the Influence of Typology, Data, and Model Architecture on Ranking Transfer Languages for Cross-Lingual POS Tagging
Enora Rice, Ali Marashian, Hannah Haynie, Katharina Wense and Alexis Palmer

Caption Generation in Cultural Heritage: Crowdsourced Data and Tuning Multimodal Large Language Models
Artem Reshetnikov and Maria-Cristina Marinescu

Preserving Cultural Identity with Context-Aware Translation Through Multi-Agent AI Systems
Mahfuz Anik, Abdur Rahman, Azmine Wasi and Md Ahsan

Enhancing Small Language Models for Cross-Lingual Generalized Zero-Shot Classification with Soft Prompt Tuning
Fred Philippy, Siwen Guo, Cedric Lothritz, Jacques Klein and Tegawendé Bissyandé

Cognate and Contact-Induced Transfer Learning for Hamshentsnag: A Low-Resource and Endangered Language
Onur Keleş, Baran Günay and Berat Doğan

On Tables with Numbers, with Numbers
Konstantinos Kogkalidis and Stergios Chatzikyriakidis

Direct Preference Optimization with Unobserved Preference Heterogeneity
Keertana Chidambaram, Karthik Seetharaman and Vasilis Syrgkanis

15:30 - 16:30 *(Hybrid) Poster Session*

16:30 - 17:00 *(Virtual) Awards Ceremony and Closing Remarks: Sanmi Koyejo*

Enhance Contextual Learning in ASR for Endangered Low-resource Languages

Zhaolin Li, Jan Niehues
Karlsruhe Institute of Technology, Germany
{zhaolin.li, jan.niehues}@kit.edu

Abstract

Automatic Speech Recognition (ASR) facilitates documenting endangered low-resource languages. While recent advances in acoustic modelling have been substantial, contextual learning remains underexplored. This study investigates the main factors that influence the integration of knowledge from language models (LMs) into state-of-the-art ASR models for endangered low-resource languages. Through experiments on five diverse low-resource languages, we find: 1) Fine-grained tokenization effectively improves ASR performance by addressing the prevalent unknown words and improving data usage efficiency; 2) The integration of transformer-based LMs into ASR systems surpasses that of N-gram LMs only in one language, even though they consistently achieve better results in language modelling tasks. 3) ASR performance is highly sensitive to language-specific optimization, as shown by a 43% performance degradation in one language due to parameter transfer across languages. We open-source our scripts to support further research and applications [1].

1 Introduction

The threat of language endangerment continues to grow due to various external pressures, prompting linguists to actively document vulnerable languages. However, manual documentation processes are often impractical and time-intensive. Automatic Speech Recognition (ASR) models offer valuable support for language documentation, yet their effectiveness is hindered by the limited availability of supervised data.

Recent advancements indicate that multilingual self-supervised learning holds promise for developing ASR systems tailored to endangered low-resource languages(Mihajlik et al., 2023; Li et al., 2024; Taguchi et al., 2024; Mainzinger and Levow, 2024; Taguchi and Chiang, 2024). Among these approaches, fine-tuning the pre-trained Wav2Vec2 models (Conneau et al., 2020) with Connectionist Temporal Classification (CTC) loss (Graves et al., 2006) has emerged as a popular and effective strategy. Compared to other pre-trained ASR models, such as Whisper (Radford et al., 2023), this approach often achieves superior performance, particularly in reducing character-level errors (Le Ferrand et al., 2024; He et al., 2024). This advantage can be attributed to its smaller parameter set and the extensive pre-training data, making it especially effective for low-resource settings.

Despite its strengths in acoustic modelling, this approach lacks contextual learning capabilities due to the conditional independence assumption inherent in CTC (Graves et al., 2006; Lu and Chen, 2023; Higuchi et al., 2022). To address this, previous research has integrated ASR models with language models (LMs) at the word level (Conneau et al., 2020; San et al., 2023; Liu et al., 2024; He et al., 2024; Pratap et al., 2024; Arisaputra et al., 2024). However, word-level integration struggles with the high prevalence of unknown words in low-resource settings, where limited text data further impedes performance.

Additionally, prior studies have predominantly employed statistical N-gram LMs for integration. However, transformer-based LMs have demonstrated superior contextual learning capabilities compared to N-gram models for high-resource languages. While few studies have explored combining transformer-based LMs with Wav2Vec2 and CTC fine-tuning (Conneau et al., 2020), these investigations have focused on high-resource languages, leaving their potential for low-resource languages unexplored. Differences in data availability and linguistic complexity underscore the need for further investigation.

To fill these gaps, we explore LM integration for five low-resource languages from diverse language

[1] https://github.com/ZL-KA/LM-LR-ASR

Proceedings of the 1st Workshop on Language Models for Underserved Communities (LM4UC 2025), pages 1–7
May 4, 2025 ©2025 Association for Computational Linguistics

families, considering differences in data size and source. Our main contributions are:

1. Fine-grained tokenizations at subword and character levels generally improve performance, except for Khinalug, a language where minimal data availability imposes constraints.

2. The transformer-based method outperforms the N-gram approach only with one language, unlike high-resource languages where transformer models consistently excel (Conneau et al., 2020), highlighting challenges in low-resource settings.

3. Parameter optimization is highly language-specific, with parameter transferring from one language to another resulting in a significant performance gap from optimal outcomes.

2 Language Model in ASR

2.1 Language Model Integration

The popular ASR system for low-resource languages leverages self-supervised pre-training followed by CTC-based fine-tuning. Due to the independence assumption inherent in CTC, the ASR system incorporates LMs during decoding to enhance contextual learning[2]. Specifically, LM integration occurs during inference-only decoding in an auto-regressive manner [3]. In accordance with the CTC algorithm, the character-level acoustic representations accumulate based on the space separator. The corresponding sequence of characters is collapsed using the CTC algorithm, and the LM assigns scores to the resulting text. The total score is computed using Equation 1:

$$score = \log P(\text{text}) + \alpha * LM(\text{text}) + \beta \quad (1)$$

Here, $\log P(\text{text})$ represents the acoustic hidden representation, and $LM(\text{text})$ denotes the LM score. The parameters α and β control the contribution of the LM and adjust the length of the generated sequences, respectively. LM integration enables the CTC-based ASR model to perform beam search, where the candidate sequence with the highest score is returned as the final prediction.

[2]https://huggingface.co/blog/wav2vec2-with-ngram

[3]https://github.com/kensho-technologies/pyctcdecode/tree/main

2.2 Tokenization Granularity

Since CTC-based fine-tuning operates at the character level, current word-level integration overlooks the fine-grained knowledge provided by CTC, leaving room for potential improvement. Additionally, word-level LMs struggle to handle the prevalence of unknown words in low-resource languages, leading to performance degradation.

This work proposes integrating LMs at the subword and character levels. We encode the transcript with space markers ("_") to denote word boundaries. Tokenization-specific ASR models and LMs are built using corresponding encoded text, enabling the models to leverage encoded knowledge effectively. This encoding increases the frequency of sequence patterns, improving data utilization efficiency for LMs. Furthermore, unknown words are decomposed into recognizable subwords or characters, reducing their negative impact on performance.

The study also investigates the impact of transformer-based LMs on LM integration. The integration process is adapted by modifying the scoring function to accommodate the transformer-based approach. Similar to N-gram LMs, log probabilities are used as LM scores.

3 Experimental Setups

3.1 Datasets

To address the unique challenges of building ASR systems for low-resource languages, such as language complexity, limited corpus size, and sparse audio sources, this study conducts experiments on five linguistically diverse languages to explore their practical application in language documentation.: Khinalug (Li et al., 2024), Kichwa (Taguchi et al., 2024), Mboshi (Godard et al., 2018), Japhug (Guillaume et al., 2022), and Bemba (Sikasote et al., 2023). Four of the selected languages are recognized as endangered, while Bemba is included to examine the impact of collecting additional supervised data. Table 1 illustrates the occurrence of unknown words in the development and test splits, highlighting the potential risks of overlooking them when using word-level LMs.

3.2 Modelling

Acoustic Model: We utilize the state-of-the-art version of Wav2Vec2 model mms-300 [4]. Pre-trained

[4]https://huggingface.co/facebook/mms-300m

Language	ISO code	Language Family	Audio source	Train (h)	Dev+Test (h)	Unknown words
Khinalug	kjj	Northeast Caucasian	Spontaneous	2.14	0.49	25.12%
Kichwa	que	Quechuan	Radio	3.05	0.77	27.28%
Mboshi	mdw	Bantu ZoneC	Reading	3.93	0.53	16.57%
Japhug	jya	Sino-Tibetan	Spontaneous	27.74	7.00	5.23%
Bemba	bem	Bantu ZoneM	Reading	116.32	11.43	7.41%

Table 1: Dataset descriptive statistic

with over 1400 languages, it provides extensive linguistic coverage and adaptability for low-resource settings. In addition, its lightweight design, with fewer parameters than other checkpoints, ensures faster and more efficient performance.

Language Model: We utilize 5-gram LMs for word and subword tokenization, and 10-gram LMs for character tokenization. For transformer-based LMs, we employ GPT-2 tailored to causal language modelling tasks[5]. The vocabulary sizes vary based on the tokenization approach: the number of distinct words for word-level, 2000 tokens for subword-level, and the number of distinct characters for character-level tokenization. These configurations are based on insights from preliminary experiments.

Pre- & Post-processing: We investigate LM integration across various tokenization levels and adapt ASR modelling accordingly. Training labels are generated by preprocessing transcripts into string sequences, embedding tokenization details directly into the training pipeline, as described in Section 2.2. This method allows the ASR model to produce outputs consistent with the chosen tokenization level. After prediction, post-processing is used to reverse the encoding steps and reconstruct the original sentence.

4 Results and Analysis

4.1 Fine-grained Tokenization Benefits

We experiment with different tokenization granularity with N-gram LMs. As shown in Table 2, compared with the coarse word-level tokenization, fine-grained tokenization improves performance for Kichwa, Mboshi, Japhug, and Bemba with Relative Word Error Rate (Relative WER) reduction of 6.5%, 7.3%, 8.4% and 9.8%, respectively. However, for Khinalug, the fine-grained approach shows comparable results but no clear gains, likely due to limited data and the spontaneous nature of the audio source.

Besides, we find the character level tokenization leads to the best performance for most languages, indicating character tokenization as a more effective choice. Regarding the outlier Mboshi, we notice its character ASR model struggles due to fast speaking speed or morphological complexity (Appendices A), complicating direct comparisons with subword models. Despite this challenge, the character-based approach shows greater relative improvements when transitioning from no LM to LM integration compared to the subword approach.

	No LM	Word	Subword	Char
Khinalug	42.2	**34.2**	37.9	35.8
Kichwa	17.7	15.4	15.3	**14.4**
Mboshi	31.4	27.3	**25.3**	30.1
Japhug	26.5	23.6	24.0	**21.3**
Bemba	40.0	38.6	35.5	**34.8**

Table 2: Experimental results for integrations granularity with N-gram LMs. Word, subword and char indicate the tokenization granularity. The evaluation metric is WER.

	No LM	N-gram	Transformer
Khinalug	45.5	35.9	40.5
Kichwa	18.6	**15.0**	17.1
Mboshi	33.4	**27.5**	28.5
Japhug	26.8	23.0	**21.8**
Bemba	39.0	**36.3**	37.2

Table 3: Experimental results for comparison between N-gram and transformer-based LMs. The resulted WER represents the average across experiments using word, subword, and character tokenization.

4.2 N-gram Integration Outperforms

Transformer-based LMs demonstrate notable strengths in perplexity evaluation, as detailed in

[5]https://huggingface.co/docs/transformers/tasks/language_modeling

	Text	WER	N-gram PPL	Trans PPL
Gold	alcaldesa juzgadomanta llukshikta rikukuni	-	7.5	5.4
No LM	alcaldesa husgadomanta llukshikta rikukuni	25.0	9.3	5.3
N-gram	alcaldesa juzgadomanta llukshikta rikukuni	0	7.5	5.4
Trans	alcaldesa huskadomanta llukshikta rikukuni	25.0	8.9	4.8

Table 4: An example of Kichwa with character-level tokenization is presented. Note that all hypotheses are considered during decoding in all experiments, but only one is selected as the final prediction with Equation 1 in each experiment.

Appendix B. We investigate transformer-based integration across all tokenization types and report the average scores. Surprisingly, as shown in Table 3, transformer-based LMs outperform N-gram LMs only for a single language, Japhug.

A closer examination of prediction samples reveals a misalignment between ASR performance and language modelling under the current integration approach. As shown in Table 4, the N-gram and transformer-based approaches do select the candidates with the lowest perplexity, and the perplexity values from transformer LM are indeed higher than that of N-gram LM, indicating the superior performance in causal language modelling. However, inconsistencies arise in how different LMs rank these candidates.

Specifically, the ASR gold transcript aligns more with the N-gram ranking than the transformer-based LM in this example. Although both models share the same vocabulary, allowing direct perplexity comparisons, their rankings might differ due to variations in architecture and evaluation. This suggests the current integration approach lacks robustness for low-resource languages, as it does not consistently improve ASR performance across models.

4.3 Language Optimization Matters

In developing ASR systems, prior research has predominantly focused on ASR training optimization, with limited attention to integrating LMs. In this study, we observe that the optimal tokenization granularity for five languages spans all three tokenization types and that the integration parameters vary significantly across languages. To highlight the importance of language-specific optimization, we experiment with reasonable parameter adaptation from Kichwa to Mboshi, which has a similar amount of supervised data, and Japhug, which has the same optimal tokenization type. As shown in Table 5, direct parameter transfer results in performance degradations of 32.0% and 43.2%, respectively.

	Token	(Alpha, Beta)	WER
Kichwa	char	(0.9, 5.0)	14.4
Mboshi	subword	(0.6, 2.0)	25.3
Transferred	char	(0.9, 5.0)	33.4
Japhug	char	(0.6, 1.0)	21.3
Transferred	char	(0.9, 5.0)	30.5

Table 5: Experiment results of parameter transferring from Kichwa to Mboshi and Japhug. Transferred means inferencing with the parameters optimized for Kichwa; Token indicates the tokenization type; Alpha and Beta indicate the parameters in decoding (Equation 1).

Moreover, we find that customizing beam size could improve inference speed while maintaining performance, demonstrating the practical benefits of tailored ASR systems (Appendix C.1). Additionally, our results indicate that ASR performance in low-resource languages is highly sensitive to training hyperparameters; even small adjustments in the learning rate can lead to significant performance differences (Appendix C.2). These findings emphasize the critical importance of language-specific settings in building effective ASR systems for low-resource languages.

5 Conclusion

This study focuses on improving contextual learning in ASR models for low-resource languages by examining tokenization granularity and the integration of transformer-based LMs. The findings show that fine-grained tokenization enhances ASR performance by addressing unknown words and increasing data usage efficiency. Moreover, integrating transformer-based LMs does not consistently outperform N-gram LMs in boosting ASR accuracy. Finally, our results indicate that directly applying experimental settings to new languages harms performance, emphasizing the importance of language-specific optimizations.

References

Panji Arisaputra, Alif Tri Handoyo, and Amalia Zahra. 2024. Xls-r deep learning model for multilingual asr on low-resource languages: Indonesian, javanese, and sundanese. *arXiv preprint arXiv:2401.06832*.

Alexis Conneau, Alexei Baevski, Ronan Collobert, Abdelrahman Mohamed, and Michael Auli. 2020. Unsupervised cross-lingual representation learning for speech recognition. *arXiv preprint arXiv:2006.13979*.

Pierre Godard, Gilles Adda, Martine Adda-Decker, Juan Benjumea, Laurent Besacier, Jamison Cooper-Leavitt, Guy-Noel Kouarata, Lori Lamel, Hélène Maynard, Markus Mueller, Annie Rialland, Sebastian Stueker, François Yvon, and Marcely Zanon-Boito. 2018. A very low resource language speech corpus for computational language documentation experiments. In *Proceedings of the Eleventh International Conference on Language Resources and Evaluation (LREC 2018)*, Miyazaki, Japan. European Language Resources Association (ELRA).

Alex Graves, Santiago Fernández, Faustino Gomez, and Jürgen Schmidhuber. 2006. Connectionist temporal classification: labelling unsegmented sequence data with recurrent neural networks. In *Proceedings of the 23rd international conference on Machine learning*, pages 369–376.

Séverine Guillaume, Guillaume Wisniewski, Cécile Macaire, Guillaume Jacques, Alexis Michaud, Benjamin Galliot, Maximin Coavoux, Solange Rossato, Minh-Châu Nguyên, and Maxime Fily. 2022. Fine-tuning pre-trained models for automatic speech recognition, experiments on a fieldwork corpus of japhug (trans-himalayan family). In *Proceedings of the Fifth Workshop on the Use of Computational Methods in the Study of Endangered Languages*, pages 170–178, Dublin, Ireland. Association for Computational Linguistics.

Taiqi He, Kwanghee Choi, Lindia Tjuatja, Nathaniel Robinson, Jiatong Shi, Shinji Watanabe, Graham Neubig, David Mortensen, and Lori Levin. 2024. Wav2Gloss: Generating interlinear glossed text from speech. In *Proceedings of the 62nd Annual Meeting of the Association for Computational Linguistics (Volume 1: Long Papers)*, pages 568–582, Bangkok, Thailand. Association for Computational Linguistics.

Yosuke Higuchi, Brian Yan, Siddhant Arora, Tetsuji Ogawa, Tetsunori Kobayashi, and Shinji Watanabe. 2022. BERT meets CTC: New formulation of end-to-end speech recognition with pre-trained masked language model. In *Findings of the Association for Computational Linguistics: EMNLP 2022*, pages 5486–5503, Abu Dhabi, United Arab Emirates. Association for Computational Linguistics.

Eric Le Ferrand, Zoey Liu, Antti Arppe, and Emily Prud'hommeaux. 2024. Are modern neural ASR architectures robust for polysynthetic languages? In *Findings of the Association for Computational Linguistics: EMNLP 2024*, pages 2953–2963, Miami, Florida, USA. Association for Computational Linguistics.

Zhaolin Li, Monika Rind-Pawlowski, and Jan Niehues. 2024. Speech recognition corpus of the khinalug language for documenting endangered languages. In *Proceedings of the 2024 Joint International Conference on Computational Linguistics, Language Resources and Evaluation (LREC-COLING 2024)*, pages 15171–15180, Torino, Italia. ELRA and ICCL.

Zoey Liu, Nitin Venkateswaran, Eric Le Ferrand, and Emily Prud'hommeaux. 2024. How important is a language model for low-resource ASR? In *Findings of the Association for Computational Linguistics: ACL 2024*, pages 206–213, Bangkok, Thailand. Association for Computational Linguistics.

Ke-Han Lu and Kuan-Yu Chen. 2023. A context-aware knowledge transferring strategy for ctc-based asr. In *2022 IEEE Spoken Language Technology Workshop (SLT)*, pages 60–67.

Julia Mainzinger and Gina-Anne Levow. 2024. Fine-tuning ASR models for very low-resource languages: A study on mvskoke. In *Proceedings of the 62nd Annual Meeting of the Association for Computational Linguistics (Volume 4: Student Research Workshop)*, pages 76–82, Bangkok, Thailand. Association for Computational Linguistics.

Peter Mihajlik, Mate Kadar, Gergely Dosinszky, Yan Meng, Meng Kedalai, Julian Linke, Tibor Fegyo, and Katalin Mady. 2023. What kind of multi- or cross-lingual pre-training is the most effective for a spontaneous, less-resourced asr task? 2nd Annual Meeting of the Special Interest Group on Under-resourced Languages: SIGUL 2023 ; Conference date: 18-08-2023 Through 20-08-2023.

Vineel Pratap, Andros Tjandra, Bowen Shi, Paden Tomasello, Arun Babu, Sayani Kundu, Ali Elkahky, Zhaoheng Ni, Apoorv Vyas, Maryam Fazel-Zarandi, et al. 2024. Scaling speech technology to 1,000+ languages. *Journal of Machine Learning Research*, 25(97):1–52.

Alec Radford, Jong Wook Kim, Tao Xu, Greg Brockman, Christine McLeavey, and Ilya Sutskever. 2023. Robust speech recognition via large-scale weak supervision. In *International conference on machine learning*, pages 28492–28518. PMLR.

Nay San, Martijn Bartelds, Blaine Billings, Ella de Falco, Hendi Feriza, Johan Safri, Wawan Sahrozi, Ben Foley, Bradley McDonnell, and Dan Jurafsky. 2023. Leveraging supplementary text data to kick-start automatic speech recognition system development with limited transcriptions. In *Proceedings of the Sixth Workshop on the Use of Computational Methods in the Study of Endangered Languages*, pages 1–6, Remote. Association for Computational Linguistics.

Claytone Sikasote, Eunice Mukonde, Md Mahfuz Ibn Alam, and Antonios Anastasopoulos. 2023. BIG-C: a multimodal multi-purpose dataset for Bemba. In *Proceedings of the 61st Annual Meeting of the Association for Computational Linguistics (Volume 1: Long Papers)*, pages 2062–2078, Toronto, Canada. Association for Computational Linguistics.

Chihiro Taguchi and David Chiang. 2024. Language complexity and speech recognition accuracy: Orthographic complexity hurts, phonological complexity doesn't. In *Proceedings of the 62nd Annual Meeting of the Association for Computational Linguistics (Volume 1: Long Papers)*, pages 15493–15503, Bangkok, Thailand. Association for Computational Linguistics.

Chihiro Taguchi, Jefferson Saransig, Dayana Velásquez, and David Chiang. 2024. Killkan: The automatic speech recognition dataset for kichwa with morphosyntactic information. In *Proceedings of the 2024 Joint International Conference on Computational Linguistics, Language Resources and Evaluation (LREC-COLING 2024)*, pages 9753–9763, Torino, Italia. ELRA and ICCL.

Silero Team. 2024. Silero vad: pre-trained enterprise-grade voice activity detector (vad), number detector and language classifier. https://github.com/snakers4/silero-vad.

A ASR Performance analysis

A.1 ASR Performance without Language Models

This section evaluates the performance of the ASR model using different tokenization methods without including language models (LMs). As outlined in Table 6, subword- and character-level tokenizations demonstrate slightly lower performance than word-level tokenization. This decline can be attributed to the added task of predicting the word boundary symbol "_." Nonetheless, this trade-off enables the incorporation of a more robust LM at the subword and character levels, enhancing the overall ASR performance during LM integration.

Lang	Word	Subwrod	Char
Khinalug	42.2	47.0	47.4
Kichwa	17.7	18.1	19.9
Mboshi	31.4	29.5	39.4
Japhug	26.5	26.5	27.5
Bemba	40.0	38.7	38.5

Table 6: ASR model performance of different tokenization types without LMs

A.2 Character Density Analysis

The Mboshi ASR model with character-level tokenization performs noticeably worse compared to word- and subword-level models. To investigate the outliers, we examine the character density of the corpus and find that the Mboshi corpus has a significantly higher number of characters per second than others, even though all audio files are sampled at 16 kHz (see Table 7).

We specifically use Voice Activity Detection (VAD) (Team, 2024) to measure the speaking duration and count the number of characters in the corresponding transcripts. We argue that the high character density negatively impacts character-level tokenization, as it leaves limited space for detecting separators between characters, resulting in information loss. Additionally, we suspect that the morphological complexity of Mboshi could be another contributing factor, but we are unable to evaluate this hypothesis due to a lack of linguistic expertise.

Lang	Train	Valid	Test
Khinalug	0.75	0.75	0.74
Kichwa	0.84	0.85	0.83
Mboshi	1.08	1.1	1.06
Japhug	0.83	0.84	0.84
Bemba	0.75	0.75	0.75

Table 7: Analytical statistic on character per second

B Causal Language Modelling

In this section, we compare N-gram and transformer-based language models (LMs) in the context of causal language modelling, which focuses on predicting the next token. This analysis supports our discussion in Section 4.2. As shown in Table 8, transformer-based LMs consistently achieve lower perplexity than N-gram LMs across all languages. This aligns with our expectation that transformer-based models outperform N-gram models in causal language modelling tasks due to their superior ability to capture contextual information. Additionally, we observe that larger datasets amplify the performance gap between the two types of models.

C Language Specific optimization

C.1 Integration Parameters

This section highlights the importance of language-specific parameters in language model integration.

	Word		Subword		Char	
	N-gram	Trans	N-gram	Trans	N-gram	Trans
Khinalug	1619.9	1243.2	709.5	604.7	10.3	8.8
Kichwa	1770.2	1271.7	550.2	313.7	6.9	4.0
Mboshi	1015.7	673.7	343.4	173.8	9.83	5.5
Japhug	699.6	448.0	181.7	75.1	7.3	3.5
Bemba	2915.9	1439.5	238.6	79.0	6.2	2.9

Table 8: Perplexity comparison for difference tokenization of N-gram and transformer-based LMs

	Beam	(α, β)	WER
Kichwa			
word	10	0.2/0	15.5
word	100	0.2/0	15.4
subword	10	0.9/5.0	15.7
subword	100	0.9/5.0	15.3
char	10	0.8/2.0	14.8
char	100	0.8/2.0	14.4
Japhug			
word	10	0/0	25.3
word	100	0.1/0	23.6
subword	10	0.1/2	24.2
subword	100	0.1/2	24.0
char	10	0.5/1	21.9
char	100	0.6/1	21.3

Table 9: Experimental results about beam searching and the selection of alpha and beta for Kichwa and Japhug

As illustrated in Table 9, a beam size of 10 performs comparably to a beam size of 100, demonstrating that this smaller value can reduce computational costs and hardware requirements. Additionally, we observe that the parameters alpha and beta require tailored values for optimal performance.

C.2 ASR Training Parameters

In this study, we explore various training hyperparameters to highlight their significance in low-resource scenarios. Specifically, we experiment with learning rates of 5e-4, 1e-4, 5e-5, 1e-5, 5e-6, and 1e-6. Our findings reveal that using the same hyperparameters across different languages or applying parameters optimized for one language to another results in noticeable performance degradation (as shown in Table 10). This underscores the importance of language-specific optimization when developing ASR systems for low-resource languages, in contrast to high-resource scenarios where the abundance of supervised data mitigates the influence of training hyperparameters.

Lang	Learning rate	CER	WER
Khinalug	1e-4	13.35	55.85
	1e-5	11.40	47.00
Japhug	1e-4	14.41	28.41
	1e-5	12.95	26.47

Table 10: Impact of learning rate on building ASR models

Empowering Low-Resource Languages: TraSe Architecture for Enhanced Retrieval-Augmented Generation in Bangla

Atia Shahnaz Ipa, Mohammad Abu Tareq Rony*, Mohammad Shariful Islam
Department of Mechatronics Engineering, Khulna University of Engineering & Technology, Khulna, Bangladesh.
Department of Statistics, Noakhali Science & Technology University, Bangladesh
Department of Computer Science & Telecommunication Engineering, Noakhali Science & Technology University, Bangladesh
atia.s.ipa@gmail.com, abutareqrony@gmail.com, shariful.cse43@gmail.com

Abstract

Research on Retrieval-Augmented Generation for low-resource languages has been sparse because of limited resources. To address this, we focus on Bangla, a low-resource language, and have created a dataset of 200 question-answer pairs as a basis for our study from Bangla Wikipedia dump data. This paper introduces the TraSe architecture, which enhances RAG for Bangla using Translative prompting. Our experiments demonstrate that TraSe improves answer selection accuracy, achieving 34% with automatic retrieval and 63% with Human-in-the-Loop retrieval, outperforming baseline methods. The TraSe architecture marks a significant advancement in RAG for low-resource languages and has the potential to enhance question-answering systems for Bangla and similar languages. Future research could explore additional low-resource languages. The code is available at the following GitHub repository: `https://github.com/Atia6/TraSe-Bangla-RAG`.

1 Introduction

The rapid advancements in natural language processing (NLP) have led to the development of sophisticated models that can perform a wide range of tasks with high accuracy(Bird, 2024). Among these, Retrieval-Augmented Generation (RAG) has emerged as a powerful approach that combines the strengths of information retrieval and generative models to produce more informed and contextually accurate responses. While RAG has been extensively explored in languages like English, its application in low-resource languages, such as Bangla, remains significantly underdeveloped(Cuconasu et al., 2024).

The scarcity of research and resources in Bangla RAG presents a critical gap in the NLP field, particularly given the language's extensive use by over 230 million speakers worldwide(Bhattacharjee et al., 2022a). Existing systems struggle to meet the nuanced demands of Bangla language processing, often unable to retrieve (Rony et al., 2024) and generate contextually relevant information effectively (Ipa et al., 2024). This gap not only limits the practical applications of NLP in Bangla but also highlights the need for tailored architectures to address the unique challenges posed by this language.

In response to this need, we propose the TraSe architecture, a novel approach specifically designed for the RAG in Bangla. TraSe integrates advanced retrieval mechanisms with generative capabilities, optimizing performance across various tasks by leveraging both pre-existing knowledge and contextual information. This paper presents a detailed examination of TraSe's architecture, its comparative performance against existing systems, and its potential to enhance Bangla language processing. Through this research, we aim to contribute a significant step forward in the development of effective NLP tools for Bangla, bridging the gap in RAG research for this important language.

1.1 Main Contributions

We achieved significant advancements in RAG for the low-resource Bangla language through the Translative method and further enhanced performance using the TraSe method. Our main contributions are as follows:

1. Created a Bangla question-answering dataset consisting of 200 question-answer pairs.

2. Introduced the Translative prompting method specifically designed for Bangla

Proceedings of the 1st Workshop on Language Models for Underserved Communities (LM4UC 2025), pages 8–15
May 4, 2025

question answering.

3. Developed the TraSe architecture and demonstrated its superior performance compared to baseline prompting methods.

2 Related Work

Retrieval-Augmented Generation (RAG) has emerged as a powerful framework for addressing key limitations of large language models (LLMs), such as hallucination, outdated knowledge, and lack of transparency (Gao et al., 2023; Huang and Huang, 2024). By integrating external knowledge into the generation process, RAG enhances accuracy, reliability, and contextual relevance (Zhao et al., 2024). Over time, the paradigm has evolved from simple retrieval-based augmentation to more sophisticated modular architectures that optimize retrieval, generation, and augmentation processes (Gao et al., 2023). A notable advancement in this direction is FLARE, an active retrieval mechanism that continuously gathers relevant information throughout the generation process to improve response quality (Jiang et al., 2023). Beyond traditional text-based applications, RAG has demonstrated versatility across multimodal tasks and knowledge-intensive scenarios, reinforcing its potential in various domains (Zhao et al., 2024).

Despite these advancements, RAG still faces challenges in evaluation, retrieval quality, and real-world implementation. Researchers are actively working to develop comprehensive benchmarks and refine methodologies to improve retrieval accuracy, optimize integration with LLMs, and enhance system adaptability (Zhao et al., 2024; Huang and Huang, 2024). Several recent innovations have focused on addressing these limitations. Corrective RAG, introduced by (Yan et al., 2024), incorporates a retrieval evaluator to assess document quality and dynamically trigger different retrieval actions, such as web searches, thereby improving the reliability of retrieved content. SelfMem (Cheng et al., 2023) takes a different approach by iteratively using a retrieval-augmented generator to build an unbounded memory pool, leveraging past model outputs as a self-referential knowledge base. Meanwhile, Iter-RetGen (Shao et al., 2023) adopts an iterative retrieval-generation cycle where model-generated content informs subsequent retrieval steps, refining relevance and coherence. These methods specifically address issues related to retrieval precision, fixed corpus constraints, and complex information needs, demonstrating improved performance across various NLP tasks, including question answering, summarization, and dialogue generation.

Further developments continue to push the boundaries of RAG optimization. Stochastic RAG (Zamani and Bendersky, 2024) introduces an end-to-end optimization framework that utilizes straight-through Gumbel-top-k selection, enhancing retrieval and generation efficiency while achieving state-of-the-art results across multiple tasks. Blended RAG (Sawarkar et al., 2024) improves retrieval effectiveness by leveraging hybrid query strategies and semantic search, surpassing conventional fine-tuning approaches on datasets like SQuAD. Additionally, Graph Retrieval-Augmented Generation (GRAG) (Hu et al., 2024) presents a divide-and-conquer strategy for retrieving structured textual subgraphs, facilitating multi-hop reasoning, and significantly outperforming standard RAG models in handling networked document structures.

Beyond these techniques, other research efforts have sought to refine RAG's adaptability and evaluation. R^2AG (Ye et al., 2024) aims to bridge the semantic gap between retrievers and LLMs by embedding retrieval information directly into the generation process. RAGAs (Shahul et al., 2023) introduces a reference-free evaluation framework to assess retrieval relevance, LLM faithfulness, and overall generation quality, providing a more holistic assessment of RAG pipelines. The RAGGED framework (Hsia et al., 2024) analyzes different RAG configurations, revealing that optimal performance depends on varying model architectures and context utilization strategies. Additionally, MemoRAG (Qian et al., 2024) pioneers a memory-augmented approach that employs a dual-system architecture—where a lightweight LLM manages global memory while a more expressive LLM handles final answer generation—enabling better handling of ambiguous queries and long-term knowledge retention.

Together, these advancements illustrate the increasing sophistication of RAG techniques and their transformative potential for LLMs. By improving retrieval strategies, optimizing generative integration, and expanding to new application areas, RAG continues to evolve as a fundamental enabler of more accurate, contextually aware, and reliable AI-generated content.

3 Methodology

In this study, we developed TraSe architecture, a selection-based process to improve the performance of RAG for Bangla question answering with the help of the translative method. We further compared the performance of our model with existing techniques.

3.1 Dataset

We created 200 questions from the Bangla Wikipedia dump for our experiment. The raw Bangla dataset that we utilized consisted of 27 topics in 27 articles. The dataset is preprocessed to convert to chunks of 5 sentences. Along with 200 questions, 3 related contexts are accompanied by each question for human-in-the-loop (HIL) context insertion in the LLM. Dataset details are given in Table 1. In Table 2, several question-answer pairs along with their corresponding answer types are presented.

3.2 Baselines

The baseline methods for comparison are described below.

Zero Shot: The zero-shot method involves assigning a task to a model without prior examples or specific training, relying solely on the model's pre-existing knowledge. This approach is useful for generalization in low-data scenarios. (Arora et al., 2023) explored the use of zero-shot retrieval in their work.

2 Shot: The two-shot method provides the model with two examples before a new task, helping it better understand the task structure and improve performance. (Brown et al., 2020) explored the few-shot technique in their work on GPT-3.

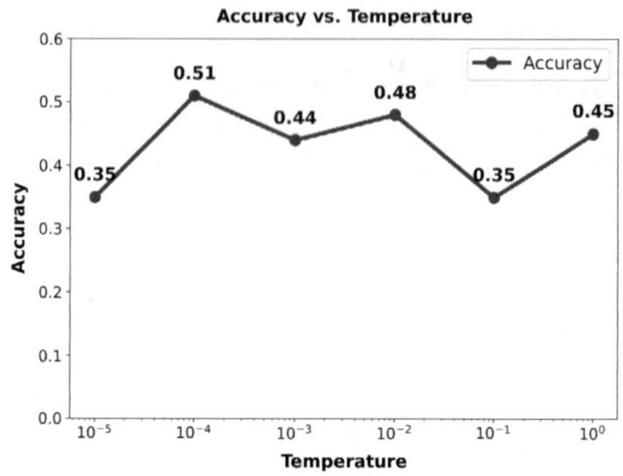

Figure 1: Temperature vs accuracy for the zero-shot method with HIL context.

Self-Ask: Self-Ask encourages the model to ask clarifying questions before answering, breaking down complex queries for more accurate responses. (Press et al., 2023) discussed this method in their study.

ReAct: ReAct (Reasoning and Acting) alternates between reasoning and action steps, allowing the model to iteratively refine its understanding and outputs, which is particularly useful in complex tasks. This method was introduced by (Yao et al., 2023).

3.3 LLM Parameter

For this experiment, we used the Llama 2 7B model, which supports over 260 languages, in a text generation pipeline via the transformers[1] library. The model, optimized with bfloat16 data and automatic device mapping, generates sequences of up to 3000 tokens. Sampling with a 'top_k' of 10 promotes diverse yet coherent outputs. Zero-shot direct prompting and HIL context were applied as shown in Figure 1, and after testing temperatures from 0.00001 to 1, the most accurate results were achieved at a temperature of 0.0001, which was selected for the final setup. In this research, we used LangChain[2] to integrate the Hugging Face pipeline, allowing us to efficiently apply prompting techniques with pre-trained models.

[1]https://pypi.org/project/transformers/
[2]https://www.langchain.com/

Table 1: Dataset description

Dataset	No of Articles	No. of Words	No. of Chunks	Question Answer Pair	Text Based Answer	Number Based Answer
Bangla Wikipedia Dump	27	53,575	710	200	70	130

Table 2: Question-answer pairs with answer type

Question	Answer	Answer Type
ঢাকা শহর কতটি সংসদীয় এলাকায় বিভক্ত? *(How many parliamentary constituencies is Dhaka city divided into?)*	২৫ টি *(25)*	Number-based
সচিবালয় কোথায় অবস্থিত? *(Where is the Secretariat located?)*	রমনায় *(In Ramna)*	Text-based
জাতীয় সংসদ ভবনের স্থপতি কে ছিলেন? *(Who was the architect of the National Parliament Building?)*	লুইস কান *(Louis Kahn)*	Text-based
বাংলাদেশের জাতীয় সংসদ ভবন কয় কক্ষবিশিষ্ট? *(How many chambers does the National Parliament Building of Bangladesh have?)*	এক কক্ষ *(Single chamber)*	Text-based
বাংলাদেশের জাতীয় মসজিদ কোনটি? *(What is the national mosque of Bangladesh?)*	বায়তুল মুকাররম *(Baitul Mukarram)*	Text-based
ঢাকায় প্রতিবছর কত টন কঠিন বর্জ্য উৎপন্ন হয়? *(How many tons of solid waste are generated in Dhaka each year?)*	৯৭ লক্ষ টন *(9.7 million tons)*	Number-based
বাংলাদেশের প্রধান বাণিজ্যিক কেন্দ কোনটি? *(What is the main commercial hub of Bangladesh?)*	ঢাকা *(Dhaka)*	Text-based

3.4 Translative Prompting

Llama 2 has not been trained on a large amount of Bangla data. Therefore, its performance is not that great in the case of Bangla. The translative method instructs the model to translate the query and context to English, then find the answer, and then translate the answer to Bangla, as depicted in Figure 2. This method has been seen to be useful for text-based answers in this study.

3.5 TraSe Architecture

The TraSe architecture can be seen in Figure 3. BanglaBERT (Bhattacharjee et al., 2022b) and bert base multilingual case (Devlin et al., 2018) embedding models have been used to embed query and document. Cosine similarity is used to retrieve the top 3 contexts. We have also used accurate 3 contexts along with the query for HIL context to evaluate the performance of the model when the retrieval process is accurate.

As Translative prompting is more useful for text-based answers than the others, a selective model has been proposed. In the model, query, contexts, answers generated from Translative prompting, and answers generated from one of the other methods (zero-shot, 2-shot, Self Ask, and ReAct) are inserted into the LLM pipeline and asked to select one of the answers based on the query and context.

3.6 Evaluation Metrics

Accuracy: Accuracy is the percentage of correct answers. The generated answers were manually evaluated and assigned as right or wrong answers. Based on manual evaluation the accuracy has been determined. We have taken an answer to be accurate if the information is correct, whether it is answered

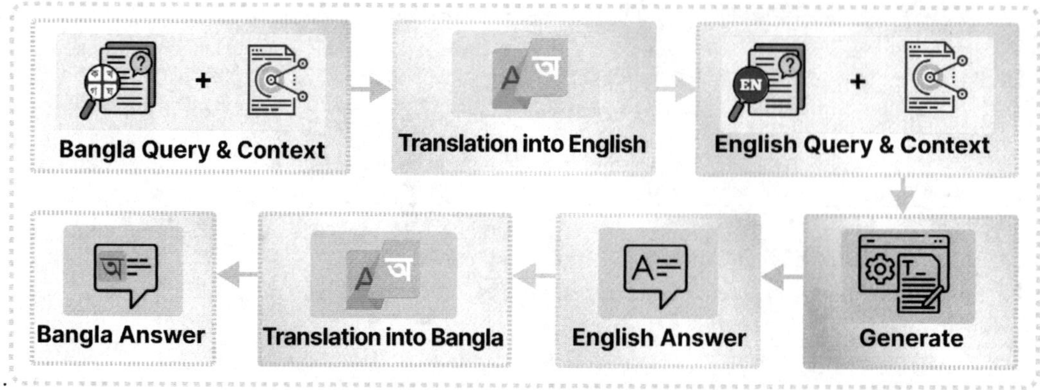

Figure 2: Flowchart of Translative method.

in Bangla or English. In the equation, TP means true positives (correct positives), TN means true negatives (correct negatives), FP means false positives (incorrect positives), and FN means false negatives (incorrect negatives). The formula for accuracy is given by:

$$\text{Accuracy} = \frac{TP + TN}{TP + TN + FP + FN} \quad (1)$$

F1 Score: The F1 score is the harmonic mean of precision and recall, making it a more reliable metric than accuracy when dealing with imbalanced datasets. The formula for F1 Score is:

$$F1 \text{ Score} = 2 \cdot \frac{\text{Recall} \cdot \text{Precision}}{\text{Precision} + \text{Recall}} \quad (2)$$

Exact Match is an important evaluation metric for question answering. However, in our case, it is not useful as the generated answer is not always in Bangla. One example is given below.
Query: 'রাষ্ট্রপতি এরশাদ কত খিস্টাব্দ পর্যন্ত দেশ শাসন করেন?' *Until when President Ershad ruled the country?*
Actual Answer: ১৯৯১ খ্রিস্টাব্দ *1999 AC*
Generated Answer: The answer to the query is 1991.

So, the generated answer is correct but not an exact match with the actual answer.

4 Result and Discussion

The efficiency of the translative method for text-based question answering is evident in Figure 4. With an accuracy of 0.28 for BanglaBERT, 0.24 for Bert-base-multilingual-case, and 0.61 for the HIL context, this method consistently outperforms the other four methods for text-based answering. Additionally, the translative method demonstrates competitive accuracy in number-based answers.

Table 3 presents the F1 scores and accuracy for various models, including baseline methods and the Translative prompting technique, with and without retrieval using BanglaBERT embeddings, Bert-base-multilingual-case embeddings, and Human-in-the-Loop (HIL) retrieval. The results show that the Translative model generally outperforms baseline models across different retrieval methods. Notably, all TraSe models demonstrate significant improvements over the baselines. For instance, the combination of zero-shot and Translative prompting achieves a 33% accuracy with Bert-base-multilingual-case, a substantial improvement over the 22% accuracy of the baseline 0-shot direct method. Similarly, in the HIL retrieval context, the TraSe method with zero-shot and Translative prompting achieves a 63% accuracy, compared to 51% for the baseline, indicating a notable improvement. Additionally, the 2-shot Translative combination is competitive with the zero-shot Translative method for BanglaBERT embeddings, achieving a 34% accuracy compared to 33%. Overall, when retrieval is accurate, the combination of zero-shot and Translative prompting with the TraSe architecture consistently achieves higher accuracy, with up to 63% in the HIL retrieval setting, showcasing the effectiveness of the TraSe approach.

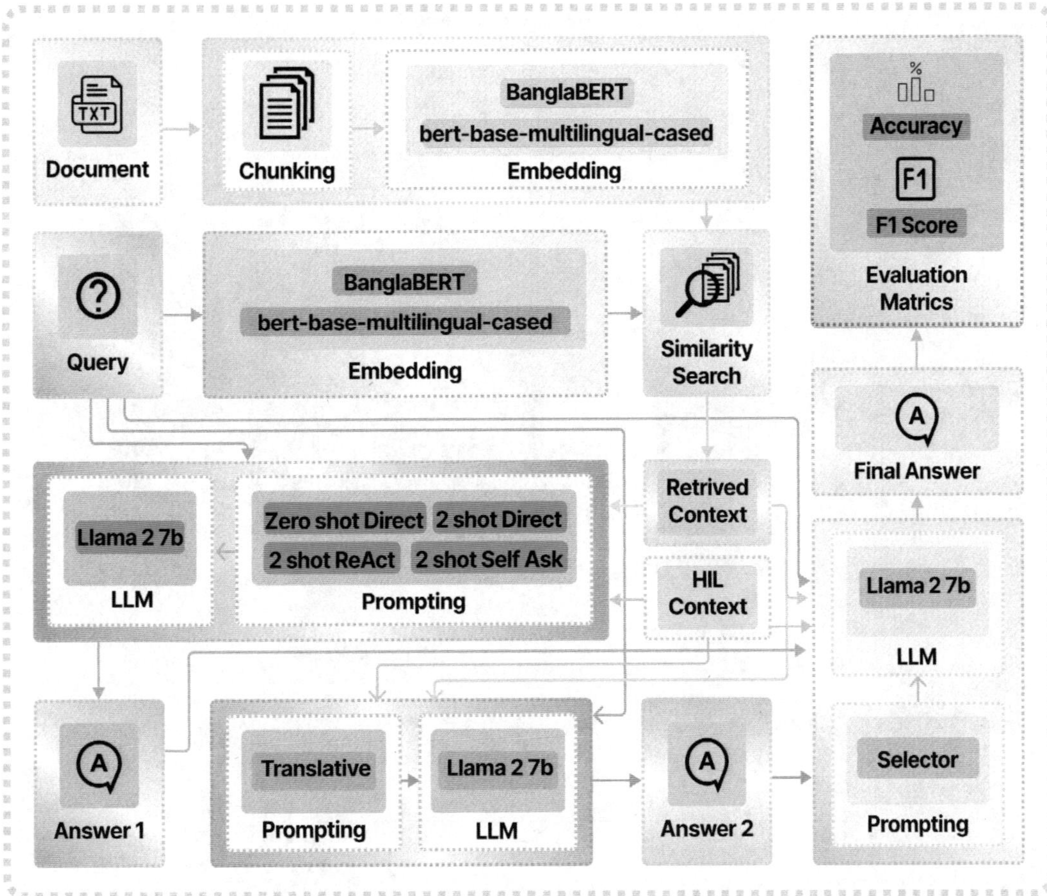

Figure 3: Flowchart of TraSe method.

5 Conclusion

In this study, we introduced the Translative prompting model, which demonstrated strong performance in both number-based and text-based answers for Bangla RAG. Building on this, we developed the TraSe model, leveraging the strengths of Translative prompting to enhance answer selection from previously generated responses. The TraSe model achieved notable accuracy improvements, reaching 34% accuracy with automatic retrieval and 63% accuracy with Human-in-the-Loop (HIL) retrieval, underscoring its effectiveness in both automated and human-assisted retrieval contexts.

Future research should prioritize incorporating a variety of language models, larger and more diverse datasets, and an expanded set of low-resource languages to validate and build upon these findings, ultimately contributing to a deeper and more generalizable understanding of language model performance.

Limitations

A limitation of this study is that it utilizes a single language model, which may not capture the full spectrum of performance across different models. Additionally, the smaller sample size may affect the generalizability of the results. Future research could benefit from incorporating a variety of models and larger datasets to validate and extend these findings. Furthermore, investigating other low-resource languages could provide additional insights and enhance the robustness of the conclusions. Investigating additional languages would not only enhance the robustness of the conclusions but also provide a more comprehensive understanding of how language models perform in diverse linguistic contexts.

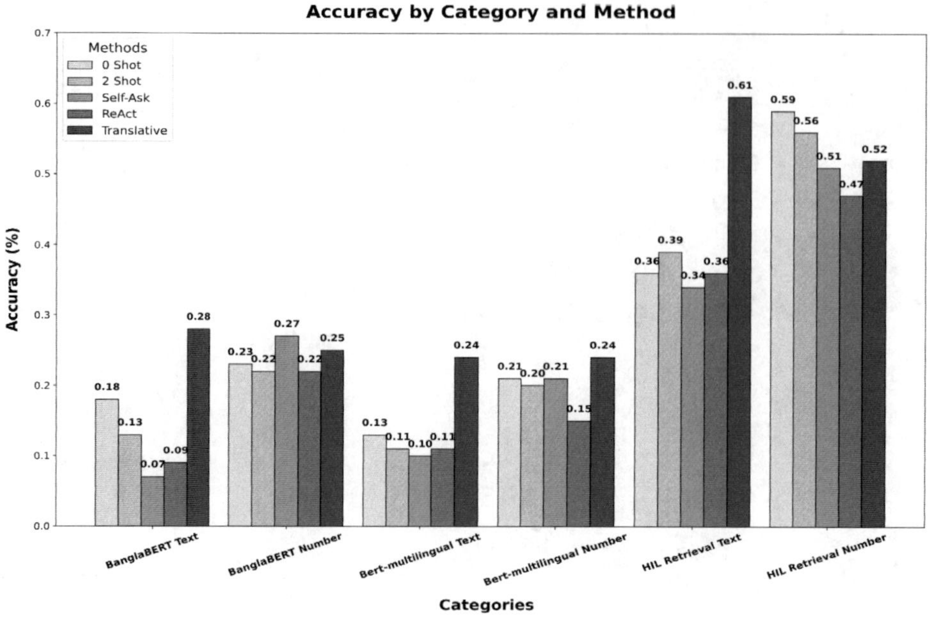

Figure 4: Accuracy of text-based and number-based answers

Table 3: Performance comparison between methods with and without retrieval across different models.

Method	Without Retrieval		With Retrieval					
			BanglaBERT		Bert-base-multilingual-case		Human In the loop Retrieval	
	F1 Score	Accuracy	F1 Score	Accuracy	F1 Score	Accuracy	F1 Score	Accuracy
0 shot direct	.06	.03	.36	.22	.31	.18	.68	.51
2 shot direct	.13	.07	.32	.19	.28	.16	.67	.50
Self-Ask	-	-	.33	.20	.29	.17	.62	.45
ReAct	-	-	.29	.17	.25	.14	.60	.43
Translative	-	-	.41	.26	.39	.24	.71	.55
	TraSe Method							
0shot+ Translative	-	-	.50	.33	.45	.29	.77	.63
2shot+ Translative	-	-	.51	.34	.41	.26	.75	.60
SelfAsk+ Translative	-	-	.46	.30	.43	.27	.76	.61
ReAct + Translative	-	-	.45	.29	.36	.22	.74	.59

References

Daman Arora, Anush Kini, Sayak Ray Chowdhury, Nagarajan Natarajan, Gaurav Sinha, and Amit Sharma. 2023. Gar-meets-rag paradigm for zero-shot information retrieval. *ArXiv*, abs/2310.20158.

Abhik Bhattacharjee, Tahmid Hasan, Wasi Ahmad, Kazi Samin Mubasshir, Md Saiful Islam, Anindya Iqbal, M. Sohel Rahman, and Rifat Shahriyar. 2022a. BanglaBERT: Language model pretraining and benchmarks for low-resource language understanding evaluation in Bangla. In *Findings of the Association for Computational Linguistics: NAACL 2022*, pages 1318–1327, Seattle, United States. Association for Computational Linguistics.

Abhik Bhattacharjee, Tahmid Hasan, Wasi Ahmad, Kazi Samin Mubasshir, Md Saiful Islam, Anindya Iqbal, M. Sohel Rahman, and Rifat Shahriyar. 2022b. BanglaBERT: Language model pretraining and benchmarks for low-resource language understanding evaluation in Bangla. In *Findings of the Association for Computational Linguistics: NAACL 2022*, pages 1318–1327, Seattle, United States. Association for Computational Linguistics.

Steven Bird. 2024. Must nlp be extractive? In *Proceedings of the 62nd Annual Meeting of the Association for Computational Linguistics (Volume 1: Long Papers)*, pages 14915–14929.

Tom B. Brown, Benjamin Mann, Nick Ryder, Melanie Subbiah, Jared Kaplan, Prafulla Dhariwal, Arvind Neelakantan, Pranav Shyam, Girish Sastry, Amanda Askell, Sandhini Agarwal, Ariel Herbert-Voss, Gretchen Krueger, Tom Henighan, Rewon Child, Aditya Ramesh, Daniel M. Ziegler, Jeffrey Wu, Clemens Winter, Christopher Hesse, Mark Chen, Eric Sigler, Mateusz Litwin, Scott Gray, Benjamin Chess, Jack Clark, Christopher Berner, Sam McCandlish, Alec Radford, Ilya Sutskever, and Dario Amodei. 2020. Language models are few-shot learners.

Xin Cheng, Di Luo, Xiuying Chen, Lemao Liu, Dongyan Zhao, and Rui Yan. 2023. Lift yourself up: Retrieval-augmented text generation with self memory. *ArXiv*, abs/2305.02437.

Florin Cuconasu, Giovanni Trappolini, Federico Siciliano, Simone Filice, Cesare Campagnano, Yoelle Maarek, Nicola Tonellotto, and Fabrizio Silvestri. 2024. The power of noise: Redefining retrieval for rag systems. In *Proceedings of the 47th International ACM SIGIR Conference on Research and Development in Information Retrieval*, pages 719–729.

Jacob Devlin, Ming-Wei Chang, Kenton Lee, and Kristina Toutanova. 2018. BERT: pre-training of deep bidirectional transformers for language understanding. *CoRR*, abs/1810.04805.

Yunfan Gao, Yun Xiong, Xinyu Gao, Kangxiang Jia, Jinliu Pan, Yuxi Bi, Yi Dai, Jiawei Sun, Qianyu Guo, Meng Wang, and Haofen Wang. 2023. Retrieval-augmented generation for large language models: A survey. *ArXiv*, abs/2312.10997.

Jennifer Hsia, Afreen Shaikh, Zhiruo Wang, and Graham Neubig. 2024. Ragged: Towards informed design of retrieval augmented generation systems. *ArXiv*, abs/2403.09040.

Yuntong Hu, Zhihan Lei, Zhengwu Zhang, Bo Pan, Chen Ling, and Liang Zhao. 2024. Grag: Graph retrieval-augmented generation. *ArXiv*, abs/2405.16506.

Yizheng Huang and Xiangji Huang. 2024. A survey on retrieval-augmented text generation for large language models. *ArXiv*, abs/2404.10981.

Atia Shahnaz Ipa, Priyo Nath Roy, Mohammad Abu Tareq Rony, Ali Raza, Norma Latif Fitriyani, Yeonghyeon Gu, and Muhammad Syafrudin. 2024. Bdsentillm: A novel llm approach to sentiment analysis of product reviews. *IEEE Access*.

Zhengbao Jiang, Frank F. Xu, Luyu Gao, Zhiqing Sun, Qian Liu, Jane Dwivedi-Yu, Yiming Yang, Jamie Callan, and Graham Neubig. 2023. Active retrieval augmented generation. *ArXiv*, abs/2305.06983.

Ofir Press, Muru Zhang, Sewon Min, Ludwig Schmidt, Noah A. Smith, and Mike Lewis. 2023. Measuring and narrowing the compositionality gap in language models.

Hongjin Qian, Peitian Zhang, Zheng Liu, Kelong Mao, and Zhicheng Dou. 2024. Memorag: Moving towards next-gen rag via memory-inspired knowledge discovery. *ArXiv*, abs/2409.05591.

Mohammad Abu Tareq Rony, Mohammad Shariful Islam, Tipu Sultan, Samah Alshathri, and Walid El-Shafai. 2024. Medigpt: Exploring potentials of conventional and large language models on medical data. *IEEE Access*.

Kunal Sawarkar, Abhilasha Mangal, and Shivam Raj Solanki. 2024. Blended rag: Improving rag (retriever-augmented generation) accuracy with semantic search and hybrid query-based retrievers. *2024 IEEE 7th International Conference on Multimedia Information Processing and Retrieval (MIPR)*, pages 155–161.

ES Shahul, Jithin James, Luis Espinosa Anke, and Steven Schockaert. 2023. Ragas: Automated evaluation of retrieval augmented generation. In *Conference of the European Chapter of the Association for Computational Linguistics*.

Zhihong Shao, Yeyun Gong, Yelong Shen, Minlie Huang, Nan Duan, and Weizhu Chen. 2023. Enhancing retrieval-augmented large language models with iterative retrieval-generation synergy.

Shi-Qi Yan, Jia-Chen Gu, Yun Zhu, and Zhen-Hua Ling. 2024. Corrective retrieval augmented generation.

Shunyu Yao, Jeffrey Zhao, Dian Yu, Nan Du, Izhak Shafran, Karthik Narasimhan, and Yuan Cao. 2023. React: Synergizing reasoning and acting in language models.

Fuda Ye, Shuangyin Li, Yongqi Zhang, and Lei Chen. 2024. R2ag: Incorporating retrieval information into retrieval augmented generation. In *Conference on Empirical Methods in Natural Language Processing*.

Hamed Zamani and Michael Bendersky. 2024. Stochastic rag: End-to-end retrieval-augmented generation through expected utility maximization. *ArXiv*, abs/2405.02816.

Penghao Zhao, Hailin Zhang, Qinhan Yu, Zhengren Wang, Yunteng Geng, Fangcheng Fu, Ling Yang, Wentao Zhang, and Bin Cui. 2024. Retrieval-augmented generation for ai-generated content: A survey. *ArXiv*, abs/2402.19473.

ABDUL: a new Approach to Build language models for Dialects Using formal Language corpora only

Yassine Toughrai[1,2], Kamel Smaïli[1,2], David Langois[1,2]
[1]Université de Lorraine
[2] Laboratoire lorrain de recherche en informatique et ses applications
{yassine.toughrai, smaili, david.langlois}@loria.fr

Abstract

Arabic dialects present major challenges for natural language processing (NLP) due to their diglossic nature, phonetic variability, and the scarcity of resources. To address this, we introduce a phoneme-like transcription approach that enables the training of robust language models for North African Dialects (NADs) using only formal language data, without the need for dialect-specific corpora. Our key insight is that Arabic dialects are highly phonetic, with NADs particularly influenced by European languages. This motivated us to develop a novel approach in which we convert Arabic script into a Latin-based representation, allowing our language model, ABDUL, to benefit from existing Latin-script corpora. Our method demonstrates strong performance in multi-label emotion classification and named entity recognition (NER) across various Arabic dialects. ABDUL achieves results comparable to or better than specialized and multilingual models such as DarijaBERT, DziriBERT, and mBERT. Notably, in the NER task, ABDUL outperforms mBERT by 5% in F1-score for Modern Standard Arabic (MSA), Moroccan, and Algerian Arabic, despite using a vocabulary four times smaller than mBERT.

1 Introduction

NADs, including Moroccan, Algerian, and Tunisian, introduce additional complexities. Influenced by Berber languages and colonial languages such as French and Spanish, these dialects display notable phonetic variability, including vowel inconsistency and the adoption of phonemes absent in MSA, such as /p/ and /v/ (Barkat-Defradas et al., 2003). In addition, their lexicons are enriched by extensive borrowing from French and Spanish and often incorporating them with phonetic modifications (Owens, 2013).

In this article, we introduce a phoneme-like transcription approach that bridges formal Arabic with dialectal varieties through linguistic normalization. Inspired by the Buckwalter (Buckwalter, 2002) transliteration system, our method simplifies and adapts transliteration by clustering phonetically similar sounds, improving alignment with dialectal phonetic patterns. To highlight consonants and long vowels (e.g., the "ā" in the word kitāb for "book" which is pronounced with an extended duration of the vowel /a/), this approach deliberately omits diacritization and even removes preexisting diacritics from the text, reducing phonetic variability (Al-Mozainy, 1981).

By transforming Arabic script into a standardized phoneme-like Latin representation, this preprocessing pipeline promotes cross-script and cross-dialect generalization, allowing for the development of robust NLP models trained solely on formal language data. In this article, we will focus exclusively on transliterating MSA to handle Arabic dialects, with the future goal of including French and code-switched text, given their significance in NADs.

2 Linguistic Justification

NADs are low-resource languages with no formal or standardized grammatical rules, relying mainly on direct phonetic transcription. Alongside MSA vocabulary, they feature extensive lexical borrowings from French, Spanish, Turkish, and Italian, reflecting the historical and colonial influence of these languages in the region. The lexical resemblance between Algerian Arabic (ALG) and MSA has been quantitatively analyzed using computational methods. Abukwaik et al. (Abu Kwaik et al., 2018) employed Latent Semantic Indexing (LSI) to assess lexical overlap between MSA and various Arabic dialects, reporting an LSI similarity score of 0.68 for Algerian Arabic. This score indicates a moderate lexical divergence, suggesting that while some vocabulary is shared, directly applying MSA-

Proceedings of the 1st Workshop on Language Models for Underserved Communities (LM4UC 2025), pages 16–21
May 4, 2025

trained models to Algerian Arabic could result in significant tokenization mismatches. Harrat et al. (Harrat et al., 2014) found that approximately 20% of Algerian dialectal words originate from Arabic, while 34% are derived from MSA. Studies estimate that loanwords make up around 30–40% of the vocabulary in these dialects, particularly in technical, educational, and governmental contexts (Owens, 2013; Barkat-Defradas et al., 2003). In (Harrat et al., 2016), the authors argue that significant variations between and MSA occur in vocalization, along with the omission or modification of certain letters, particularly the Hamza[1]. Despite the influence of foreign lexicons, NADs preserve core linguistic structures from MSA. However, in terms of pronunciation, Menacer et al. (Menacer et al., 2017) found that 46% of MSA-derived words in NADs exhibit phonetic variations compared to their standard MSA counterparts. Another key characteristic of NADs is their strong dependence on consonantal structures for lexical and semantic distinctions, as vowel patterns vary significantly across regions (Barkat-Defradas et al., 2003). Given these linguistic properties, ABDUL leverages stable consonantal structures, which serve as robust subword units for training NLP models, reducing variability caused by inconsistent usage of vowels.

3 Related Work

NADs are low-resource languages that lack formalized grammatical rules and primarily rely on phonetic transcription. In this work, we propose a novel paradigm for training language models for NADs using only formal language corpora, eliminating the need for dialect-specific datasets. To evaluate the effectiveness of our approach, we compare it against several key baselines in Arabic NLP, particularly those designed for Arabic dialects:

- **AraBERT** [2]: A pretrained BERT model for MSA (Antoun et al., 2020), serving as a foundational model for Arabic NLP. It is trained on a mix of MSA corpora and Arabic Wikipedia, capturing linguistic nuances in formal Arabic.
- **mBERT** [3]: A multilingual BERT model pretrained on 100+ languages (Devlin et al., 2019). While not specifically optimized for Arabic, it provides a multilingual perspective on cross-lingual transfer.
- **DarijaBERT** [4]: A BERT model fine-tuned for Moroccan Arabic (Darija) (Gaanoun et al., 2023), leveraging localized datasets to capture dialect-specific nuances.
- **TunBERT** [5]: A Tunisian Arabic BERT model (Messaoudi et al., 2021), highlighting the lexical and phonological idiosyncrasies of this dialect.
- **DziriBERT** [6]: A pretrained model for Algerian Arabic (Dziri) (Abdaoui et al., 2022), providing a benchmark for North African dialectal NLP.

Beyond these baselines, our approach is further inspired by the study "Consonant is All You Need" (Al-shaibani and Ahmad, 2023), which highlights the benefits of reducing reliance on vowels for more efficient NLP models. This work demonstrates how selectively omitting certain lexical features can lead to smaller vocabularies, lower computational complexity, and improved training efficiency. These insights align with our dediacritization and consonant-centric transcription strategy, reinforcing the scalability and effectiveness of our method.

Through a rigorous comparative analysis, we aim to underscore the advantages of our approach. By pretraining a language model from scratch on data processed via our pipeline, we establish a fair and consistent benchmark to demonstrate the benefits of phoneme-like transcription for Arabic dialectal NLP. Our work contributes to the broader goal of improving low-resource language modeling through linguistically informed methodologies.

4 Methodology

To effectively adapt formal Arabic resources for dialectal NLP, we develop a preprocessing pipeline that normalizes phonetic variability while preserving linguistically significant features. In the following, we outline the key steps in our phoneme-like transcription process.

4.1 Phoneme-like Transcription Pipeline

Our preprocessing pipeline transforms Arabic text into a phoneme-like Latin representation by:

[1] The Hamza is a letter in the Arabic alphabet representing the glottal stop

[2] https://huggingface.co/aubmindlab/bert-base-arabertv2

[3] https://huggingface.co/google-bert/bert-base-multilingual-uncased

[4] https://huggingface.co/SI2M-Lab/DarijaBERT

[5] https://huggingface.co/tunis-ai/TunBERT

[6] https://huggingface.co/alger-ia/DziriBERT

1. **Dediacritization**: We remove short vowels and diacritics, treating them as having a minimal impact to normalize phonetic variations and highlight consonant structures. This approach aligns with the principle that consonants encode the fundamental semantic meaning of words in Arabic (Watson, 2002).

2. **Retention of Long Vowels**: long vowels are preserved to capture essential phonetic cues while reducing ambiguity, reflecting their phonemic stability in Arabic dialects (Al-Mozainy, 1981).

3. **Simplified Transliteration**: Inspired by the Buckwalter transliteration system, our simplified Latin-script transcription ensures phonetic consistency across dialects. This improves tokenization efficiency and allows models trained with formal Arabic corpora to generalize better to dialects, particularly by unifying phonetically similar sounds under a shared representation.

4.2 Model Training

We pretrain a BERT model from scratch using the Arabic split of the OSCAR corpus (Ortiz Suárez et al., 2019), applying our preprocessing pipeline. We utilize a WordPiece tokenizer with a vocabulary size of 30,522 tokens. The model undergoes training for 9 epochs using the Adam optimizer, with a learning rate of 5e-5, a batch size of 64, and a maximum sequence length of 512. Training is conducted on a single NVIDIA A100, with a masked language modeling (MLM) probability of 0.15.

The choice of vocabulary size plays a crucial role in language model training, especially for morphologically rich languages like Arabic. To ensure fair comparison, we adopt the BERT architecture, aligning with benchmark models such as DarijaBERT, DziriBERT, TunBERT, AraBERT, and mBERT. The 30,522-token vocabulary was selected to match the lowest vocabulary size among these benchmarks (Table 1), allowing for an equitable evaluation of efficiency across different pretraining settings.

5 Datasets

In this section, we describe the datasets used for pretraining and benchmarking ABDUL, covering MSA and NADs. Our selection includes a large-scale corpus in MSA for pretraining and multiple dialect-specific datasets for downstream tasks, ensuring a comprehensive evaluation across emotion classification and named entity recognition (NER).

Table 1: Vocabulary size comparison between the ABDUL trained BERT model and the models it will be benchmarked against

Language	Model	Vocab Size
Moroccan	DarijaBERT	80,000
Algerian	DziriBERT	50,000
Tunisian	TunBERT	30,522
MSA	arabert	64,000
Multilingual	mBERT	119,547
MSA	ABDUL	30,522

5.1 Pretraining Dataset

We use the Arabic subset of the OSCAR corpus (Ortiz Suárez et al., 2019) for pretraining our model. This dataset contains approximately 8.7 million documents and 6.1 billion words, totaling around 84.2 GB of text. Derived from web sources such as news articles, blogs, and forums, OSCAR provides a diverse representation of MSA. Its scale and domain diversity make it well-suited for training transformer-based language models, ensuring broad linguistic coverage.

5.2 Emotion Classification Datasets

For text classification, we employ the SemEval 2025 [7] Task 11-A dataset, which focuses on emotion detection in Moroccan and Algerian Arabic. The dataset consists of approximately 900 labeled instances per dialect, annotated with four emotion categories: joy, anger, sadness, and fear. This dataset serves as a benchmark for evaluating emotion classification in different research works concerning NADs, which pose unique linguistic challenges due to their phonetic variations and lexical borrowings.

5.3 Named Entity Recognition (NER) Datasets

For NER evaluation, we utilize three datasets: WikiFANE(Alotaibi and Lee, 2014), DzNER (Dahou and Cheragui, 2023), and DarNER (Moussa and Mourhir, 2023), which cover different dialects and entity types, providing a comprehensive benchmark for dialectal Arabic NER.

[7] https://semeval.github.io/SemEval2025/

- **WikiFANE**: Covers MSA and NADs, providing a general-purpose dataset.
- **DzNER**: Focuses on Algerian Arabic, with a broader range of entity types.
- **DarNER**: Specializes in Moroccan Arabic and includes date entities in addition to standard entity categories.

Table 2 summarizes the dataset attributes.

6 Results

The performance of ABDUL is evaluated on two tasks: emotion classification and named entity recognition (NER), across multiple Arabic variants. The results demonstrate ABDUL's ability to generalize effectively across dialects while maintaining competitive performance against specialized models.

6.1 Emotion Classification Performance

Table 3 presents the emotion classification results for Algerian Arabic. ABDUL achieves a macro-F1 score of **0.5315**, ranking second behind DziriBERT (**0.5573**). It outperforms DarijaBERT (**0.5107**), the specialized Moroccan Arabic model, and significantly surpasses TunBERT (**0.2473**), which struggles in this dialect.

Table 3: Emotion classification results for Algerian Arabic.

Model	Precision	Recall	Macro-F1	Accuracy
DarijaBERT	0.6454	0.4289	0.5107	0.2747
DziriBERT	**0.6560**	0.4928	**0.5573**	**0.3186**
TunBERT	0.4220	0.2210	0.2473	0.2087
arabert	0.6369	0.4159	0.4964	0.2417
mBERT	0.5295	0.3434	0.4071	0.2197
ABDUL	0.6000	**0.5014**	0.5315	0.2088

Table 4 presents the emotion classification results for Moroccan Arabic. ABDUL achieves a macro-F1 score of **0.4519**, closely matching AraBERT (**0.4518**), a model trained on MSA. It outperforms DarijaBERT (**0.4648**) and significantly surpasses TunBERT (**0.1020**).

Table 4: Emotion classification results for Moroccan Arabic.

Model	Precision	Recall	Macro-F1	Accuracy
DarijaBERT	0.5399	**0.4122**	**0.4648**	**0.5280**
DziriBERT	0.5057	0.3589	0.4157	0.4410
TunBERT	0.1538	0.0797	0.1020	0.2981
arabert	**0.7039**	0.3775	0.4518	0.4907
mBERT	0.4109	0.2777	0.3254	0.3727
ABDUL	0.5266	0.4035	0.4519	0.4596

Table 5 presents the averaged classification results across dialects. ABDUL achieves an overall macro-F1 score of **0.4915**, outperforming DarijaBERT (**0.4878**) and DziriBERT (**0.4865**). This highlights ABDUL's ability to generalize across NADs despite being trained exclusively on MSA.

Table 5: Average emotion classification results across dialects.

Model	Precision	Recall	Macro-F1	Accuracy
DarijaBERT	0.5926	0.4205	0.4878	**0.4013**
DziriBERT	0.5808	0.4258	0.4865	0.3798
TunBERT	0.2879	0.1503	0.1746	0.2535
arabert	**0.6704**	0.3967	0.4741	0.3662
mBERT	0.4702	0.3106	0.3662	0.2962
ABDUL	0.5633	**0.4524**	**0.4915**	0.3342

These results suggest that ABDUL's phoneme-like transcription preprocessing effectively captures dialectal features while avoiding reliance on extensive dialect-specific data. Its particularly strong performance in Algerian Arabic underscores its suitability for handling underrepresented dialects in emotion classification.

6.2 Named Entity Recognition (NER) Performance

Table 6 presents the results for NER in MSA. ABDUL achieves an F1 score of **0.4646**, performing on par with mBERT (**0.4647**), the top-performing model. It surpasses arabert (**0.4427**), demonstrating its effectiveness in formal Arabic settings. The results assess ABDUL's ability to generalize across different Arabic variants and effectively capture named entities despite phonetic and lexical variability.

Table 2: NER datasets for Arabic and North African dialects.

Dataset	Language/Dialect	Entities	Size in tokens
WikiFANE	MSA and North African Dialects	102 different entities	490k
DzNER	Algerian Arabic (Darija)	PER, LOC, ORG, MISC	220k
DarNER	Moroccan Arabic (Darija)	PER, LOC, ORG, DATE	65,905

Table 6: NER performance on MSA.

Model	Precision	Recall	F1	Accuracy
DarijaBERT	0.4922	0.4112	0.4481	0.8927
DziriBERT	0.4825	0.3854	0.4285	0.8911
TunBERT	0.4416	0.0068	0.0134	0.8633
arabert	0.5016	0.3962	0.4427	0.8954
mBERT	0.5152	**0.4233**	**0.4647**	0.8977
ABDUL	**0.5180**	0.4212	0.4646	**0.8979**

For NER in Algerian Arabic (Table 7), ABDUL achieves the highest F1 score of **0.6828**, significantly outperforming DziriBERT (**0.5461**), which is specifically trained for this dialect.

Table 7: NER performance on Algerian Arabic.

Model	Precision	Recall	F1	Accuracy
DarijaBERT	0.5556	0.5615	0.5585	0.9384
DziriBERT	0.5361	0.5565	0.5461	0.9382
TunBERT	0.4286	0.0071	0.0140	0.9104
arabert	0.5104	0.5841	0.5448	0.9389
mBERT	0.4975	0.5727	0.5325	0.9343
ABDUL	**0.6601**	**0.7071**	**0.6828**	**0.9553**

For NER in Moroccan Arabic (Table 8), ABDUL attains an F1 score of **0.6557**, ranking just behind mBERT (**0.7192**), the best-performing model overall. However, it surpasses DarijaBERT (**0.6246**), that was designed especially for Morrocan. A qualitative analysis of the DarNER corpus revealed that many words were transcribed in a way that closely aligns with their Arabic root rather than reflecting phonetic pronunciation. This likely explains mBERT's and arabert's superior performance, as these models benefit from their extensive pretraining on MSA.

Table 8: NER performance on Moroccan Arabic.

Model	Precision	Recall	F1	Accuracy
DarijaBERT	0.6077	0.6424	0.6246	0.9272
DziriBERT	0.5875	0.5516	0.5690	0.9193
TunBERT	0.1928	0.0548	0.0853	0.8436
arabert	0.6491	0.6761	0.6623	0.9290
mBERT	**0.7140**	**0.7246**	**0.7192**	**0.9403**
ABDUL	0.6415	0.6706	0.6557	0.9346

Table 9 presents the averaged NER performance across MSA, Algerian, and Moroccan Arabic. ABDUL achieves an overall F1 score of **0.6010**, outperforming both DarijaBERT (**0.5437**) and DziriBERT (**0.5145**). This demonstrates ABDUL's ability to generalize effectively across dialects while maintaining strong performance in both formal and informal Arabic varieties.

Table 9: Average NER performance across Arabic variants.

Model	Precision	Recall	F1	Accuracy
DarijaBERT	0.5518	0.5384	0.5437	0.9194
DziriBERT	0.5354	0.4978	0.5145	0.9162
TunBERT	0.3543	0.0229	0.0376	0.8724
arabert	0.5564	0.5521	0.5500	0.9211
mBERT	0.5756	0.5735	0.5721	0.9241
ABDUL	**0.6065**	**0.5996**	**0.6010**	**0.9293**

7 Conclusion

ABDUL consistently matches or exceeds the performance of specialized models for certain dialects in tasks such as emotion classification and named entity recognition (NER), despite being trained exclusively on MSA. It notably outperforms DarijaBERT and DziriBERT in several scenarios, showcasing its strong adaptability to NADs. By utilizing a phoneme-like transcription approach, ABDUL effectively bridges the gap between formal and dialectal Arabic, improving tokenization efficiency and enhancing generalization across dialects with shared linguistic features. Its ability to compete with dialect-specific models while relying solely on widely available, high-quality MSA data underscores its scalability and potential for low-resource Arabic NLP.

8 Limitations and Future Work

While ABDUL demonstrates strong performance in dialectal NLP tasks, several limitations remain. Currently, our approach does not support Latin-script Arabizi dialects, which are widely used in informal settings. Expanding ABDUL to handle Arabizi is a key part of our future work. Additionally, we plan to investigate how vocabulary size impacts performance, as well as how different formal languages used in pretraining (e.g., French, Spanish, and English) influence the model's ability to generalize across dialects.

Overall, the results are low for state-of-the-art models, including ABDUL. The task will be to test other architectures to improve the results and not settle for the current ones.

Finally, we aim to expand ABDUL's applicability to a broader set of NLP tasks, including machine translation and text generation, to further assess its scalability and effectiveness in diverse linguistic contexts. As a long-term objective, we seek to build the first large language model (LLM) for Arabic dialects, leveraging the high availability and quality of formal languages data to address the low-resource status of Arabic dialects and advance the field of dialectal Arabic NLP.

References

Amine Abdaoui, Mohamed Berrimi, Mourad Oussalah, and Abdelouahab Moussaoui. 2022. Dziribert: a pre-trained language model for the algerian dialect. *arXiv preprint arXiv:2109.12346*.

Kathrein Abu Kwaik, Motaz Saad, Stergios Chatzikyriakidis, and Simon Dobnik. 2018. A lexical distance study of arabic dialects. *Procedia Computer Science*, 142:2–13.

Hamza Al-Mozainy. 1981. *Vowel Alternations in a Bedouin Hijazi Arabic Dialect: Abstractness and Stress*. Ph.D. thesis, University of Texas at Austin.

Maged S. Al-shaibani and Irfan Ahmad. 2023. Consonant is all you need: a compact representation of english text for efficient NLP. In *The 2023 Conference on Empirical Methods in Natural Language Processing*.

Fahd Alotaibi and Mark Lee. 2014. A hybrid approach to features representation for fine-grained Arabic named entity recognition. In *Proceedings of COLING 2014, the 25th International Conference on Computational Linguistics: Technical Papers*, pages 984–995, Dublin, Ireland. Dublin City University and Association for Computational Linguistics.

Wissam Antoun, Fady Baly, and Hazem Hajj. 2020. Arabert: Transformer-based model for arabic language understanding. *arXiv preprint arXiv:2003.00104*.

Melissa Barkat-Defradas, Jalal Al-Tamimi, and Thami Benkirane. 2003. Phonetic variation in production and perception of speech: a comparative study of two Arabic dialects. In *Proceedings of the 15th International Congress of Phonetic Sciences ((ICPhS), Barcelona 3-9 August 2003*, pages pp. 857–860, Barcelona, Spain.

Tim Buckwalter. 2002. Arabic transliteration. *URL http://www. qamus. org/transliteration. htm.*

Abdelhalim Hafedh Dahou and Mohamed Amine Cheragui. 2023. Dzner: A large algerian named entity recognition dataset. *Natural Language Processing Journal*, 3:100005.

Jacob Devlin, Ming-Wei Chang, Kenton Lee, and Kristina Toutanova. 2019. Bert: Pre-training of deep bidirectional transformers for language understanding. *NAACL-HLT*, pages 4171–4186.

Kamel Gaanoun, Abdou Mohamed Naira, Anass Allak, and Imade Benelallam. 2023. Darijabert: a step forward in nlp for the written moroccan dialect.

Salima Harrat, Karima Meftouh, Mourad Abbas, Walid-Khaled Hidouci, and Kamel Smaïli. 2016. An Algerian dialect: Study and Resources. *International journal of advanced computer science and applications (IJACSA)*, 7(3):384–396.

Salima Harrat, Karima Meftouh, Mourad Abbas, and Kamel Smaïli. 2014. Building Resources for Algerian Arabic Dialects. In *15th Annual Conference of the International Communication Association Interspeech*, Singapour, Singapore. ISCA.

Mohamed Amine Menacer, Odile Mella, Dominique Fohr, Denis Jouvet, David Langlois, and Kamel Smaïli. 2017. Development of the Arabic Loria Automatic Speech Recognition system (ALASR) and its evaluation for Algerian dialect. In *ACLing 2017 - 3rd International Conference on Arabic Computational Linguistics*, pages 1–8, Dubai, United Arab Emirates.

Abir Messaoudi, Ahmed Cheikhrouhou, Hatem Haddad, Nourchene Ferchichi, Moez BenHajhmida, Abir Korched, Malek Naski, Faten Ghriss, and Amine Kerkeni. 2021. Tunbert: Pretrained contextualized text representation for tunisian dialect.

Hanane Nour Moussa and Asmaa Mourhir. 2023. Darnercorp: An annotated named entity recognition dataset in the moroccan dialect. *Data in Brief*, 48:109234.

Pedro Javier Ortiz Suárez, Benoit Sagot, and Laurent Romary. 2019. Asynchronous pipelines for processing huge corpora on medium to low resource infrastructures. Proceedings of the Workshop on Challenges in the Management of Large Corpora (CMLC-7) 2019. Cardiff, 22nd July 2019, pages 9 – 16, Mannheim. Leibniz-Institut f"ur Deutsche Sprache.

Jonathan Owens. 2013. *Arabic as a Minority Language*.

Janet Watson. 2002. *Phonology and morphology of Arabic (the phonology of the world's languages)*.

Untangling the Influence of Typology, Data and Model Architecture on Ranking Transfer Languages for Cross-Lingual POS Tagging

Enora Rice[1] **Ali Marashian**[1] **Hannah Haynie**[1] **Katharina von der Wense**[1,2]
Alexis Palmer[1]
[1]University of Colorado Boulder [2] Johannes Gutenberg University Mainz
enora.rice@colorado.edu

Abstract

Cross-lingual transfer learning is an invaluable tool for overcoming data scarcity, yet selecting a suitable transfer language remains a challenge. The precise roles of linguistic typology, training data, and model architecture in transfer language choice are not fully understood. We take a holistic approach, examining how both dataset-specific and fine-grained typological features influence transfer language selection for part-of-speech tagging, considering two different sources for morphosyntactic features. While previous work examines these dynamics in the context of bilingual biLSTMS, we extend our analysis to a more modern transfer learning pipeline: zero-shot prediction with **pretrained multilingual models**. We train a series of transfer language ranking systems and examine how different feature inputs influence ranker performance across architectures. Word overlap, type-token ratio, and genealogical distance emerge as top features across all architectures. Our findings reveal that a combination of **typological** and **dataset-dependent** features leads to the best rankings, and that good performance can be obtained with either feature group on its own.

1 Introduction

Despite being trained on 100+ languages, pretrained multilingual language models (MLMs) fail to cover the vast majority of the world's languages. Finetuning MLMs for zero-shot cross-lingual transfer is a useful technique to extend their reach by circumventing the lack of task-specific labeled data in low-resource languages. Effective zero-shot transfer hinges on choosing an appropriate source language (Eronen et al., 2023, 2022; Layacan et al., 2024), but it is still not well understood how to make this selection. Most analyses of successful source/target pairs fall into one of two categories: typological or dataset-dependent. The typological view investigates the role of linguistic similarity, with studies showing that more "similar" languages tend to form better source/target pairs (Eronen et al., 2023; de Vries et al., 2022; Lauscher et al., 2020). Much of this typological analysis is coarse-grained, focusing on features like language family or abstract distance measures. The dataset-dependent view focuses on comparing source and target datasets based on features like sub-word overlap (Wu and Dredze, 2019; Pires et al., 2019; K et al., 2020). Few papers consider both views, and those that do focus on older methods of crosslingual transfer like bilingual LSTMS (Lin et al., 2019). Additionally, previous analyses shed little light on the linguistic question of which fine-grained typological features are especially relevant for the task.

This primary goal of this paper is to offer a deeper understanding of effective transfer language selection across architectures, comparing crosslingual transfer with biLSTMs to XLM-R (Conneau et al., 2020) and M-BERT (Devlin et al., 2019). We aim to identify which features contribute to selecting a successful source/target pair for part-of-speech (POS) tagging. We focus on POS tagging because it directly reflects typological features such as word order. Our analysis addresses the following key questions:

Q1. Which features are most important for cross-lingual transfer?

Q2. Do these features differ between biLSTMs and MLMs?

Q3. How does the granularity of typological features—whether fine or coarse—affect transfer language selection?

Q4. Is it necessary to consider data set features in selecting a transfer language?

We train a series of gradient-boosted decision tree models to rank transfer languages for POS

Proceedings of the 1st Workshop on Language Models for Underserved Communities (LM4UC 2025), pages 22–31
May 4, 2025

tagging, with separate rankers for the two architectures. During training, we generate feature importance scores and identify the most salient features for each architecture (Q1, Q2). To examine the role of fine-grained typological features, we compare two typological inputs: source/target distance measures, and full finegrained feature vectors (Q3). We also evaluate how the source and quality of typological data affects ranker performance by swapping between URIEL (Littell et al., 2017) and Grambank (Skirgård et al., 2023a) feature vectors. Last, we investigate whether typological information alone can effectively determine suitable source/target language pairs by experimenting with the exclusion of dataset-specific features (Q4).

We find that impressive performance can be achieved when relying primarily on either feature category, without the need for the other, indicating that both "typological" and "dataset-dependent" views of transfer language choice represent independently viable strategies. However, peak performance is achieved by combining dataset-dependent and fine-grained typological features. Crucially, our analysis reveals that key features such as word overlap, type-token ratio, and genealogical distance remain consistently important across architectures, suggesting that the relevance of these features may transcend specific model designs, offering broader insights into cross-lingual transfer that could enable us to better leverage MLMs for low-resource applications.

2 Related Works

2.1 Ranking Transfer Languages

Lin et al. (2019) rank transfer languages using both dataset-dependent and linguistic features from the URIEL knowledge base (Littell et al., 2017). We build on their work with key adaptations: 1) Instead of varying dataset size, which obscures the role of fine-grained features, we hold corpus size constant across all language pairs. 2) In addition to bilingual biLSTMs, we examine zero-shot transfer with finetuned MLMs. 3) We replace typological distance measures with element-wise comparisons of typological feature vectors, following Dolicki and Spanakis (2021).

Khan et al. (2025) build on the work in Littell et al. (2017) to enhance the coverage of URIEL and lang2vec with novel linguistic databases and customizable distance calculations. We follow suit by comparing the impact of incorporating URIEL syntactic vectors versus Grambank syntactic vectors on the transfer language ranking task

2.2 Transfer Language Choice for Zero-shot Cross-lingual Transfer with MLMs

Lauscher et al. (2020) show a correlation between linguistic proximity and successful zero-shot transfer, but only test English as the source language. We experiment with 18 source languages. de Vries et al. (2022) find that XLM-R finetuned on a suitable transfer language performs almost three times better than when using a suboptimal transfer language. They highlight the influence of linguistic similarity but do not consider dataset features.

3 Experiments

3.1 Languages

We experiment with a total of 20 target and 18 source languages across seven language families. We determine our set of target and source languages based on the availability of sufficient data in Universal Dependencies 2.0 (UD) (de Marneffe et al., 2021). We consider target languages that have a training corpus with at least 500 lines and source languages with at least 2000. Justification for this threshold is described in 3.2.1. We also eliminate languages that are not present in URIEL and/or Grambank. Our full set of target languages is given in Table 1. Languages that also serve as source languages are italicized. While many of the languages covered by our experiments are high-resource, several others fall into a middle range and are underserved by the NLP research community at large.

3.2 Testbed Tasks

We generate gold ranking-data by training a suite of biLSTMs and finetuned XLM-R and M-BERT models for POS tagging across all possible source/target language pairs. To remove the influence of dataset size, we cap each source language training set at 2000 lines. Then, for each target language, we create a ranking of all potential source languages based on the relative performance of each model on a held out test set. Model details are outlined in following sections.

3.2.1 biLSTMs

We train a suite of 378 biLSTMs using Stanza (Qi et al., 2020)– one for each target/source pair. We train each model on 500 instances of UD data in the target language and 2000 instances in the source language. We choose this split to simulate a setting where limited training data is available in the target language but comparatively greater data is available in the source language. We set the data thresholds to ensure that sufficient training data is present for model convergence, but training data in the target language is still limited enough to make the task non-trivial. All models are trained on default Stanza hyperparameters *without* pre-trained word embeddings for a maximum of 6000 steps. We evaluate each model on a held out test set drawn from the same corpus as the target training data.

3.2.2 Fine-tuned XLM-R and M-BERT

We finetune XLM-R and M-BERT equivalently on each of our 18 source languages with a modified implementation[1] from de Vries et al. (2022). Each model is trained on the same 2000 instance UD dataset that we use to train our biLSTM models. All models are trained for 1,000 batches of 10 samples with a linearly decreasing learning rate starting at 5e-5. We use 10% dropout between transformer layers and 10% self-attention dropout.

Language	Treebank
Basque	UD_Basque-BDT
Czech	UD_Czech-PDT
Danish	UD_Danish-DDT
Dutch	UD_Dutch-LassySmall
Finnish	UD_Finnish-FTB
Hindi	UD_Hindi-HDTB
Hungarian	UD_Hungarian-Szeged
Indonesian	UD_Indonesian-GSD
Galician	UD_Galician-CTG
Italian	UD_Italian-PoSTWITA
Korean	UD_Korean-GSD
Latin	UD_Latin-ITTB
Latvian	UD_Latvian-LVTB
Turkish	UD_Turkish-IMST
Polish	UD_Polish-LFG
Portuguese	UD_Portuguese-Bosque
Russian	UD_Russian-SynTagRus
Catalan	UD_Catalan-AnCora
French	UD_French-Sequoia
English	UD_English-LinES
Ukrainian	UD_Ukrainian-IU

Table 1: Full list of target languages and their corresponding treebanks. Languages that also serve as source languages are italicized.

[1]https://github.com/wietsedv/xpos

3.3 Our Ranking System

Given a target language t and a list of n potential source languages $S = [s_1, s_2 ... s_n]$, our goal is to rank all source languages in S based on the expected performance of POS-tagging models trained on each source/target pair (s_i,t). Building on Lin et al. (2019), we train a series of gradient boosted decision trees using the LightGBM implementation (MIT License) (Ke et al., 2017) of the LambdaRank algorithm. Models are trained on gold ranking-data described in Section 3.2.

Input to our ranking system consists of vector representations of each source/target pair. Vectors are defined as a set of features, categorized into two types. We calculate **dataset-dependent** features by comparing source and target corpora using four metrics: word overlap, type-token ratio in the source language corpus, type-token ratio in the target language corpus, and the difference between the source and target language type-token ratios. **Dataset-independent** features capture linguistic similarity between the source and target languages using five measures: *genetic*, *syntactic*, *phonological*, (phonetic) *inventory*, and *geographic*. *Syntactic*, *phonological* and *inventory* features are defined using binary feature vectors sourced from typological databases. We call these our *Typology-Vector* features. By default, Typology-Vector features are represented by distance measures computed as the cosine difference between URIEL (Littell et al., 2017) vectors representing source and target, but we experiment with different representations (described in Sections 3.3.1 and 3.3.2). All features are briefly summarized in Table 2 and feature vector lengths are given in Table 3. For more detailed descriptions, refer to Lin et al. (2019).

3.3.1 Distance-Measure vs. Fully Featured

By default, we express the linguistic similarity between *syntactic*, *phonological*, and *inventory* features as a series of distance measures. We call these **distance** Typology-Vector representations. At predict time, the ranker receives a feature vector a representing the target and a feature vector b representing the source and computes the cosine distance: $1 - cos(a, b) = d$. We concatenate d to the final ranking model input vector.

To analyze the impact of fine-grained features on transfer language suitability, we experiment with an expanded representation, using an element-wise *and* operation to compare a and b: $a \wedge b = v$. We refer to v as the **full** Typology-Vector representation.

Feature Type	Description
Genetic Distance	Genealogical distance derived from language descent trees described in Glottolog.
Geographic Distance	Defined as the orthodromic distance divided by the antipodal distance between rough locations of source and target languages on the surface of the Earth.
Syntactic, *Phonological*, and *Inventory* Distances (**distance** Typology-Vector)	Computed as the cosine difference between corresponding URIEL (Littell et al., 2017) or Grambank (Skirgård et al., 2023a) feature vectors representing source and target languages.
Syntactic, *Phonological*, and *Inventory* Vectors (**full** Typology-Vector)	Computed as element-wise AND operation between corresponding URIEL (Littell et al., 2017) or Grambank (Skirgård et al., 2023a) feature vectors representing source and target languages.
Dataset-Dependent Features	Word overlap, transfer type-token ration, source type-token ration, type-token ratio distance

Table 2: All possible ranker features

Vector Type	Description
URIEL Syntactic	104
Grambank Syntactic	113
Phonological	28
Inventory	158

Table 3: Typological feature vector lengths

We concatenate v to ranker input.

3.3.2 URIEL vs. Grambank

Many typological analyses of crosslingual transfer rely on URIEL (CC BY-SA 4.0) feature vectors, which are heavily based on the World Atlas of Language Structures (CC BY 4.0) (Dryer and Haspelmath, 2013). WALS has incomplete genealogical coverage and over 80% missing data (Skirgård et al., 2023a). As such, we experiment with switching to Grambank (CC BY 4.0) (Skirgård et al., 2023a), which addresses some of WALS' shortcomings. We impute all undefined features in either database as follows.

URIEL. We use URIEL vectors that have been pre-imputed by Littell et al. (2017) using k-nearest-neighbors.[2]

Grambank. 24% of total feature values in Grambank 1.0.3 (across all languages in the database) are undefined. In order to produce fully defined feature vectors for our experiments, we first eliminate any features that are undefined for greater than 25% of languages and any languages that have greater than 25% missing data. After cropping, only 4.03% of values are missing. We impute the remaining values with the MissForest algorithm for nonparametric missing value imputation (Stekhoven and Bühlmann, 2012). We adapt our imputation procedure from Skirgård et al. (2023b).

[2]vectors available at https://github.com/antonisa/lang2vec

3.3.3 Dataset Features

We experiment with the inclusion and exclusion of dataset dependent features to assess the impact the training corpus might have on successful cross-lingual transfer. We control for training corpus size in our gold rankings, but we do not control for any other corpus features across source languages. Therefore, it is necessary to evaluate the relevance of features like type-token ratio and word overlap.

3.3.4 Evaluation

As in Lin et al. (2019), we evaluate our ranking models with leave-one-out cross-validation. For each cross-validation fold, we exclude one target language from our test set of n languages, and train our ranking model using gold transfer language rankings for each $n-1$ remaining languages. We then evaluate the model's performance on the held-out language. We evaluate our ranking models using Normalized Distributed Cumulative Gain (NCDG)(Järvelin and Kekäläinen, 2002).

Specifically, we use NCDG@p, a metric that considers the top-p elements, which is defined by:

$$NDCG@p = \frac{DCG@p}{IDCG@p},$$

where the Discounted Cumulative Gain (DCG) at position p is defined as

$$DCG@p = \sum_{i=1}^{p} \frac{2^{\gamma_i} - 1}{log_2(i+1)}.$$

γ_i is a relevance score corresponding to the language at position i of the predicted ranking that we are evaluating. For all $i \leq p$, $\gamma_i = p - i$, where p represents the number of ranked items we wish to assign relevance. We set $p = 5$, meaning that the true best transfer language has a relevance score of $\gamma = 5$. All languages below the top-5 are assigned

Syntactic Feature-Src		Dataset Features	Typology-Vector Representation	NDCG@5 *biLSTMs*	*XLM-R*	M-BERT
URIEL	a	✓	distance	**0.799**	0.755	0.654
	b	-	distance	0.385	0.643	0.625
	c	✓	full	0.776	**0.782**	0.680
	d	-	full	0.721	0.670	**0.689**
	Avg			0.670	0.713	0.662
Grambank	a	✓	distance	0.768	0.826	0.653
	b	-	distance	0.447	0.574	0.638
	c	✓	full	**0.788**	**0.827**	0.665
	d	-	full	0.721	0.707	**0.692**
	Avg			0.681	0.734	0.662
Avg *(std)*				0.676 *(0.153)*	0.723 *(0.085)*	0.662 *(0.023)*

Table 4: Average NDCG@5 for all model configurations trained on gold rankings. Every model configuration includes *genetic* and *geographic* features.

$\gamma = 0$. The Ideal Discounted Cumulative Gain (IDCG) is calculated the same as DCG except it is calculated over the gold-standard ranking. An NCDG@p of 1 indicates that the top-p predicted elements match the top-p gold elements exactly. We report the average NDCG@5 across all N leave-one-out models.

3.4 Analyzing Feature Importance

To compare the most relevant features for transfer in POS tagging across architectures, we use our most full featured ranking model, incorporating dataset-dependent features, *syntactic* features from Grambank, and **full** Typology-Vectors. We train three rankers, one for each architecture. During training, each feature is assigned an importance score based on the gain resulting from splits made on that feature. For a given split, we calculate gain as the reduction in squared error from the parent node to the child nodes, summed across all trees in the ranking model. We report average gain over all cross-validation folds and identify the top-5 most important features for each model.

4 Results

4.1 Dataset vs. Typological Features

In Table 4, we observe that regardless of *syntactic* vector source, models trained with **distance** Typology-Vector representations and *without* dataset features (setting **b**) perform relatively poorly. This suggests that coarse grained information from **distance** Typology-Vector representations may not be sufficient for choosing a transfer language. However, when we replace **distance** Typology-Vector representations with **full**, performance increases substantially. On average, NDCG@5 jumps by 0.148 between settings **b** and **d** over all 6 architecture/feature-source pairings. The performance gains from including dataset features are even more significant. On average, NDCG@5 jumps by 0.19 between settings **b** and **a**.

These findings suggest that both fine-grained typological features *and* dataset-dependent features support more accurate transfer language ranking. Both feature sources provide meaningful signals to the ranker, but setting **c** results in the best average ranker performance, suggesting that an integrated view of transfer language choice is most effective.

M-BERT stands out as a notable outlier, as setting **d** produces the highest-performing M-BERT rankers. It is unclear why excluding dataset features benefits transfer language ranking for M-BERT. However, it is noteworthy that M-BERT exhibits by far the lowest standard deviation in performance, suggesting its rankers are less sensitive to variations in feature configuration. We leave further analysis of this phenomenon to future work.

4.2 Grambank vs. URIEL

Rankers leveraging Grambank *syntactic* features outperform those trained with URIEL *syntactic* features in ranking biLSTMs and XLM-R on average, suggesting that the typological information captured by Grambank may be more informative for selecting a transfer language. However, M-BERT is yet again an outlier– on average, M-BERT rankers perform equivalently regardless of *syntactic* feature-source.

XLM-R		M-BERT		BiLSTM	
Feature	**Gain**	**Feature**	**Gain**	**Feature**	**Gain**
genetic	272.95	*genetic*	283.41	*word_overlap*	264.24
word_overlap	102.82	*word_overlap*	130.90	*transfer_ttr*	118.17
transfer_ttr	67.60	*transfer_ttr*	42.49	*genetic*	100.78
distance_ttr	25.74	*distance_ttr*	24.67	*distance_ttr*	12.66
GB093	11.96	*task_ttr*	10.06	*INV_VOW_10_MORE*	7.90
Standard Deviation	17.08		17.96		17.42

Table 5: Feature importance for top-5 features by model for ranker trained *with* dataset features and full Grambank vectors.

4.3 Feature Importance

We investigate feature importance within our most fully-featured ranking model, which incorporates dataset-dependent features, *syntactic* features from Grambank, and full Typology-Vectors. Though this is not always the highest performing setting, it enables us to elucidate the interplay between the dataset-dependent and typological features most clearly. We identify the top-5 most important features for each of our models in Table 5. Four out of five features are shared across architectures: genetic, word_overlap, transfer_ttr, and distance_ttr. Notably, these are primarily dataset-dependent features. This consistency in relative feature importance across models suggests that the features that determine a suitable transfer language choice may not be architecture-dependent. On the other hand, it is interesting that *genetic* is most important for XLM-R and M-BERT but not for biLSTMs. It is possible that the shared representation space built during multilingual pretraining already contains features like word-overlap making them less relevant for selecting a finetuning dataset.

Feature	Gain
XLM-R	
genetic	362.93
GB020	11.62
GB080	8.90
GB093	7.68
INV_OPEN_FRONT_UNROUNDED_VOWEL	7.48
Standard Deviation	20.93
M-BERT	
genetic	407.08
GB022	8.44
GB093	7.07
INV_PALATAL_LATERAL_APPROXIMANT	6.42
GB020	6.39
GB114	5.32
Standard Deviation	23.46
biLSTM	
genetic	342.61
INV_OPEN_MID_CENTRAL_UNROUNDED_VOWEL	21.75
GB172	19.12
INV_MID_CENTRAL_UNROUNDED_VOWEL	17.66
INV_LABIODENTAL_NASAL	12.22
Standard Deviation	19.83

Table 6: Feature importance for rankers Trained with full Grambank vectors and *without* dataset features

5 Supplementary Analyses

5.1 Excluding Dataset Features

For the sake of comparison, we also analyze the top-5 features for a ranking model trained with *syntactic* features from Grambank and **full** Typology-Vectors *without* dataset-dependent features. These rankers do not consistently underperform their dataset-dependent counterparts, raising the question of which dataset-independent features carry the most weight.

Looking at Table 6, we find that the *genetic* feature yields substantially more gain than any other feature. It is possible that *genetic* scores so highly because it serves as a proxy for many of the other features. This intuition is supported by Skirgård et al. (2023a), who show that phylogenetic relationships explain a majority of the variance in all but a few Grambank features.

Other than *genetic*, M-BERT and XLM-R seem to share more top features with each other than with biLSTMs– GB093 and GB020 both ranking highly. However, this does not necessarily indicate a meaningful difference between the architectures. Excluding *genetic*, gain is relatively low and consistent across features. This finding suggests that it may not be possible to identify especially salient fine-grained features, because relevance is distributed over the full feature set. In a sense, the

Src/Tgt	XLM-R Rank	BiLSTM Rank	Diff.	Src/Tgt	XLM-R Rank	BiLSTM Rank	Diff.
eus/cat	354	22	332	ukr/pol	10	339	329
kor/cat	360	29	331	ces/pol	8	302	294
kor/glg	339	13	326	rus/pol	32	324	292
kor/fra	359	54	305	dan/fin	66	345	279
pol/cat	323	24	299	rus/lav	26	304	278
eus/glg	301	12	289	lav/pol	86	337	251
eus/fra	334	46	288	eng/fin	96	347	251
pol/fra	331	49	282	ces/rus	15	258	243
tur/cat	305	27	278	ukr/lav	56	297	241
pol/glg	282	7	275	fra/fin	108	348	240

Table 7: Greatest difference in relative performance differences between XLM-R and biLSTM. Better biLSTM performance (left) vs. better XLM-R performance (right).

XLM-R		biLSTM	
Language Family Pair	**Count**	**Language Family Pair**	**Count**
Indo-European/Indo-European	125	Basque/Indo-European	13
Indo-European/Uralic	14	Koreanic/Indo-European	14
Austronesian/Indo-European	5	Indo-European/Indo-European	71
Basque/Uralic	1	Turkic/Indo-European	12
Turkic/Uralic	1	Koreanic/Uralic	1
Austronesian/Uralic	1	Koreanic/Austronesian	1
Indo-European/Turkic	14	Indo-European/Uralic	14
Indo-European/Basque	6	Basque/Uralic	1
Turkic/Indo-European	3	Indo-European/Koreanic	14
Basque/Indo-European	2	Indo-European/Austronesian	14
Koreanic/Uralic	1	Turkic/Austronesian	1
Austronesian/Turkic	1	Turkic/Koreanic	1
Basque/Turkic	1	Basque/Austronesian	1
Koreanic/Indo-European	1	Austronesian/Uralic	1
Koreanic/Turkic	1	Austronesian/Indo-European	10
		Austronesian/Koreanic	1
		Basque/Koreanic	1
		Koreanic/Basque	1
		Turkic/Basque	1
		Indo-European/Basque	8
		Austronesian/Basque	1
		Turkic/Uralic	1

Table 8: Distribution of language family pairs that ranked relatively higher in XLM-R performance rankings (left) vs. those that ranked relatively higher in biLSTM performance rankings (right)

whole may be greater than the sum of its parts.

5.2 Ranking Analysis: BiLSTMs vs. XLM-R

To contextualize our findings, we conducted a comparative analysis of gold transfer language rankings for biLSTMs and XLM-R. For each architecture, we generated an ordered list of source-target pairs based on performance. We then compared rank differences across architectures for each pair. Table 7 highlights the top-10 language pairs with the most divergent rankings.

XLM-R performs best on language pairs within the same family or subfamily, such as Slavic pairs, likely due to better typological alignment. Meanwhile, biLSTMs excel on pairs with weaker genetic ties. To further explore these trends, we counted occurrences of language family pairs where either XLM-R or biLSTM had a relative ranking advantage in Table 8.

We see that XLM-R comparatively excels on

Indo-European/Indo-European pairs, while biLSTMs perform relatively better on unrelated or weakly related pairs. These results align with expectations: XLM-R's zero-shot approach benefits from well-matched transfer pairs, whereas biLSTMs can make effective use of small amounts of target language training data.

6 Conclusion

We find that features such as word overlap, type-token ratio, and genealogical distance are consistently influential in transfer language selection regardless of model architecture; their importance may be somewhat model-agnostic.

Our findings also highlight the crucial role of dataset-dependent features in ranking transfer languages for cross-lingual transfer. Rankers trained with these features outperform those relying solely on coarse-grained typological features.

At the same time, while coarse-grained typological features alone are insufficient, rankers trained with *fine-grained* typological features achieve impressive results even without dataset-dependent features. The most successful ranking performance comes from combining both dataset-dependent and fine-grained typological features, underscoring the value of a comprehensive approach to transfer language selection.

Crucially, these insights enable us to better support languages that are not well-represented in MLM pretraining. By identifying effective transfer languages with interpretable features, we can improve cross-lingual transfer for lower-resource languages, expanding the reach of NLP beyond those languages that benefit from large-scale pretraining.

Limitations

Since the scope of this paper is limited to crosslingual transfer for POS tagging, it would be interesting to explore whether our results are extensible to other tasks. We are also limited in that we consider a set of just 20 target languages, 13 of which are Indo-European. This paper represents a step forward in explaining the dynamics at play in successful crosslingual transfer, but more work is necessary to determine whether our findings generalize across diverse linguistic contexts.

References

Alexis Conneau, Kartikay Khandelwal, Naman Goyal, Vishrav Chaudhary, Guillaume Wenzek, Francisco Guzmán, Edouard Grave, Myle Ott, Luke Zettlemoyer, and Veselin Stoyanov. 2020. Unsupervised cross-lingual representation learning at scale. In *Proceedings of the 58th Annual Meeting of the Association for Computational Linguistics*, pages 8440–8451, Online. Association for Computational Linguistics.

Marie-Catherine de Marneffe, Christopher D. Manning, Joakim Nivre, and Daniel Zeman. 2021. Universal dependencies. *Computational Linguistics*, 47(2):255–308.

Wietse de Vries, Martijn Wieling, and Malvina Nissim. 2022. Make the best of cross-lingual transfer: Evidence from POS tagging with over 100 languages. In *Proceedings of the 60th Annual Meeting of the Association for Computational Linguistics (Volume 1: Long Papers)*, pages 7676–7685, Dublin, Ireland. Association for Computational Linguistics.

Jacob Devlin, Ming-Wei Chang, Kenton Lee, and Kristina Toutanova. 2019. BERT: Pre-training of deep bidirectional transformers for language understanding. In *Proceedings of the 2019 Conference of the North American Chapter of the Association for Computational Linguistics: Human Language Technologies, Volume 1 (Long and Short Papers)*, pages 4171–4186, Minneapolis, Minnesota. Association for Computational Linguistics.

Blazej Dolicki and Gerasimos Spanakis. 2021. Analysing the impact of linguistic features on cross-lingual transfer. *CoRR*, abs/2105.05975.

Matthew S. Dryer and Martin Haspelmath, editors. 2013. *WALS Online (v2020.3)*. Zenodo.

Juuso Eronen, Michal Ptaszynski, and Fumito Masui. 2023. Zero-shot cross-lingual transfer language selection using linguistic similarity. *Information Processing & Management*, 60(3):103250.

Juuso Eronen, Michal Ptaszynski, Fumito Masui, Masaki Arata, Gniewosz Leliwa, and Michal Wroczynski. 2022. Transfer language selection for zero-shot cross-lingual abusive language detection. *Information Processing & Management*, 59(4):102981.

Kalervo Järvelin and Jaana Kekäläinen. 2002. Cumulated gain-based evaluation of ir techniques. *ACM Trans. Inf. Syst.*, 20(4):422–446.

Karthikeyan K, Zihan Wang, Stephen Mayhew, and Dan Roth. 2020. Cross-lingual ability of multilingual bert: An empirical study. In *International Conference on Learning Representations*.

Guolin Ke, Qi Meng, Thomas Finley, Taifeng Wang, Wei Chen, Weidong Ma, Qiwei Ye, and Tie-Yan Liu.

2017. Lightgbm: A highly efficient gradient boosting decision tree. In *Neural Information Processing Systems*.

Aditya Armaan Khan, Mason Stephen Shipton, David Anugraha, Kaiyao Duan, Phuong H. Hoang, Eric Khiu, A. Seza Doğruöz, and Annie Lee. 2025. URIEL+: Enhancing linguistic inclusion and usability in a typological and multilingual knowledge base. In *Proceedings of the 31st International Conference on Computational Linguistics*, pages 6937–6952, Abu Dhabi, UAE. Association for Computational Linguistics.

Anne Lauscher, Vinit Ravishankar, Ivan Vulić, and Goran Glavaš. 2020. From zero to hero: On the limitations of zero-shot language transfer with multilingual transformers. In *Proceedings of the 2020 Conference on Empirical Methods in Natural Language Processing (EMNLP)*, page 4483–4499, Online. Association for Computational Linguistics.

Jimson Layacan, Isaiah Edri W. Flores, Katrina Tan, Ma. Regina E. Estuar, Jann Montalan, and Marlene M. De Leon. 2024. Zero-shot cross-lingual POS tagging for Filipino. In *Proceedings of the 3rd Workshop on NLP Applications to Field Linguistics (Field Matters 2024)*, pages 69–77, Bangkok, Thailand. Association for Computational Linguistics.

Yu-Hsiang Lin, Chian-Yu Chen, Jean Lee, Zirui Li, Yuyan Zhang, Mengzhou Xia, Shruti Rijhwani, Junxian He, Zhisong Zhang, Xuezhe Ma, Antonios Anastasopoulos, Patrick Littell, and Graham Neubig. 2019. Choosing transfer languages for cross-lingual learning. In *Proceedings of the 57th Annual Meeting of the Association for Computational Linguistics*, pages 3125–3135, Florence, Italy. Association for Computational Linguistics.

Patrick Littell, David R. Mortensen, Ke Lin, Katherine Kairis, Carlisle Turner, and Lori Levin. 2017. URIEL and lang2vec: Representing languages as typological, geographical, and phylogenetic vectors. In *Proceedings of the 15th Conference of the European Chapter of the Association for Computational Linguistics: Volume 2, Short Papers*, pages 8–14, Valencia, Spain. Association for Computational Linguistics.

Telmo Pires, Eva Schlinger, and Dan Garrette. 2019. How multilingual is multilingual BERT? In *Proceedings of the 57th Annual Meeting of the Association for Computational Linguistics*, pages 4996–5001, Florence, Italy. Association for Computational Linguistics.

Peng Qi, Yuhao Zhang, Yuhui Zhang, Jason Bolton, and Christopher D. Manning. 2020. Stanza: A python natural language processing toolkit for many human languages. In *Proceedings of the 58th Annual Meeting of the Association for Computational Linguistics: System Demonstrations*, pages 101–108, Online. Association for Computational Linguistics.

Hedvig Skirgård, Hannah J. Haynie, Damián E. Blasi, Harald Hammarström, Jeremy Collins, Jay J. Latarche, Jakob Lesage, Tobias Weber, Alena Witzlack-Makarevich, Sam Passmore, Angela Chira, Luke Maurits, Russell Dinnage, Michael Dunn, Ger Reesink, Ruth Singer, Claire Bowern, Patience Epps, Jane Hill, Outi Vesakoski, Martine Robbeets, Noor Karolin Abbas, Daniel Auer, Nancy A. Bakker, Giulia Barbos, Robert D. Borges, Swintha Danielsen, Luise Dorenbusch, Ella Dorn, John Elliott, Giada Falcone, Jana Fischer, Yustinus Ghanggo Ate, Hannah Gibson, Hans-Philipp Göbel, Jemima A. Goodall, Victoria Gruner, Andrew Harvey, Rebekah Hayes, Leonard Heer, Roberto E. Herrera Miranda, Nataliia Hübler, Biu Huntington-Rainey, Jessica K. Ivani, Marilen Johns, Erika Just, Eri Kashima, Carolina Kipf, Janina V. Klingenberg, Nikita König, Aikaterina Koti, Richard G. A. Kowalik, Olga Krasnoukhova, Nora L. M. Lindvall, Mandy Lorenzen, Hannah Lutzenberger, Tânia R. A. Martins, Celia Mata German, Suzanne van der Meer, Jaime Montoya Samamé, Michael Müller, Saliha Muradoglu, Kelsey Neely, Johanna Nickel, Miina Norvik, Cheryl Akinyi Oluoch, Jesse Peacock, India O. C. Pearey, Naomi Peck, Stephanie Petit, Sören Pieper, Mariana Poblete, Daniel Prestipino, Linda Raabe, Amna Raja, Janis Reimringer, Sydney C. Rey, Julia Rizaew, Eloisa Ruppert, Kim K. Salmon, Jill Sammet, Rhiannon Schembri, Lars Schlabbach, Frederick W. P. Schmidt, Amalia Skilton, Wikaliler Daniel Smith, Hilário de Sousa, Kristin Sverredal, Daniel Valle, Javier Vera, Judith Voß, Tim Witte, Henry Wu, Stephanie Yam, Jingting Ye, Maisie Yong, Tessa Yuditha, Roberto Zariquiey, Robert Forkel, Nicholas Evans, Stephen C. Levinson, Martin Haspelmath, Simon J. Greenhill, Quentin D. Atkinson, and Russell D. Gray. 2023a. Grambank reveals the importance of genealogical constraints on linguistic diversity and highlights the impact of language loss. *Science Advances*, 9(16):eadg6175.

Hedvig Skirgård, Hannah J. Haynie, Harald Hammarström, Damián E. Blasi, Jeremy Collins, Jay Latarche, Jakob Lesage, Tobias Weber, Alena Witzlack-Makarevich, Michael Dunn, Ger Reesink, Ruth Singer, Claire Bowern, Patience Epps, Jane Hill, Outi Vesakoski, Noor Karolin Abbas, Sunny Ananth, Daniel Auer, Nancy A. Bakker, Giulia Barbos, Anina Bolls, Robert D. Borges, Mitchell Browen, Lennart Chevallier, Swintha Danielsen, Sinoël Dohlen, Luise Dorenbusch, Ella Dorn, Marie Duhamel, Farah El Haj Ali, John Elliott, Giada Falcone, Anna-Maria Fehn, Jana Fischer, Yustinus Ghanggo Ate, Hannah Gibson, Hans-Philipp Göbel, Jemima A. Goodall, Victoria Gruner, Andrew Harvey, Rebekah Hayes, Leonard Heer, Roberto E. Herrera Miranda, Nataliia Hübler, Biu H. Huntington-Rainey, Guglielmo Inglese, Jessica K. Ivani, Marilen Johns, Erika Just, Ivan Kapitonov, Eri Kashima, Carolina Kipf, Janina V. Klingenberg, Nikita König, Aikaterina Koti, Richard G. A. Kowalik, Olga Krasnoukhova, Kate Lynn Lindsey, Nora L. M. Lindvall, Mandy Lorenzen, Hannah Lutzenberger, Alexandra Marley, Tânia R. A. Martins, Celia Mata German, Suzanne van der Meer, Jaime Montoya, Michael Müller, Saliha Muradoğlu, HunterGatherer, David Nash, Kelsey

Neely, Johanna Nickel, Miina Norvik, Bruno Olsson, Cheryl Akinyi Oluoch, David Osgarby, Jesse Peacock, India O.C. Pearey, Naomi Peck, Jana Peter, Stephanie Petit, Sören Pieper, Mariana Poblete, Daniel Prestipino, Linda Raabe, Amna Raja, Janis Reimringer, Sydney C. Rey, Julia Rizaew, Eloisa Ruppert, Kim K. Salmon, Jill Sammet, Rhiannon Schembri, Lars Schlabbach, Frederick W. P. Schmidt, Dineke Schokkin, Jeff Siegel, Amalia Skilton, Hilário de Sousa, Kristin Sverredal, Daniel Valle, Javier Vera, Judith Voß, Daniel Wikalier Smith, Tim Witte, Henry Wu, Stephanie Yam, Jingting Ye, Maisie Yong, Tessa Yuditha, Roberto Zariquiey, Robert Forkel, Nicholas Evans, Stephen C. Levinson, Martin Haspelmath, Simon J. Greenhill, Quentin D. Atkinson, and Russell D. Gray. 2023b. Grambank v1.0. Dataset.

Daniel J. Stekhoven and Peter Bühlmann. 2012. Missforest—non-parametric missing value imputation for mixed-type data. *Bioinformatics*, 28(1):112–118.

Shijie Wu and Mark Dredze. 2019. Beto, bentz, becas: The surprising cross-lingual effectiveness of BERT. In *Proceedings of the 2019 Conference on Empirical Methods in Natural Language Processing and the 9th International Joint Conference on Natural Language Processing (EMNLP-IJCNLP)*, pages 833–844, Hong Kong, China. Association for Computational Linguistics.

Serving the Underserved: Leveraging BARTBahnar Language Model for Bahnaric-Vietnamese Translation

Long S. T. Nguyen, Tran T. B. Le, Huong P. N. Nguyen, Quynh T. N. Vo, Phong H. N. Nguyen, Tho T. Quan*

URA Research Group, Ho Chi Minh City University of Technology, VNU-HCM

***Correspondence:** qttho@hcmut.edu.vn

Abstract

The Bahnar people, one of Vietnam's ethnic minorities, represent an underserved community with limited access to modern technologies. Developing an effective Bahnaric-Vietnamese translation system is essential for fostering linguistic exchange, preserving cultural heritage, and empowering local communities by bridging communication barriers. With advancements in Artificial Intelligence (AI), Neural Machine Translation (NMT) has achieved remarkable success across various language pairs. However, the low-resource nature of Bahnaric, characterized by data scarcity, vocabulary constraints, and the lack of parallel corpora, poses significant challenges to building an accurate and efficient translation system. To address these challenges, we propose a novel hybrid architecture for Bahnaric-Vietnamese translation, with BARTBahnar as its core language model. BARTBahnar is developed by continually training a pre-trained Vietnamese model, BARTPho, on augmented monolingual Bahnaric data, followed by fine-tuning on bilingual datasets. This transfer learning approach reduces training costs while effectively capturing linguistic similarities between the two languages. Additionally, we implement advanced data augmentation techniques to enrich and diversify training data, further enhancing BARTBahnar's robustness and translation accuracy. Beyond leveraging the language model, our hybrid system integrates rule-based and statistical methods to improve translation quality. Experimental results show substantial improvements on bilingual Bahnaric-Vietnamese datasets, validating the effectiveness of our approach for low-resource translation. To support further research, we open-source our code and related materials at `https://github.com/ura-hcmut/BARTBahnar`.

1 Introduction

The Bahnar people, one of Vietnam's 54 ethnic minorities, account for approximately 0.3% of the country's population. As one of the larger minority groups, they possess a rich cultural heritage reflected in unique traditions, festivals, clothing, cuisine, and, most notably, their distinct Bahnaric languages (Bui et al., 2024). This linguistic diversity is a cornerstone of their identity, necessitating dedicated efforts for preservation and promotion. Recognizing this, the Vietnamese government has implemented various policies to safeguard the cultural and linguistic heritage of ethnic minorities, including the Bahnar people. Language preservation plays a pivotal role in maintaining the identity of ethnic groups worldwide. Facilitating linguistic interaction between the Bahnaric and Vietnamese-speaking communities is essential for fostering cultural exchange, mutual understanding, and the preservation of minority identities. Thus, developing an efficient Bahnaric-Vietnamese machine translation system would significantly enhance communication, granting Vietnamese speakers access to the wealth of Bahnaric cultural texts while enabling deeper cross-cultural interactions.

The rapid advancements in Artificial Intelligence, particularly in *Neural Machine Translation* (NMT), have significantly improved translation quality across various language pairs (Qin, 2022). The introduction of the *Transformer* architecture (Vaswani et al., 2017) and subsequent developments in *Large Language Models* (LLMs) have revolutionized *Natural Language Processing* (NLP) applications, including NMT (Wang et al., 2024). Transformer-based models can be broadly categorized into three primary architectures, namely encoder-only, decoder-only, and encoder-decoder. The *encoder-only* type is primarily designed for powerful understanding tasks, making it unsuitable for non-trivial applications such as NMT. Meanwhile, the *decoder-only* architecture excels in text generation but requires large-scale training datasets and lacks explicit encoder support for source language comprehension, making it sub-

Proceedings of the 1st Workshop on Language Models for Underserved Communities (LM4UC 2025), pages 32–41
May 4, 2025

optimal for NMT (Qorib et al., 2024). Additionally, decoder-only models rely on autoregressive generation, which demands substantial computational resources and extensive parallel corpora—both of which are severely lacking for low-resource languages. In contrast, the *encoder-decoder* architecture is inherently suited for NMT, as the encoder effectively captures the semantic and syntactic structure of the source language, while the decoder generates the corresponding translation. However, despite these advantages, building an encoder-decoder-based NMT system for an extremely low-resource language such as Bahnaric remains highly challenging due to severe data scarcity and vocabulary limitations (Ngo et al., 2019). To the best of our knowledge, no prior research has been conducted on Bahnaric-Vietnamese translation.

Given these challenges, it is crucial to examine the linguistic characteristics of Bahnaric and its relationship to Vietnamese. Both languages belong to the *Austroasiatic* family and are considered low-resource in the linguistic landscape (Alves, 2006). Moreover, as both languages coexist within the same country and share a common historical and cultural background, they exhibit notable syntactic similarities and structural overlaps. Additionally, Bahnaric speakers frequently incorporate Vietnamese loanwords, particularly in cases where native Bahnaric vocabulary lacks equivalents (Bui et al., 2024). These linguistic overlaps serve as critical insights for designing an effective translation system.

To leverage these shared linguistic features, we adopt *BARTPho* (Tran et al., 2022), a pre-trained encoder-decoder language model built upon the *Bidirectional and Auto-Regressive Transformers* (BART) (Lewis et al., 2020) architecture, trained on large-scale Vietnamese corpora. This model effectively captures the linguistic characteristics of Vietnamese, making it a strong foundation for adaptation to Bahnaric. To enhance its ability to model the syntactic and lexical properties of Bahnaric, we continually train BARTPho on augmented monolingual Bahnaric data. The model is then fine-tuned on an augmented bilingual Bahnaric-Vietnamese dataset, producing an optimized translation system, which we refer to as *BARTBahnar*. To address the issue of data scarcity in Bahnaric, we implement various *Data Augmentation* (DA) techniques (Li et al., 2022) specifically designed for NMT. These techniques enrich and diversify the training data, improving translation performance. Furthermore, to fully exploit the unique linguistic characteristics of Bahnaric, we propose a novel hybrid approach that integrates BARTBahnar with rule-based and statistical methods. This hybrid strategy enhances translation reliability, particularly in handling loanwords and resolving cases where direct model-generated translations may be inaccurate, ultimately improving translation quality and supporting linguistic preservation.

Our key contributions are summarized as follows.

- We introduced BARTBahnar, an encoder-decoder language model fine-tuned for Bahnaric-Vietnamese translation, leveraging *transfer learning* from BARTPho and various DA techniques. This approach significantly reduces training costs while effectively utilizing linguistic similarities between the two languages to enhance translation performance.
- We designed a robust hybrid system that integrates BARTBahnar with rule-based and statistical methods, effectively handling loanwords and improving translation accuracy.
- We achieved promising translation results on bilingual Bahnaric-Vietnamese datasets, demonstrating the effectiveness of our approach in preserving linguistic heritage and fostering cultural exchange within underserved communities.

2 Related Works

2.1 NMT for Low-resource Languages

NMT has emerged as the dominant paradigm in machine translation, leveraging deep learning models to achieve state-of-the-art performance. However, its reliance on large-scale parallel corpora poses significant challenges for low-resource languages. Existing works addressing these limitations can be broadly categorized into three primary directions: utilizing monolingual data, auxiliary languages, and multi-modal data (Wang et al., 2021).

Monolingual Data Monolingual data, being more abundant and easier to collect than parallel corpora, serves as a critical resource for NMT in low-resource scenarios. Key methodologies include: *(1) Back and Forward Translation*, where pseudo-parallel data is generated by translating monolingual sentences in reverse or the same direction (Sennrich et al., 2016), *(2) Joint Training*, which leverages monolingual data from both source and target languages simultaneously (He et al., 2016), *(3) Unsupervised NMT*, relying on bilingual alignment and iterative back translation (Lample et al., 2018), and *(4) Language Model Pre-training*, where self-supervised training on monolingual data, as demonstrated by models like (Hwang and Jeong, 2023), significantly boosts translation performance. Although these methods effectively exploit monolingual corpora, they heavily depend on high-quality data and often struggle with linguistically distant language pairs, limiting their generalizability.

Auxiliary Languages Closely related languages can facilitate knowledge transfer in low-resource scenarios. Common strategies include: *(1) Multilingual Training*, which shares parameters across multiple language pairs (Johnson et al., 2017), *(2) Transfer Learning*, where models pre-trained on high-resource languages are fine-tuned for low-resource settings (Hujon et al., 2023), and *(3) Pivot Translation*, using an intermediate language to create pseudo-parallel corpora or to combine source-pivot and pivot-target models (Cheng et al., 2017). While these methods leverage linguistic similarities effectively, their success is sensitive to the choice of auxiliary languages, data balancing, and error propagation in pivot-based setups. Moreover, multilingual training can be computationally demanding, posing challenges in resource-constrained contexts.

Multi-modal Data Multi-modal data, such as images and speech, expands the capabilities of NMT by integrating non-textual information. Techniques include: *(1) Image Data*, where image captions generate pseudo-parallel corpora or image features are incorporated into NMT models (Chen et al., 2019), and *(2) Speech-Text Pairs*, supporting translation for languages without written scripts (Zhang et al., 2021). While multi-modal approaches provide valuable support for languages with limited textual resources, they rely on high-quality aligned datasets and face inherent complexity in fusing diverse modalities.

Despite these advancements, most approaches still require large, high-quality datasets, whether monolingual or bilingual, which are unavailable for extremely low-resource languages like Bahnaric. This highlights the critical role of DA techniques in improving NMT performance for low-resource languages.

2.2 Data Augmentation in NMT

To alleviate data scarcity in low-resource NMT, extensive research has focused on DA, which can be grouped into three categories, namely paraphrasing-based methods, noising-based methods, and sampling-based methods (Li et al., 2022).

Paraphrasing-based Methods These methods generate augmented data by altering the original text at lexical, phrase, or sentence levels. For instance, tools like WordNet (Miller, 1994) replace words with synonyms, while *Easy Data Augmentation* (EDA) (Wei and Zou, 2019) offers simple substitution-based strategies. More advanced techniques utilize word embeddings (Wang and Yang, 2015) for enhanced semantic consistency. Although these approaches increase data diversity, they often struggle with preserving sentence meaning, especially in languages with limited lexical resources.

Noising-based Methods These approaches introduce random changes to the original data without maintaining semantic fidelity. Word swapping (Wei and Zou, 2019), sentence-level swapping (Yan et al., 2019), and insertion/deletion (Wei and Zou, 2019) are common examples. While easy to implement, these methods risk disrupting sentence coherence and may be unsuitable for languages with complex syntactic structures.

Sampling-based Methods These methods typically require task-specific knowledge or annotations, such as altering grammatical structures (e.g., converting active to passive voice) (Min et al., 2020) or constructing pseudo-parallel sentences (Zhang et al., 2020). Although effective in generating richer training data, they demand substantial linguistic resources, which are rarely available for extreme low-resource languages.

While DA can significantly boost translation performance, its efficacy for Bahnaric, where grammatical and semantic resources are scarce, remains unknown. Grammar-based approaches can be particularly challenging and may reduce translation accuracy if applied without a deep understanding of the language's structure.

Another standout DA technique is back-translation, which generates entirely new sentences by translating target sentences back into the source language, thus enriching data diversity. For example, (Fabbri et al., 2021) use English-French models to augment French data before training

French-English NMT. Moreover, with the rise of LLMs, (Mai and Luong, 2023) apply GPT-3.5 to augment Vietnamese data, achieving notable improvements in NLP tasks. Nevertheless, deploying back-translation or LLM-based methods for languages like Bahnaric remains challenging due to the lack of pre-trained models and high-quality parallel corpora.

3 Proposed Hybrid Architecture for Bahnaric-Vietnamese NMT

3.1 Overall Pipeline

We propose a comprehensive hybrid system for Bahnaric-Vietnamese translation, consisting of five main phases: Loanword Detection, Word Segmentation, Lexical Mapping, BARTBahnar Translation, and Post-Processing, as illustrated in Figure 1.

The pipeline begins with *Loanword Detection*, which identifies and extracts shared loanwords that appear in both Bahnaric and Vietnamese. These words do not require translation and are excluded from further processing. The remaining words are passed to the *Word Segmentation* phase, where Bahnaric sentences are segmented into meaningful phrases using statistical methods. The segmented phrases are then mapped to their Vietnamese equivalents in the *Lexical Mapping* phase via a bilingual dictionary. Words and phrases that cannot be mapped directly are handled by *BARTBahnar*, which generates Vietnamese translations for the remaining content. Finally, the translated output undergoes *Post-Processing*, ensuring proper sentence structure, punctuation, and grammatical refinements to enhance fluency and accuracy.

3.1.1 Loanword Detection

Loanword detection plays a crucial role in improving translation efficiency by identifying words that are shared between Bahnaric and Vietnamese. This module employs rule-based methods to filter out punctuation marks, special symbols, and numeric characters. Additionally, we utilize a *Named Entity Recognition* (NER) model from a well-established open-source Vietnamese NLP toolkit to detect proper nouns, such as place names and personal names. The identified loanwords are excluded from further translation and directly transferred to the output.

3.1.2 Word Segmentation

As Bahnaric lacks explicit word boundaries, statistical segmentation is necessary to split sentences into meaningful phrases. To construct a phrase dictionary from our monolingual Bahnaric corpus, we employ *Pointwise Mutual Information* (PMI) (Roussinov et al., 2007), a statistical measure that quantifies the strength of association between words. Given an n-gram $(x_1, x_2, .., x_n)$ and $\mathcal{X}^n$ as the set of all possible n-grams extracted from the corpus, the PMI score is computed as shown in Equation 1.

$$\text{PMI}(x_1, x_2, .., x_n) = \log_2 \left(\frac{P(x_1, x_2, .., x_n)}{\prod_{i=1}^{n} P(x_i)} \right), \quad (1)$$

where

$$P(x_1, x_2, .., x_n) = \frac{\text{count}(x_1, x_2, .., x_n)}{\sum_{(x_1, x_2, .., x_n) \in \mathcal{X}^n} \text{count}(x_1, x_2, .., x_n)},$$

$$P(x_i) = \frac{\text{count}(x_i)}{\sum_{x_i \in \mathcal{X}^1} \text{count}(x_i)}.$$

A higher PMI value indicates a stronger association between words, suggesting that they are more likely to form a valid phrase. An n-gram is considered a valid phrase if it satisfies both a minimum frequency threshold and a minimum PMI threshold, as defined in Equation 2 and Equation 3.

$$\text{count}(x_1, x_2, .., x_n) \geqslant \text{min\_freq}, \quad (2)$$

$$\text{PMI}(x_1, x_2, .., x_n) \geqslant \text{min\_pmi}. \quad (3)$$

All valid n-grams are stored in the phrase dictionary. The Bahnaric input is then segmented into phrase units based on this dictionary, facilitating accurate lexical mapping and translation.

3.1.3 Lexical Mapping

This phase employs a bilingual Bahnaric-Vietnamese dictionary to map commonly used words and phrases to their corresponding Vietnamese translations. To efficiently retrieve the most relevant Vietnamese equivalents, we index the dictionary using *Solr* (Tahiliani and Bansal, 2018), an open-source search engine optimized for fast lookup operations. Segments that can be directly mapped are substituted with their Vietnamese counterparts, while unmapped segments are passed to the next translation phase using BARTBahnar.

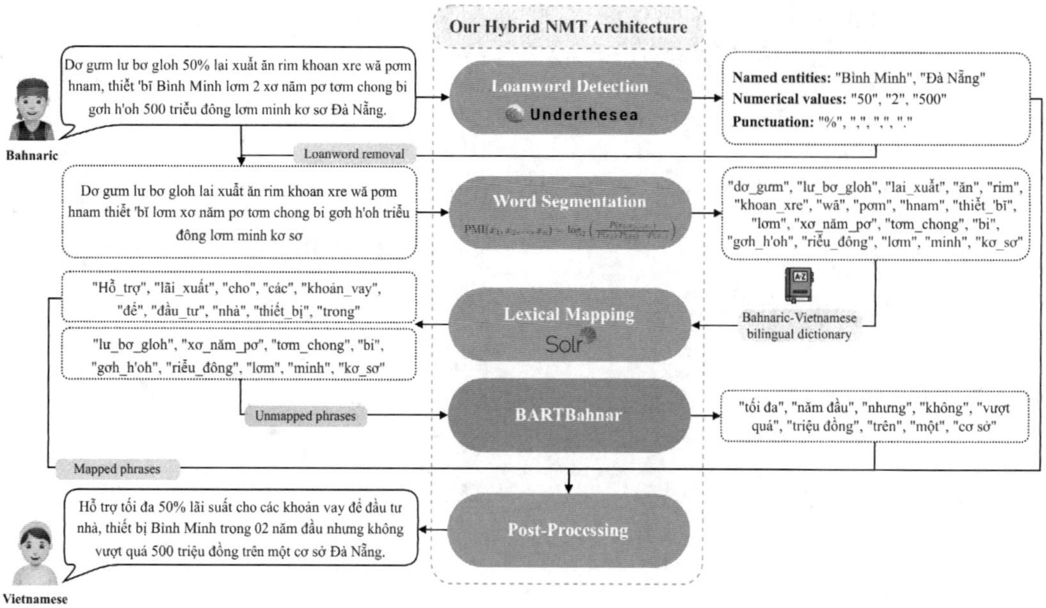

Figure 1: Illustration of our hybrid NMT architecture, integrating BARTBahnar with rule-based and statistical components. The figure outlines the step-by-step translation process from Bahnaric to Vietnamese. For reference, the English equivalent of the original Bahnaric sentence is *"Support up to 50% interest rate for loans to invest in housing and Binh Minh equipment for the first two years, but not exceeding 500 million VND per facility in Da Nang."*.

3.1.4 BARTBahnar Translation

Unmapped segments that lack direct dictionary translations are processed by *BARTBahnar*, our encoder-decoder language model fine-tuned for Bahnaric-Vietnamese translation. The details of BARTBahnar are elaborated in Section 3.2.

3.1.5 Post-Processing

A critical challenge in *Lexical Mapping* is ambiguity, where multiple Vietnamese candidates may correspond to a single Bahnaric phrase. To resolve this, we implement a scoring mechanism that selects the most contextually appropriate translation, as formulated in Equation 4.

$$v_c = \underset{v_c \in \{v_{c_1}, v_{c_2}, \dots, v_{c_k}\}}{\operatorname{argmax}} \operatorname{Score}(y_{\text{partial}}, v_c), \tag{4}$$

where v_c is the chosen translation candidate, y_{partial} represents the current state of the translated sentence, and $\operatorname{Score}(y_{\text{partial}}, v_c)$ is computed using a pre-trained language model to ensure fluency and semantic coherence.

After resolving ambiguities, the post-processing module further standardizes punctuation, capitalization, and word order, producing the final Vietnamese translation and completing the pipeline.

3.2 Our BARTBahnar Language Model

We propose a training strategy to effectively adapt a pre-trained language model for low-resource translation, with a specific focus on Bahnaric-Vietnamese. Our approach builds upon *BART*, a sequence-to-sequence model trained as a denoising autoencoder (Lewis et al., 2020), which enhances its ability to reconstruct text under noisy conditions. The model employs a *Bidirectional Encoder* for richer contextual understanding and an *Autoregressive Decoder* for coherent text generation. During training, a random subset of tokens is masked, and the model must autoregressively recover the original sequence, as illustrated in Figure 2.

Our training strategy comprises three main phases: *(1) Pre-training on monolingual Vietnamese data* to capture Vietnamese linguistic features, *(2) Continual pre-training on monolingual Bahnaric data* to adapt the model to Bahnaric text, and *(3) Fine-tuning on bilingual Bahnaric-Vietnamese datasets* for the translation task.

3.2.1 Pre-training on Vietnamese Language

To leverage prior knowledge from a closely related language, we utilize *BARTPho*, a BART model pre-trained on 145 million word-segmented Viet-

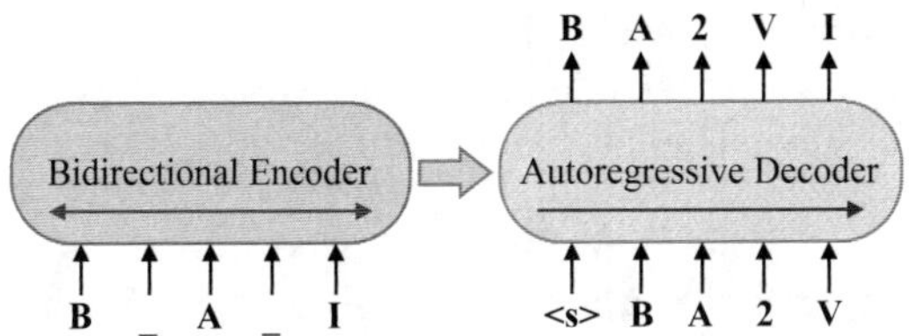

Figure 2: The architecture of BART and its training process as an autoregressive masked language model.

namese sentences. During this stage, two types of noise are introduced, namely *random token masking* and *sentence shuffling*, to enhance the model's ability to handle diverse syntactic structures. Having already learned fundamental properties of Vietnamese grammar and syntax, BARTPho provides a robust foundation for further adaptation to Bahnaric.

3.2.2 Continual Pre-training on Bahnaric Language

We further adapt BARTPho to Bahnaric by training it on a monolingual Bahnaric corpus using an autoregressive *Masked Language Modeling* (MLM) objective, similar to the original pre-training approach. Since Bahnaric is an extremely low-resource language, constructing a high-quality dataset poses a significant challenge.

To address this, we conducted extensive field surveys in Bahnar-speaking regions across Vietnam to gather rare but valuable linguistic materials. Our data sources include: *(1) Direct interviews* with native Bahnar speakers for documenting grammar and vocabulary, *(2) Printed texts* such as religious books, newspapers, song lyrics, and *(3) Local news* bulletins and historical documents. After digitizing and cleaning these materials, we employed a team of annotators to normalize the content, creating a high-quality bilingual Bahnaric-Vietnamese dataset (referred to as the *Original* dataset). Additionally, we applied back-translation techniques to augment this dataset by reconstructing synthetic Bahnaric text from high-quality Vietnamese sentences obtained from *Vietnamese Wikipedia*, leveraging an existing Vietnamese-Bahnaric translation model (Vo et al., 2024). The final dataset statistics are summarized in Table 1.

In this phase, we use only the monolingual Bahnaric portion of the dataset to allow the model to effectively learn Bahnaric syntax and semantics.

Table 1: Statistics of our Bahnaric-Vietnamese bilingual dataset.

Data Source	Sentence Pairs
Original	53,942
Back-Translation	270,587
Total	324,529

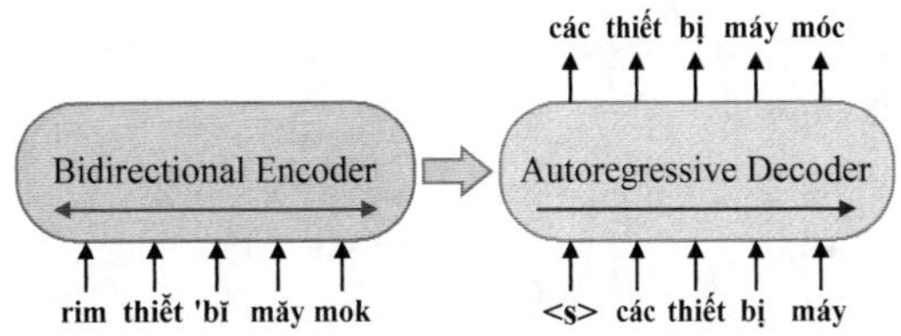

Figure 3: The fine-tuning process for the Bahnaric-Vietnamese translation task.

3.2.3 Fine-tuning for Bahnaric-Vietnamese Translation

After pre-training, we adapt the model for direct translation using a bilingual Bahnaric-Vietnamese dataset. Unlike the MLM phase, where input sequences are partially corrupted, this stage follows a *supervised translation* approach: the encoder takes an unmasked Bahnaric sentence, and the decoder generates the corresponding Vietnamese translation, as shown in Figure 3. During this step, we employ various DA techniques but apply them selectively to the *Original* subset to maintain high-quality supervision, detailed in Section 4.4. We exclude the back-translated data to avoid introducing potential errors, which could otherwise undermine the reliability of the training set.

4 Experimentations

We conduct two main experiments. In the first, we compare our BARTBahnar model against various baselines on the Bahnaric-Vietnamese translation task using only the Original dataset, providing a fair evaluation under limited data conditions. In the second, we examine how different DA techniques affect both BARTBahnar's training process, introduced in Section 3.2.3, and the performance of our end-to-end translation pipeline.

4.1 Dataset

From the Original dataset described in Table 1, we allocate 90% for training and 10% for testing. Although this corpus is relatively small, it is sourced from diverse domains (e.g., economics, social, politics, sports), ensuring a broad range of vocabulary and grammatical constructions.

4.2 Baselines

We select four baselines to compare against BART-Bahnar, as described below.

Transformer We replicate the standard Transformer architecture introduced by (Vaswani et al., 2017), following its original hyperparameter configuration.

PhoBERT-Fused NMT Based on (Zhu et al., 2020), we integrate a Bidirectional Encoder into each layer of an encoder-decoder NMT system. In our setup, we replace the baseline's encoder with *PhoBERT*, the encoder component of BARTPho.

ViT5 This is a pretrained Transformer-based encoder-decoder model for Vietnamese (Phan et al., 2022), trained on a large, high-quality Vietnamese corpus using T5-style self-supervision.

BARTPho We employ BARTPho directly, without any Bahnaric-focused continual pre-training.

All baselines are fine-tuned on the Original dataset for 15 epochs with a learning rate of $2e{-}05$, using the `AdamW` optimizer (Loshchilov and Hutter, 2019) and hyperparameters $\beta_1 = 0.9$, $\beta_2 = 0.999$, and $\varepsilon = 1\text{e}{-}08$.

4.3 Evaluation Metrics

We evaluate translation quality using the *BiLingual Evaluation Understudy* (BLEU) and *Metric for Evaluation of Translation with Explicit ORdering* (METEOR). Both metrics measure lexical and syntactic similarity between the model's output and a reference translation, making them suitable for the Bahnaric-Vietnamese language pair.

4.4 Data Augmentation Methods

Inspired by EDA techniques (Wei and Zou, 2019) and various approaches in the literature, we designed a set of augmentation methods that preserve sentence meaning, maintain grammatical correctness, and introduce controlled variations. This approach balances linguistic diversity with data integrity, ensuring that augmented samples remain useful for training.

Swapping Method Reorders sentence segments within paragraphs or compound sentences, helping the model generalize across varying syntactic patterns.

Combining Method Merges semantically related sentences into more cohesive structures, reducing ambiguities and enriching training examples.

Replacing Method Uses external lexical resources to substitute words with contextually suitable synonyms while preserving semantic consistency. Thematic labels and *part-of-speech* (POS) tagging guide valid replacements.

Insertion and Deletion Methods The insertion method selectively adds thematic words (e.g., locations, time references), providing extra context. The deletion method removes non-essential words, forcing the model to infer missing information and improving robustness against noisy input.

Sliding Window Method Extracts overlapping sub-sequences from sentences, generating samples of varying lengths. By capturing both local and long-range dependencies, it enhances the model's ability to handle diverse input structures.

4.5 Results and Analysis

Table 2 presents the performance of BARTBahnar compared to various baselines on the Bahnaric-Vietnamese translation task. As shown, BART-Bahnar consistently outperforms all baselines, validating our transfer learning strategy. By continually pre-training on Bahnaric data, BARTBahnar effectively captures linguistic features from both Vietnamese and Bahnaric, leading to significant improvements in translation accuracy. Notably, the substantial performance drop observed when using BARTPho without Bahnaric-focused continual pre-training demonstrates the necessity of domain adaptation before fine-tuning on the bilingual corpus. These findings reinforce that relying solely on Vietnamese knowledge in BARTPho, even with monolingual Bahnaric training, is insufficient for optimal Bahnaric-Vietnamese translation.

Table 2: Performance comparison of BARTBahnar and baseline models on the Bahnaric-Vietnamese translation task.

Baselines	BLEU↑	METEOR↑
Transformer	0.26	0.0431
PhoBERT-Fused NMT	2.05	0.2648
ViT5	7.18	0.2386
BARTPho	5.73	0.2076
BARTBahnar	**10.41**	**0.2822**

Beyond baseline comparisons, we also analyze the impact of different data augmentation methods, as shown in Table 3. Notably, the Replacing method, which applies thematic or synonym-based word substitutions, yields the greatest improvements by increasing translation accuracy by up to 200% in certain configurations. This result indicates that broadening vocabulary coverage and introducing controlled lexical variation significantly enhance the model's ability to generalize and capture linguistic nuances in Bahnaric. Additionally, the Deletion method proves effective in this context, since randomly removing words trains the model to handle incomplete source sentences. However, adding excessive noise or distorting sentence structure too much can be counterproductive. For instance, combining Insertion and Swapping leads to a sharp decline in translation quality, likely due to conflicting syntactic cues or disrupted natural sentence formations, thereby undermining model reliability.

Table 3: Effect of various DA methods on our pipeline's translation performance.

DA Methods	BLEU↑	METEOR↑
Insert + Swap	7.56	0.1905
Insert + Original	12.18	0.2921
Swap	13.74	0.2758
Slide	16.37	0.2640
Combine	16.63	0.3170
Delete	19.45	**0.3323**
Replace (theme)	**20.19**	0.3210
Replace (synonym)	**21.68**	**0.3459**

These results confirm that carefully selecting data augmentation strategies can significantly improve model performance, whereas excessive or poorly suited transformations may introduce noise and reduce accuracy. By strategically applying effective augmentation techniques, particularly synonym replacement, our BARTBahnar-based pipeline achieves better generalization, enhanced robustness, and improved translation quality for Bahnaric-Vietnamese.

5 Conclusion

In this paper, we introduced a novel hybrid architecture for low-resource machine translation, focusing on Bahnaric-Vietnamese and achieving promising results. Alongside rule-based methods that leverage shared features, such as the frequent use of loanwords among Bahnaric speakers to reduce errors and improve translation quality, our key contribution is the custom language model BARTBahnar. This model undergoes a strategic training process: it is first pre-trained on Vietnamese monolingual data, then adapted to Bahnaric monolingual data, and finally fine-tuned for the Bahnaric-Vietnamese translation task. By building on the domestic language model BARTPho, we substantially reduce training costs while relying on structural commonalities between Vietnamese and Bahnaric to maintain high performance. We also investigated various data augmentation methods to identify which techniques are most beneficial for low-resource languages like Bahnaric. Our findings suggest that certain augmentations significantly increase data diversity and enhance translation accuracy, while others may introduce excessive noise, underscoring the importance of carefully selecting augmentation strategies.

Future work could involve further customizing the language model by integrating additional Bahnaric-specific linguistic properties and refining the rule-based components to handle more nuanced text. Exploring additional combinations of data augmentation methods also holds potential for further improvements.

Limitations

Although our system achieves promising results for Bahnaric-Vietnamese translation, several limitations remain. First, it relies on a pre-trained Vietnamese language model, BARTPho, which may not be available for extremely low-resource languages lacking a higher-resource "sibling" language, and training such a model from scratch could be prohibitively expensive. Second, the effectiveness of our transfer learning approach hinges on structural similarities between the two languages; adapting it to languages with drastically different syntax and grammar may pose significant challenges. Finally, the rule-based components in our hybrid system require a bilingual dictionary for phrase mapping, which must be derived from an existing corpus. This can be problematic if the corpus lacks sufficient coverage or quality, and it is labor-intensive to develop in practice.

Acknowledgement

This research is funded by Vietnam Ministry of Science and Technology under the Program "Supporting Research, Development, and Technology Application of Industry 4.0" (KC-4.0/19-25), via the project "Development of a Vietnamese-Bahnaric Machine Translation and Bahnaric Text-to-Speech System (All Dialects)" (KC-4.0-29/19-25).

References

Mark Alves. 2006. Linguistic Research on the Origins of the Vietnamese Language: An Overview. *Journal of Vietnamese Studies*, 1(1-2):104–130.

Long-Ngo-Hoang Bui, Huu-Thien-Phu Nguyen, Minh-Khoi Le, Cong-Thien Pham, and Thanh-Tho Quan. 2024. Handling imbalanced resources and loanwords in Vietnamese-Bahnaric neural machine translation. *International Journal of Intelligent Information and Database Systems*, 16(4):451–472.

Shizhe Chen, Qin Jin, and Jianlong Fu. 2019. From Words to Sentences: A Progressive Learning Approach for Zero-resource Machine Translation with Visual Pivots. In *Proceedings of the Twenty-Eighth International Joint Conference on Artificial Intelligence, IJCAI-19*, pages 4932–4938. International Joint Conferences on Artificial Intelligence Organization.

Yong Cheng, Qian Yang, Yang Liu, Maosong Sun, and Wei Xu. 2017. Joint Training for Pivot-based Neural Machine Translation. In *Proceedings of the Twenty-Sixth International Joint Conference on Artificial Intelligence, IJCAI-17*, pages 3974–3980.

Alexander Fabbri, Simeng Han, Haoyuan Li, Haoran Li, Marjan Ghazvininejad, Shafiq Joty, Dragomir Radev, and Yashar Mehdad. 2021. Improving Zero and Few-Shot Abstractive Summarization with Intermediate Fine-tuning and Data Augmentation. In *Proceedings of the 2021 Conference of the North American Chapter of the Association for Computational Linguistics: Human Language Technologies*, pages 704–717, Online. Association for Computational Linguistics.

Di He, Yingce Xia, Tao Qin, Liwei Wang, Nenghai Yu, Tie-Yan Liu, and Wei-Ying Ma. 2016. Dual learning for machine translation. In *Proceedings of the 30th International Conference on Neural Information Processing Systems*, NIPS'16, page 820–828, Red Hook, NY, USA. Curran Associates Inc.

Aiusha V Hujon, Thoudam Doren Singh, and Khwairakpam Amitab. 2023. Transfer Learning Based Neural Machine Translation of English-Khasi on Low-Resource Settings. *Procedia Computer Science*, 218:1–8. International Conference on Machine Learning and Data Engineering.

Soon-Jae Hwang and Chang-Sung Jeong. 2023. Integrating Pre-Trained Language Model into Neural Machine Translation . In *2023 2nd International Conference on Frontiers of Communications, Information System and Data Science (CISDS)*, pages 59–66, Los Alamitos, CA, USA. IEEE Computer Society.

Melvin Johnson, Mike Schuster, Quoc V. Le, Maxim Krikun, Yonghui Wu, Zhifeng Chen, Nikhil Thorat, Fernanda Viégas, Martin Wattenberg, Greg Corrado, Macduff Hughes, and Jeffrey Dean. 2017. Google's Multilingual Neural Machine Translation System: Enabling Zero-Shot Translation. *Transactions of the Association for Computational Linguistics*, 5:339–351.

Guillaume Lample, Alexis Conneau, Ludovic Denoyer, and Marc'Aurelio Ranzato. 2018. Unsupervised Machine Translation Using Monolingual Corpora Only. In *International Conference on Learning Representations*.

Mike Lewis, Yinhan Liu, Naman Goyal, Marjan Ghazvininejad, Abdelrahman Mohamed, Omer Levy, Veselin Stoyanov, and Luke Zettlemoyer. 2020. BART: Denoising Sequence-to-Sequence Pre-training for Natural Language Generation, Translation, and Comprehension. In *Proceedings of the 58th Annual Meeting of the Association for Computational Linguistics*, pages 7871–7880, Online. Association for Computational Linguistics.

Bohan Li, Yutai Hou, and Wanxiang Che. 2022. Data augmentation approaches in natural language processing: A survey. *AI Open*, 3:71–90.

Ilya Loshchilov and Frank Hutter. 2019. Decoupled Weight Decay Regularization. In *International Conference on Learning Representations*.

Hieu-Hien Mai and Ngoc Hoang Luong. 2023. Data Augmentation with GPT-3.5 for Vietnamese Natural Language Inference. In *2023 RIVF International Conference on Computing and Communication Technologies (RIVF)*, pages 435–440.

George A. Miller. 1994. WordNet: A Lexical Database for English. In *Human Language Technology: Proceedings of a Workshop held at Plainsboro, New Jersey, March 8-11, 1994*.

Junghyun Min, R. Thomas McCoy, Dipanjan Das, Emily Pitler, and Tal Linzen. 2020. Syntactic Data Augmentation Increases Robustness to Inference Heuristics. In *Proceedings of the 58th Annual Meeting of the Association for Computational Linguistics*, pages 2339–2352, Online. Association for Computational Linguistics.

Thi-Vinh Ngo, Thanh-Le Ha, Phuong-Thai Nguyen, and Le-Minh Nguyen. 2019. Overcoming the Rare Word Problem for low-resource language pairs in Neural Machine Translation. In *Proceedings of the 6th Workshop on Asian Translation*, pages 207–214, Hong Kong, China. Association for Computational Linguistics.

Long Phan, Hieu Tran, Hieu Nguyen, and Trieu H. Trinh. 2022. ViT5: Pretrained Text-to-Text Transformer for Vietnamese Language Generation. In *Proceedings of the 2022 Conference of the North American Chapter of the Association for Computational Linguistics: Human Language Technologies: Student*

Research Workshop, pages 136–142, Hybrid: Seattle, Washington + Online. Association for Computational Linguistics.

Mo Qin. 2022. Machine Translation Technology Based on Natural Language Processing. In *2022 European Conference on Natural Language Processing and Information Retrieval (ECNLPIR)*, pages 10–13.

Muhammad Qorib, Geonsik Moon, and Hwee Tou Ng. 2024. Are Decoder-Only Language Models Better than Encoder-Only Language Models in Understanding Word Meaning? In *Findings of the Association for Computational Linguistics: ACL 2024*, pages 16339–16347, Bangkok, Thailand. Association for Computational Linguistics.

Dmitri Roussinov, SzeWang Fong, and David B. Skillicorn. 2007. Detecting word substitutions: PMI vs. HMM. In *SIGIR 2007: Proceedings of the 30th Annual International ACM SIGIR Conference on Research and Development in Information Retrieval, Amsterdam, The Netherlands, July 23-27, 2007*, pages 885–886. ACM.

Rico Sennrich, Barry Haddow, and Alexandra Birch. 2016. Improving Neural Machine Translation Models with Monolingual Data. In *Proceedings of the 54th Annual Meeting of the Association for Computational Linguistics (Volume 1: Long Papers)*, pages 86–96, Berlin, Germany. Association for Computational Linguistics.

Sahitya Tahiliani and Ayush Bansal. 2018. Comparative Analysis on Big Data Tools: Apache Solr Search and Hibernate Search. In *2018 3rd IEEE International Conference on Recent Trends in Electronics, Information & Communication Technology (RTEICT)*, pages 164–170.

Nguyen Luong Tran, Duong Minh Le, and Dat Quoc Nguyen. 2022. BARTpho: Pre-trained Sequence-to-Sequence Models for Vietnamese. In *Proceedings of the 23rd Annual Conference of the International Speech Communication Association*.

Ashish Vaswani, Noam Shazeer, Niki Parmar, Jakob Uszkoreit, Llion Jones, Aidan N Gomez, Ł ukasz Kaiser, and Illia Polosukhin. 2017. Attention is All you Need. In *Advances in Neural Information Processing Systems*, volume 30. Curran Associates, Inc.

Hoang Nhat Khang Vo, Duc Dong Le, Tran Minh Dat Phan, Tan Sang Nguyen, Quoc Nguyen Pham, Ngoc Oanh Tran, Quang Duc Nguyen, Tran Minh Hieu Vo, and Tho Quan. 2024. Revitalizing Bahnaric Language through Neural Machine Translation: Challenges, Strategies, and Promising Outcomes. *Proceedings of the AAAI Conference on Artificial Intelligence*, 38(21):23360–23368.

Rui Wang, Xu Tan, Renqian Luo, Tao Qin, and Tie-Yan Liu. 2021. A Survey on Low-Resource Neural Machine Translation. In *Proceedings of the Thirtieth International Joint Conference on Artificial Intelligence, IJCAI-21*, pages 4636–4643. International Joint Conferences on Artificial Intelligence Organization. Survey Track.

William Yang Wang and Diyi Yang. 2015. That's So Annoying!!!: A Lexical and Frame-Semantic Embedding Based Data Augmentation Approach to Automatic Categorization of Annoying Behaviors using #petpeeve Tweets. In *Proceedings of the 2015 Conference on Empirical Methods in Natural Language Processing*, pages 2557–2563, Lisbon, Portugal. Association for Computational Linguistics.

Yanshu Wang, Jinyi Zhang, Tianrong Shi, Dashuai Deng, Ye Tian, and Tadahiro Matsumoto. 2024. Recent Advances in Interactive Machine Translation With Large Language Models. *IEEE Access*, 12:179353–179382.

Jason Wei and Kai Zou. 2019. EDA: Easy Data Augmentation Techniques for Boosting Performance on Text Classification Tasks. In *Proceedings of the 2019 Conference on Empirical Methods in Natural Language Processing and the 9th International Joint Conference on Natural Language Processing (EMNLP-IJCNLP)*, pages 6382–6388, Hong Kong, China. Association for Computational Linguistics.

Ge Yan, Yu Li, Shu Zhang, and Zhenyu Chen. 2019. Data Augmentation for Deep Learning of Judgment Documents. In *Intelligence Science and Big Data Engineering. Big Data and Machine Learning*, pages 232–242, Cham. Springer International Publishing.

Chen Zhang, Xu Tan, Yi Ren, Tao Qin, Kejun Zhang, and Tie-Yan Liu. 2021. UWSpeech: Speech to Speech Translation for Unwritten Languages. *Proceedings of the AAAI Conference on Artificial Intelligence*, 35(16):14319–14327.

Yi Zhang, Tao Ge, and Xu Sun. 2020. Parallel Data Augmentation for Formality Style Transfer. In *Proceedings of the 58th Annual Meeting of the Association for Computational Linguistics*, pages 3221–3228, Online. Association for Computational Linguistics.

Jinhua Zhu, Yingce Xia, Lijun Wu, Di He, Tao Qin, Wengang Zhou, Houqiang Li, and Tieyan Liu. 2020. Incorporating BERT into Neural Machine Translation. In *International Conference on Learning Representations*.

Caption generation in Cultural Heritage: Crowdsourced Data and Tuning Multimodal Large Language Models

Artem Reshetnikov
Barcelona Supercomputing Center
Barcelona, Spain
a.reflesh@gmail.com

Maria-Cristina Marinescu
School of Management, IQS
Universitat Ramon Llull
Barcelona, Spain
cristina.marinescu@iqs.url.edu

Abstract

Automated caption generation for paintings enables enhanced access and understanding of visual artworks. This work introduces a novel caption dataset, obtained by manual annotation of about 7500 images from the publicly available DEArt dataset for object detection and pose estimation. Our focus is on describing the visual scenes rather than the context or style of the artwork - more common in other existing captioning datasets. The dataset is the result of a crowdsourcing initiative spanning 13 months, with volunteers adhering to explicit captioning guidelines reflecting our requirements. We provide each artwork in the dataset with five captions, created independently by volunteers to ensure diversity of interpretation and increase the robustness of the captioning model.

In addition, we explore using the crowdsourced dataset for fine-tuning Large Language Models with vision encoders for domain-specific caption generation. The goal is to improve the performance of multimodal LLMs in the context of cultural heritage, a domain with "small data" which often struggles with the nuanced visual analysis and interpretation required for cultural objects such as paintings. The use of crowdsourced data in the domain adaptation process enables us to incorporate the collective perceptual insights of diverse annotators, resulting in an exploration of visual narratives and a observing a reduction in hallucinations otherwise created by these large language models.

1 Introduction

To offer innovative methods for engaging with and understanding visual artefacts at scale, many systems rely on rich metadata - for instance, in the form of captions or descriptions. Having access to good captions of artworks not only facilitates broader public access to these artifacts but also fosters a deeper appreciation for their cultural significance. However, the automatic generation of captions is not without challenges. Artworks often present scenes with intricate symbolism and complex narratives, where the most important elements can be hard to identify and demand nuanced caption beyond simple object recognition.

In this paper we introduce a novel dataset of captions of the visual content of artworks and showcase how it can help in the domain adaptation of state-of-art approaches such as Multimodal Large Language Models (mLLMs) (Liu et al., 2023) for the task of caption generation. The image dataset was sourced from the publicly available DEArt object detection and pose estimation dataset (Reshetnikov et al., 2022b), a curated assemblage of paintings spanning diverse European cultures, centuries and artistic movements.

Our motivation for collecting this new dataset was twofold. First, good models rely on the existence of large amounts of quality data. For reasons that are (1) technical - small data with a large variety between the representation of objects - real or imaginary, depiction of actions usually not captured in photographs, etc - but also (2) the relatively low interest in cultural heritage - which results in limited effort and financing, there is still a considerable gap between how precise multimodal LLMs perform for photographs and artworks. This gap could be narrowed by new quality datasets. Secondly, we chose to focus on the visual scene because we believe that it is necessary to identify all/most of the elements to be able to assign cultural meaning to a work; additionally, in those cases where a visual setup can consistently derive further meaning could be inferred more reliably top-down (from domain knowledge) rather than being generated based on a limited dataset.

The model adaptation work was motivated by the experiments we ran that use mMMLs to generate captions for cultural heritage (CH) artifacts; the results underlined some apparent shortcomings: on the one hand, content unrelated to the visual

Proceedings of the 1st Workshop on Language Models for Underserved Communities (LM4UC 2025), pages 42–50
May 4, 2025

scene (i.e., mistaken identity for both objects and relationships between objects), and on the other, missing elements. Our hypothesis was that these models could effectively leverage domain knowledge from datasets like ours, to overcome some of their apparent limitations.

Our crowdsourcing campaign was hosted on the Zooniverse platform and involved volunteers from various backgrounds and expertise levels, who created detailed caption annotations for about 7500 DEArt paintings during a year-long period. Given that a high percentage of the images are non-iconic (Berg and Berg, 2009), gathering 5 different annotations per image allows for a diversity of perspectives and interpretations, which can make the trained model more robust. Based on this data, we use parameter-efficient fine-tuning techniques(Xu et al., 2023) and demonstrate the possibility of mitigating hallucinations in LLM-generated captions.

2 Related work

Early efforts in image captioning, such as (Vinyals et al., 2015), laid the groundwork for later advancements. The distinctive challenges posed by cultural heritage artworks demand specialized solutions due to several important features not present in everyday pictures: anachronic objects, imaginary beings, actions not present in photographs - eg decapitations, etc. Several works have made significant contributions in the area of captioning for cultural heritage, of which we briefly present those directly related to our task - visual content captioning.

(Cetinic, 2021) highlights the complexity of describing artworks with multiple levels of interpretation and develops a captioning model based on a large-scale dataset of artwork images annotated with concepts from the Iconclass classification system. The model is fine-tuned using a transformer-based vision-language pre-trained model. Results suggest that the model could generate meaningful captions that exhibit a stronger relevance to the visual art context than those generated by the baseline (pre-trained) model.

(Bai et al., 2021) introduces a multi-topic and knowledgeable art description framework (Bai et al., 2021) which models the generated sentences according to three artistic perspectives and enhances each caption with external knowledge (from Wikipedia). The framework is validated through an exhaustive analysis, both quantitative and qualitative, as well as a comparative human evaluation.

(Stefanini et al., 2019) addresses the problem of cross-modal retrieval of images and sentences coming from the artistic domain. The authors collect and manually annotate the Artpedia dataset that contains paintings and textual sentences describing both the visual content of the paintings and other (contextual) information. They then devise a visual-textual model that jointly addresses the challenge of the retrieval of images and sentences by exploiting the visual and textual chunks.

More recently, the ArtCap dataset(Lu et al., 2024) provides 3,606 paintings, each annotated with five captions, showcasing high-quality annotations and effectiveness in benchmarking painting captioning models. The SemArt dataset(Garcia and Vogiatzis, 2018), designed for semantic art understanding, includes fine-art paintings with attributes and textual artistic comments. It also introduces the Text2Art challenge, a multi-modal retrieval task linking artistic texts and paintings.

The DEArt dataset(Reshetnikov et al., 2022a) focuses on object detection and pose estimation for 15K images of European artwork between the 12th and the 18th centuries. It includes 69 object classes, many of which are specific to cultural heritage, but does not include caption annotations. Recognizing this gap and considering the rich variety of non-iconic images in DEArt, we decided to leverage a subset to create a caption generation dataset.

Recent advances in the field of Large Language Models (LLMs) (OpenAI, 2023) have seen the successful integration of visual information into these models, giving rise to a new generation of mLLMs. Notable among these is LLaVA (Liu et al., 2023), which, along with other models such as Mini-GPT4 (OpenAI, 2023) and Instruct-BLIP (Dai et al., 2023), have shown impressive image captioning and question-answering capabilities.

Like LLMs and unlike most of the ArtCap and SemiArt works, our approach relies on crowdsourcing data. This has the advantage of training the model with a variety of interpretations of paintings, coming from volunteers with different levels of expertise in cultural heritage. We believe that this can make the trained model more flexible and accurate.

Other works in metadata generation for cultural heritage exist, but they at least partly focus on the generation of style and context information (artwork's history, author's biography etc.), which introduces noise in the captions.

3 Guidelines for caption generation

To create effective guidelines[1], we drew inspiration from established practices such as (Starr, 2022), and we discussed our proposal with several cultural heritage experts. After deciding to use Zooniverse as a platform, we received expert advice from one of their shepherds.

Our guidelines emphasize the requirements of clarity, simplicity, and objectivity. We encourage annotators to start captions with the most crucial elements, progressing from foreground to background. We recommend avoiding assumptions, e.g., the identity of characters, events or places, assumptions about time periods (which, e.g. may bias the choice of object names), or professional jargon. The focus should always be on what is visually present in the image, avoiding implications or intentions. Named entities should be identified, but only if they are clearly recognizable or convey important information. Guidelines provide specific instructions for spatial orientation, using absolute positioning and limiting the use of "background/foreground" to essential details. They also advocate for concise annotations, restricting captions to 250 characters, while encouraging multiple sentences for clarity and simplicity. The language should be straightforward and avoid comparative constructs (e.g. larger, smallest), pronouns, and unnecessary punctuation. The annotation interface included examples to illustrate the preferred style and promote clear and informative annotations in a standardized manner.

4 Crowdsourcing process and preprocessing of the annotated data

After a thorough assessment of various platforms, which included short tests for quality of annotations, we decided to use the Zooniverse platform. Zooniverse's established reputation in supporting citizen science projects with quality metadata, the possibility of hosting caption annotation tasks, and the reality that volunteers make for better annotators (possibly due to the inherent interest in the project), were decisive factors in our decision. Due to GDPR and other law restrictions, Zooniverse platform doesn't allow the collecting of data about volunteers. However, In March 2015, the Zooniverse team conducted a survey to better understand their volunteer community. The survey, part of a Master's thesis by Victoria Homsy at Oxford University, gathered responses from approximately 300 active participants. Key findings revealed a gender distribution of 60% male and 40% female volunteers. Age-wise, the community was diverse, with a slight underrepresentation of older individuals. Geographically, the user base was primarily from English-speaking countries, notably the UK and the US, each contributing about a third of the participants, while only 2% hailed from developing nations. Employment data indicated that around half of the volunteers were employed, 15% were retired, 10% unemployed, and 4% unable to work due to disability. The survey also highlighted a wide range of occupations among volunteers, including roles such as professor, administrator, guard, and various technical positions.

The crowdsourcing campaign was initiated with the design of a user-friendly interface (UI) to facilitate efficient interaction between volunteers and the paintings. We ran the campaign in batches to try to get 4-5 good annotations per image for increasingly larger subsets of DEArt, while at the same time keeping a balance between diversity and thematic consistency.

Concretely, we included images with different styles and from different time periods, while excluding most portraits and other iconic images with limited interest from a captioning perspective (e.g.images that weren't iconographic or that had low expected variability for the captions). This process was iterative and involved: (1) the gradual decrease of the size of the batches to increase the motivation of the volunteers to complete the work, and (2) the adaptation of the image selection process to propose paintings of complexity that had lead to good captions in previous batches.

The multiple captions generated for each painting by the different volunteers reflect diverse artistic interpretations and visual insights and thus help us train a more robust captioning model.

At the end of each batch annotation process, we ran a data health check; rigorous quality control mechanisms were applied to manually verify the adherence of captions to guidelines and to maintain thematic alignment. Corrections and clarifications were incorporated into our guidelines and User Interface to enhance annotation accuracy. This iterative batch approach enabled us to capitalize on the collective contributions of volunteers while preserving dataset integrity.

The total number of uploaded images was 7543.

[1]Link to guidelines

Dataset	Images	Captions per Image	Total Captions
Our Dataset	7,543	**4.57**	**34,535**
SemArt	**21,383**	1	21,383
ArtPedia	2,930	3.1	9,173

Table 1: Comparison of our dataset versus state-of-the-art caption datasets in CH. Our dataset features a balanced mix of images and captions per image, achieving the highest total caption count among the datasets.

The dataset health check was based on several rules:

1. Filter out captions with fewer than two tokens.
2. Filter out captions containing specific words. E.g. when presented with an image, some users introduce a caption of an image in the guidelines rather than the one that corresponds to the dataset image. Another (general) case was due to our campaign not allowing volunteers to skip images they didn't want to annotate.
3. Eliminate annotations by users who either didn't read the guidelines properly or intentionally chose not to follow them. Some examples we identified that fall in this class are "aN oLd DrAwInG!!!!!!!!!!!!!!!!!!!!!", "bad example".
4. Users seem to be remarkably consistent in providing useless, or high-quality, annotations. This provided us with yet another criteria to eliminate all captions from specific users.

Following the dataset health check, 34535 captions were retained. Our crowdsourced dataset stands out for its richness (i.e. number of annotations per images and total annotations) and diversity (i.e. different annotator views, given by the number of annotations per image) in comparison to the datasets that are the largest and most relevant in cultural heritage, as indicated by the metrics in Table 1. While it contains fewer images than SemArt, our dataset offers an average of 4.57 captions per image. The higher caption diversity is crucial to train more nuanced models, as it reflects how a visual scene can be described differently - which increases the power of generalization. In contrast, SemArt provides only one caption per image (although of museum-expert quality), which may limit the range of insights available for each artwork. Although ArtPedia offers a moderate number of captions per image (3.1 on average), its total image count is significantly lower, leading to a smaller pool of captions overall (9173).

This comparative analysis highlights the balance achieved in our dataset between the quantity of images and the variety of annotations. The emphasis on obtaining multiple captions per image enriches the dataset by incorporating a variety of descriptive styles, subjective interpretations, and visual details, thus providing a comprehensive base for fine-tuning models. The iterative process of data collection and quality checks ensures that our dataset maintains both breadth and depth, allowing the generation of high-quality, diverse painting captions.

To measure diversity, we calculated three metrics and compared them with the ArtCap dataset. Our choice is due to the similarity in dataset structure (e.g. multiply captions per image, focus on visual content). Diversity was measured using the following metrics:

- Lexical Diversity: Counts unique words across captions (e.g., type-token ratio).
- Semantic Diversity: Measures how semantically different the captions are using embeddings.
- Edit Distance/Overlap: Measure by counting the minimum number of operations required to transform one string into the other.

Results are shown in Table 2. We will release the caption dataset after publication.

5 Model architecture and training process

For model training and caption generation experiments, we chose an open-sourced model, the LLAVA (Large Language and Vision Assistant) llava-v1.5-7b. LLAVA is a novel end-to-end large multimodal model that combines a vision encoder and an LLM for general-purpose visual and language understanding. It represents a significant

Metric	Our dataset	ArtCap	Observation
Lexical Diversity	**0.5831**	0.4765	Our dataset has higher lexical diversity, meaning it uses a larger variety of unique words relative to its total word count. This suggests that captions in our dataset are more varied in vocabulary compared to ArtCap data.
Semantic Diversity	0.8094	**0.8236**	Both datasets exhibit high semantic diversity, but ArtCap dataset is slightly more diverse. Captions in ArtCap likely describe the images using different structure of sentences more often than in our dataset.
Edit Distance	**174.73**	44.07	Our dataset has a much higher edit distance, indicating its captions are structurally more distinct. Captions in ArtCap dataset are more similar in word arrangement and structure.

Table 2: Comparative analysis of caption diversity metrics between our dataset and ArtCap. Higher values indicate greater diversity.

advancement in the field of multimodal AI, demonstrating impressive multimodal chat capabilities - sometimes of similar quality of captions as those generated by the multimodal GPT-4 - and setting a new state-of-the-art accuracy standard for QA(Rodrigues et al., 2024).

The LLAVA pre-trained visual encoder and the LLM connect using a simple projection matrix. This setup allows the model to convert images into a word embedding space, while textual input is also transformed into the same space. The image and word tokens are then passed to a LLaMA (Touvron et al., 2023) decoder, which produces output.

Retraining or even fine-tuning LLMs typically demands extensive datasets and significant GPU hours. This process not only consumes considerable computational resources but also carries the risk of catastrophic forgetting, where the model loses the knowledge it previously acquired when too many layers of the network update their weights. To address these challenges, one of the parameter-efficient fine-tuning (PEFT) approaches (Xu et al., 2023) has been used for domain adaptation of the LLAVA model. PEFT methods are designed to adjust only a small subset of the model's parameters while keeping the majority of them fixed. This makes the fine-tuning process more efficient and less resource-intensive. By focusing on a limited number of parameters, PEFT techniques significantly reduce the computational load and the amount of data required, enabling quicker and more cost-effective adaptation to new domains. This can lead to a more agile and scalable deployment of LLMs for specialized application domains, ensuring that the model remains both accurate and efficient.

LoRA (Low-Rank Adaptation of Large Language Models) (Hu et al., 2021) is one of the PEFT techniques to train LLMs on specific tasks or domains. This technique introduces trainable rank decomposition matrices into each layer of transformer architecture and also reduces the number of trainable parameters for downstream tasks while keeping the pre-trained weights frozen.

To further optimize resource usage and fine-tuning efficiency, we employed QLoRA (Quantized Low-Rank Adaptation) instead of traditional LoRA. QLoRA was the most optimal choice because it reduces the memory footprint even further by leveraging 4-bit quantization, allowing for the fine-tuning of LLMs on consumer-grade hardware without sacrificing model performance. The use of QLoRA enables efficient memory utilization, allowing us to fine-tune larger models with fewer hardware resources, significantly lowering both the cost and time required for adaptation (Han et al., 2024).

Our QLoRA(Table 3) configuration is characterized by several key parameters such as the rank and the alpha value, which contribute to better convergence and scalability. Additionally, the use of mixed-precision training with bfloat16 (BF16) and TensorFlow32 (TF32) enables faster computation while minimizing memory requirements. To ensure

Model Architecture			
LoRA Rank (r)	128	LoRA Alpha	256
Vision Tower	clip	MM Projector Type	mlp2xgelu
MM Projector LR	2e-5	Vision Select Layer	-2
Quantization Bits	4	Image Aspect	pad
Model Max Length	2048		
Training Configuration			
Train Batch Size	4	Eval Batch Size	4
Grad. Accum. Steps	16	DataLoader Workers	4
Learning Rate	2e-4	Weight Decay	0.0
Warmup Ratio	0.03	LR Scheduler	cosine
Training Epochs	10		

Table 3: LoRA fine-tuning hyperparameters organized by model architecture and training configuration.

effective utilization of resources, the data loading process is optimized with lazy preprocessing and efficient parallelism (Rasley et al., 2020) using multiple dataloader workers. The LLAVA architecture we implement utilizes Vicuna-7B as LLM (Zheng et al., 2023) and the ViT vision transformer (Dosovitskiy et al., 2021) from OpenAI's CLIP model (Dai et al., 2023), which incorporates advanced features like multimodal projection layers and gradient checkpointing (See Figure1). See more details about model parameters and training configuration in Table 3.

6 Evaluation

We employed multiple evaluation metrics to assess the quality of the image captions generated by the baseline (LLAVA) and fine-tuned models, including Rouge1 (R1), Rouge2 (R2), RougeL (RL), and RougeLsum (RLsum), which measure n-gram overlap between generated and reference captions. Additionally, we included Meteor, Cider, and ClipScore, providing a more comprehensive view of the captioning performance. Rouge metrics are particularly useful for evaluating fluency and structure through n-gram and subsequence overlaps, while Meteor and Cider provide insights into the semantic accuracy; ClipScore assesses the alignment between the generated captions and the visual content.

Table 4 presents the comparison between results with the baseline LLAVA model and its fine-tuned version using QLoRA - for our dataset and the SemArt dataset. Fine-tuning on our dataset led to significant improvements over the baseline; for instance, the Rouge1 score increased from 0.31 to 0.43, and Rouge2 rose from 0.09 to 0.18, indicating a stronger overlap with reference captions. RougeL and RougeLsum similarly improved from 0.21 to 0.31 and 0.21 to 0.32, respectively, reflecting enhanced structural consistency and coherence of generated captions. The fine-tuned LLAVA model also demonstrated notable gains in Meteor and Cider scores, with Cider improving from 0.28 to 0.48, suggesting a better match with the overall reference data. Additionally, ClipScore increased from 0.31 to 0.42, indicating a higher alignment between captions and the visual content of the images.

However, the results on SemArt were more modest. Fine-tuning improved Rouge1 from 0.19 to 0.21 and Rouge2 from 0.027 to 0.11, while the gains in RougeL and RougeLsum were similarly limited (0.14 to 0.16). The lower ClipScore of 0.315 for the fine-tuned LLAVA on SemArt, compared to 0.42 on our dataset, indicates that the captions generated for SemArt images were less contextually aligned with the visual content. This disparity suggests that the model's ability to generate highly relevant captions is influenced by the characteristics of the dataset used for training, with our dataset providing a better foundation for capturing the nuanced relationship between text and imagery.

Overall, the evaluation demonstrates that fine-tuning using QLoRA can significantly improve the performance of mMMLs when training for specific domains, especially when these domains do not (or cannot) have extensive datasets. Moreover, the richer and more diverse the manual annotations, the higher the quality of the generated captions, as reflected by the lower ClipScore.

7 Limitations and discussion

Given the widespread excitement surrounding LLM capabilities and despite the improvements our fine-tuned model brings, we questioned whether these quantitative results also reflect a better quality of the generated captions from a *human viewpoint*. We thus embarked on an empirical exploration; our experiments with the baseline LLAVA model and the improvements that the fine-tuned LLAVA model achieved point to limitations in terms of the effectiveness of general-purpose mLLMs in the absence of domain-specific adaptations.

1. Hallucinations: One of the most notable limitations observed was the baseline model's tendency to hallucinate (invent details not present in the actual artwork). E.g., in the caption of "Palas Athena in Fight against Centaurs" (Figure 2c), the baseline LLAVA model generated incorrect elements, such

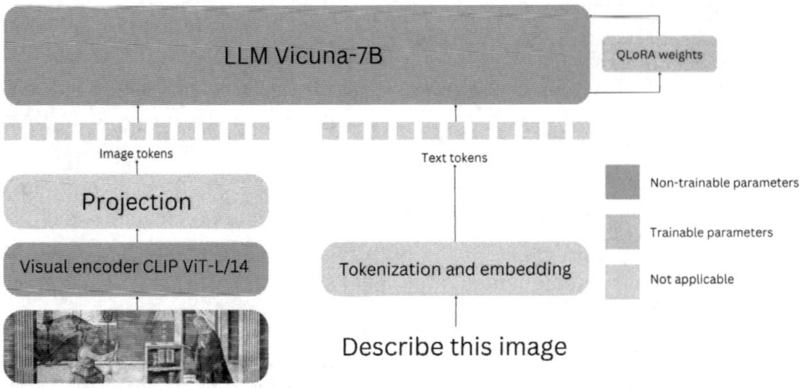

Figure 1: Architecture of LLAVA model with QLoRA layer

Model	R1	R2	RL	RLsum	Meteor	Cider	ClipScore
Baseline LLAVA (Our Dataset)	0.31	0.09	0.21	0.21	0.25	0.28	0.31
Fine-tuned LLAVA (Our Dataset)	0.43	0.18	0.31	0.32	0.31	0.48	0.42
Baseline LLAVA (SemArt)	0.19	0.027	0.14	0.14	0.12	0.19	0.21
Fine-tuned LLAVA (SemArt)	0.21	0.11	0.16	0.16	0.19	0.24	0.315

Note: R = ROUGE (R1 = ROUGE-1, R2 = ROUGE-2, RL = ROUGE-L, RLsum = ROUGE-L summary)

Table 4: Evaluation metrics for LLAVA models fine-tuned using QLoRA on two datasets (Our Dataset and SemArt).

as a dog and a bird, which do not exist in the painting. Similarly, for "Jupiter and Bellerophon" (Figure 2a), it inaccurately describes a scene involving angels when the painting actually features a man and a winged horse. This may also be interpreted to some extent as a case of mistaken identity in the case of the horse, whose wings made the baseline model believe it is an angel. On the other hand, the man on the left does not have wings, and the baseline model hallucinates angel instead. Finally, in "Annunciation" (Figure 2b), the basic model hallucinates a baby and a potted plant; this last could also be interpreted as mistaken identity since we assume the wings are interpreted as greenery. Both models hallucinate a man in white.

2. Incompleteness and mistaken identity: In several instances, the model produced captions that lacked crucial details. For example, in "Annunciation" (Figure 2b), the baseline model's caption mentions a woman and a child, omitting - or making the mistake - that the second figure is an angel and he is holding a flower; the baseline model does not see the wings, nor the flower. Both aspects are part of a significant religious interaction that is central to the meaning of the painting. Likewise, in Figure 2c, the centaurs are interpreted by the baseline model as horses; in Figure 2a, the model does not identify a horse at all.

The baseline model also mistakenly identifies crucial actions. In Figure 2a, the man *falls* rather than *being lifted*, while in Figure 2c, the woman is *killing* a beast rather than *standing* on it. Both actions are critical to understand the true meaning embedded in the artpiece, and its symbolism.

These limitations suggest that foundation models like LLAVA struggle with both accuracy and completeness in complex visual art contexts. Developing a domain-specific dataset and fine-tuning mLLM models like LLAVA for art interpretation is a more reliable approach.

8 Conclusion

This work introduces a novel dataset for caption generation of paintings sourced from a publicly available dataset. Our caption dataset was created through a year-long crowdsourcing campaign on Zooniverse, with volunteers adhering to explicit captioning guidelines. We have shown that this is a valuable resource for research and development in the field of automated caption generation for visual art. It can be used to fine-tune mLLMs - such as LLAVA - for domain adaptation, resulting in significant improvements in the quality of generated captions compared to the baseline models. The LoRA approach to fine-tuning mLLMs appears to be particularly effective in enhancing the model's ability to generate captions that are more coherent, contextually aligned, and better capture the nuances of

(a) "Jupiter and Bellerophon", unknown.
Baseline LLAVA: *The image depicts a painting of a man being lifted into the air by two angels. The man is positioned in the center of the scene, with one angel on his left side and the other on his right side. The angels are holding the man, and he appears to be flying through the sky. In the background, there are two people standing, possibly observing the scene or waiting for their turn to be lifted. The painting captures a moment of wonder and awe.*
Fine-tuned LLAVA: *The image features a painting of a man and a winged horse flying through the sky. The man falls from the horse, which is positioned towards the right side of the scene. The painting captures the dynamic and dramatic moment of the man and the horse soaring through the air. In the background, there is another man visible, on the left side of the painting. The scene appears to be set in a mountainous landscape, with a mountain visible in the background. The overall atmosphere of the painting is one of adventure and freedom.*

(b) "Annunciation", D. Ghirlandaio.
Baseline LLAVA: *The image depicts a scene from a painting, featuring a woman and a child. The woman is kneeling down, holding a baby, while the child is standing nearby. The woman appears to be dressed in a yellow gown, and the child is wearing a white gown. The painting is set in a room with a window in the background. In the room, there is a chair positioned towards the right side of the scene, and a potted plant is located on the left side. Additionally, there is a bowl placed on the floor, close to the woman and the child.*
Fine-tuned LLAVA: *The image features a painting of a woman sitting in front of an angel, who is kneeling and holding a white flower. They appear to be engaged in a conversation or a religious ceremony. The woman is wearing a yellow dress, while the man is dressed in white. In the background, there is a window with a curtain, which adds to the atmosphere of the scene. The painting is likely a religious or historical depiction, as it captures the interaction between the two individuals.*

(c) "Palas Athena in Fight against Centaurs", Milan Thomka Mitrovský.
Baseline LLAVA: *The image features a woman dressed in a warrior costume, standing on a horse and holding a shield. She appears to be engaged in a battle or a mock fight. The horse is positioned in the center of the scene, with the woman standing on its back. There are two other people in the background, one on the left side and the other on the right side of the image. The scene also includes a dog, which is located on the left side of the image, and a bird, which is flying in the sky above the woman and the horse.*
Fine-tuned LLAVA: *The image depicts a painting of a woman killing a centaur. The woman is wearing a helmet and is holding a shield, while the man appears to be holding a sword. The scene takes place in a lush green field, with a body of water in the background. There are several other centaurs in the painting, some of whom are closer to the water and others further away. The overall atmosphere of the painting suggests a battle or a moment of intense action.*

Figure 2: Comparison of generated captions between baseline and fine-tuned LLAVA models on different artworks.

artistic interpretation. We believe that this research will contribute to further advancements in automated caption generation for paintings and other forms of visual art, ultimately enhancing accessibility and understanding of these cultural artifacts.

9 Ethical and broader impact of the work

Participation in the annotation campaign was voluntary. Annotators were informed about the purpose, benefits, risks, and funding behind the study before participating. The dataset we used as a source of images has a Creative Commons license and is openly available. We pseudo-anonymized the collected data based on identifiers. We did not collect any personally identifiable data beyond user names on the Zooniverse platform. We recognize no additional potential for harm in our work beyond those already incurred by LLMs (e.g. bias), and our approach fine-tunes one such mLLM model to make it more accurate for the cultural heritage domain. AI assistants were not used in this work. Upon publication, we will release the dataset publicly for research use, which is classified as a "not high-risk" according to the EU Artificial Intelligence Act. We are not aware of any other possible ethical consequences of the proposed dataset and fine-tuned model.

10 Acknowledgement

This publication uses data generated via the Zooniverse.org platform, development of which is funded by generous support, including a Global Impact Award from Google, and by a grant from the Alfred P. Sloan Foundation.

This research has been supported by Saint-George-on-a-Bike (project 2018-EU-IA-0104), co-financed by the Connecting Europe Facility of the European Union.

References

Zechen Bai, Yuta Nakashima, and Noa Garcia. 2021. Explain me the painting: Multi-topic knowledgeable art description generation. *Preprint*, arXiv:2109.05743.

Tamara L. Berg and Alexander C. Berg. 2009. Finding iconic images. *2009 IEEE Computer Society Conference on Computer Vision and Pattern Recognition Workshops*, pages 1–8.

Eva Cetinic. 2021. Towards generating and evaluating iconographic image captions of artworks. *Journal of Imaging*, 7:123.

Wenliang Dai, Junnan Li, Dongxu Li, Anthony Meng Huat Tiong, Junqi Zhao, Weisheng Wang, Boyang Li, Pascale Fung, and Steven Hoi. 2023. Instructblip: Towards general-purpose vision-language models with instruction tuning. *Preprint*, arXiv:2305.06500.

Alexey Dosovitskiy, Lucas Beyer, Alexander Kolesnikov, Dirk Weissenborn, Xiaohua Zhai, Thomas Unterthiner, Mostafa Dehghani, Matthias Minderer, Georg Heigold, Sylvain Gelly, Jakob Uszkoreit, and Neil Houlsby. 2021. An image is worth 16x16 words: Transformers for image recognition at scale. *Preprint*, arXiv:2010.11929.

Noa Garcia and George Vogiatzis. 2018. How to read paintings: Semantic art understanding with multimodal retrieval. *Preprint*, arXiv:1810.09617.

Zeyu Han, Chao Gao, Jinyang Liu, Jeff Zhang, and Sai Qian Zhang. 2024. Parameter-efficient fine-tuning for large models: A comprehensive survey. *Preprint*, arXiv:2403.14608.

Edward J. Hu, Yelong Shen, Phillip Wallis, Zeyuan Allen-Zhu, Yuanzhi Li, Shean Wang, Lu Wang, and Weizhu Chen. 2021. Lora: Low-rank adaptation of large language models. *Preprint*, arXiv:2106.09685.

Haotian Liu, Chunyuan Li, Qingyang Wu, and Yong Jae Lee. 2023. Visual instruction tuning. *Preprint*, arXiv:2304.08485.

Yue Lu, Chao Guo, Xingyuan Dai, and Fei-Yue Wang. 2024. Artcap: A dataset for image captioning of fine art paintings. *IEEE Transactions on Computational Social Systems*, 11(1):576–587.

OpenAI. 2023. Gpt-4v(ision) system card.

Jeff Rasley, Samyam Rajbhandari, Olatunji Ruwase, and Yuxiong He. 2020. Deepspeed: System optimizations enable training deep learning models with over 100 billion parameters. In *Proceedings of the 26th ACM SIGKDD International Conference on Knowledge Discovery & Data Mining*, KDD '20, page 3505–3506, New York, NY, USA. Association for Computing Machinery.

Artem Reshetnikov, Maria-Cristina Marinescu, and Joaquim More Lopez. 2022a. Deart: Dataset of european art. *Preprint*, arXiv:2211.01226.

Artem Reshetnikov, Sergio Mendoza, and Maria-Cristina Marinescu. 2022b. Deart: Dataset of european art.

Luiz Rodrigues, Filipe Dwan Pereira, Luciano Cabral, Dragan Gašević, Geber Ramalho, and Rafael Ferreira Mello. 2024. Assessing the quality of automatic-generated short answers using gpt-4. *Computers and Education: Artificial Intelligence*, 7:100248.

Ruth Starr. 2022. Cooper hewitt guidelines for image description.

Matteo Stefanini, Marcella Cornia, Lorenzo Baraldi, Massimiliano Corsini, and Rita Cucchiara. 2019. Artpedia: A new visual-semantic dataset with visual and contextual sentences in the artistic domain.

Hugo Touvron, Thibaut Lavril, Gautier Izacard, Xavier Martinet, Marie-Anne Lachaux, Timothée Lacroix, Baptiste Rozière, Naman Goyal, Eric Hambro, Faisal Azhar, Aurelien Rodriguez, Armand Joulin, Edouard Grave, and Guillaume Lample. 2023. Llama: Open and efficient foundation language models. *Preprint*, arXiv:2302.13971.

Oriol Vinyals, Alexander Toshev, Samy Bengio, and Dumitru Erhan. 2015. Show and tell: A neural image caption generator. *Preprint*, arXiv:1411.4555.

Lingling Xu, Haoran Xie, Si-Zhao Joe Qin, Xiaohui Tao, and Fu Lee Wang. 2023. Parameter-efficient fine-tuning methods for pretrained language models: A critical review and assessment. *Preprint*, arXiv:2312.12148.

Lianmin Zheng, Wei-Lin Chiang, Ying Sheng, Siyuan Zhuang, Zhanghao Wu, Yonghao Zhuang, Zi Lin, Zhuohan Li, Dacheng Li, Eric P. Xing, Hao Zhang, Joseph E. Gonzalez, and Ion Stoica. 2023. Judging llm-as-a-judge with mt-bench and chatbot arena. *Preprint*, arXiv:2306.05685.

Preserving Cultural Identity with Context-Aware Translation Through Multi-Agent AI Systems

Mahfuz Ahmed Anik[1] Abdur Rahman[1], Azmine Toushik Wasi[1†], Md Manjurul Ahsan[2]
[1]Shahjalal University of Science and Technology, Sylhet, Bangladesh
[2]University of Oklahoma, Norman, OK 73019, USA
[†]**Correspondence:** azmine32@student.sust.edu

Abstract

Language is a cornerstone of cultural identity, yet globalization and the dominance of major languages have placed nearly 3,000 languages at risk of extinction. Existing AI-driven translation models prioritize efficiency but often fail to capture cultural nuances, idiomatic expressions, and historical significance, leading to translations that marginalize linguistic diversity. To address these challenges, we propose a multi-agent AI framework designed for culturally adaptive translation in underserved language communities. Our approach leverages specialized agents for translation, interpretation, content synthesis, and bias evaluation, ensuring that linguistic accuracy and cultural relevance are preserved. Using CrewAI and LangChain, our system enhances contextual fidelity while mitigating biases through external validation. Comparative analysis shows that our framework outperforms GPT-4o, producing contextually rich and culturally embedded translations—a critical advancement for Indigenous, regional, and low-resource languages. This research underscores the potential of multi-agent AI in fostering equitable, sustainable, and culturally sensitive NLP technologies, aligning with the AI Governance, Cultural NLP, and Sustainable NLP pillars of Language Models for Underserved Communities. Our full experimental codebase is publicly available at: github.com/ciol-researchlab/Context-Aware_Translation_MAS.

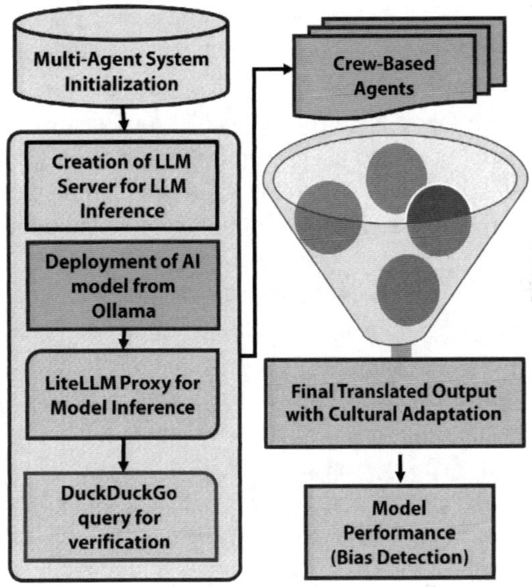

Figure 1: Our Approach for Preserving Cultural Identity with Context-Aware Translation Through Multi-Agent AI Systems

1 Introduction

Language is a vital cultural repository, transmitting traditions, values, and historical narratives across generations. It preserves oral traditions, folklore, and indigenous knowledge, shaping a community's worldview and identity (Goel). However, globalization, urbanization, and the dominance of English have led to an alarming decline in linguistic diversity, with nearly 3,000 languages projected to disappear this century (Kandler and Unger, 2023). This loss severs communities from their heritage, weakens intergenerational transmission, and marginalizes minority identities. Despite growing awareness, traditional preservation methods remain inadequate; documentation efforts fail to capture cultural complexity, while machine translation distorts contextual meaning (Hutson et al., 2024). The digital linguistic divide further excludes underrepresented languages, limiting their digital presence and corpus availability (Bella et al., 2023). Additionally, economic pressures favor dominant global languages, leading younger generations to abandon their native tongues. While technological advancements offer potential solutions, current approaches often focus on efficiency rather than cultural authenticity, overlooking the need for linguistic preservation beyond translation (Mufwene, 2005). As AI-driven methods become central to language processing, it is essential to rethink how

Proceedings of the 1st Workshop on Language Models for Underserved Communities (LM4UC 2025), pages 51–60
May 4, 2025 ©2025 Association for Computational Linguistics

these systems can adapt to cultural and contextual complexities rather than replace them.

The shortcomings of existing AI-driven language models highlight the urgent need for a more culturally aware and linguistically inclusive approach. Traditional machine translation systems, while effective in word-to-word conversion, often fail to retain cultural and historical depth, with up to 47% of contextual meaning lost in conventional translations (Tian et al., 2022). This challenge is particularly significant for tonal languages, oral traditions, and indigenous dialects, where subtleties are essential for accurate interpretation. Additionally, the dominance of English-centric AI models reinforces linguistic hierarchies, marginalizing lesser-known languages and limiting their digital accessibility (Lepp and Sarin, 2024). Compounding this issue, AI trained primarily on Western linguistic paradigms struggles to handle dialectal diversity, non-standardized orthographies, and tonal complexity, making it unsuitable for many underrepresented languages (Kshetri, 2024; Romanou et al., 2024). Beyond technological constraints, globalization and socio-economic shifts further accelerate language endangerment, as younger generations increasingly prioritize global languages over ancestral ones (Garg, 2024). These challenges necessitate a shift from isolated, monolithic AI models to collaborative, multi-agent AI systems capable of not just translation but interpretation, synthesis, and evaluation through a cultural lens (Jones et al., 2025). By integrating context-aware translation, multimodal AI, and real-time bias detection, an innovative AI-driven linguistic framework can bridge these gaps and establish a more sustainable, culturally embedded approach to language preservation.

To address these challenges, we propose a Multi-Agent AI Framework for Cross-Language Understanding, designed to enhance the linguistic, cultural, and ethical integrity of machine translations, as outlined in Figure 1. Unlike traditional NLP models, which process translation in a linear and isolated manner, our framework orchestrates multiple AI agents that collaboratively refine linguistic and cultural adaptation at different stages. The Translation Agent ensures grammatical accuracy, while the Interpretation Agent enriches outputs by embedding historical, social, and contextual markers. The Content Synthesis Agent structures the final output, preserving idiomatic expressions, ceremonial speech, and linguistic variations for readability and coherence. Finally, the Quality and Bias Evaluation Agent mitigates distortions by cross-referencing historical data, detecting biases, and ensuring fairness through real-time validation mechanisms such as DuckDuckGo search integration.

Our collaborative AI system, developed using `CrewAI` and `LangChain`, is powered by `Aya-Expanse:8b` (Dang et al., 2024) via `Ollama`, with `LiteLLM` proxying to optimize model efficiency. By leveraging this multi-agent approach, our framework bridges the gap between low-resource language communities and high-performance NLP models, offering a scalable, ethically responsible, and culturally sensitive solution. Furthermore, this paradigm not only enhances translation quality but also provides a foundation for digital language preservation, ensuring that linguistic heritage remains accessible and relevant in the AI-driven era. Our work contributes to sustainable NLP development by promoting equitable access to AI technologies, aligning with the broader mission of inclusive and ethical AI for global linguistic diversity.

2 Related Work

The preservation of linguistic diversity and cultural heritage has been a growing research focus, with studies exploring both traditional methods and AI-driven computational techniques. Early efforts emphasized community-driven documentation, while modern advancements leverage machine translation, generative AI, and multimodal learning to enhance language sustainability.

2.1 Cultural Language Preservation

Traditional language preservation often relies on linguistic documentation and community-driven efforts. Nekoto et al. introduced a participatory translation approach to enhance neural machine translation (NMT) for under-resourced languages, fostering greater involvement from native speakers. Miyagawa (2024) developed a bi-directional translation system specifically for Ainu, addressing its unique linguistic structure and revitalizing the language's usage in modern contexts. Louadi (2024) emphasized the importance of diverse and inclusive datasets to reduce biases in AI applications, particularly in language preservation. Hutson et al. (2024) proposed scalable AI models to promote the use of mother tongues, enhancing cultural identity and continuity. Furthermore, Nanduri and Bonsignore (2023) explored AI-powered language

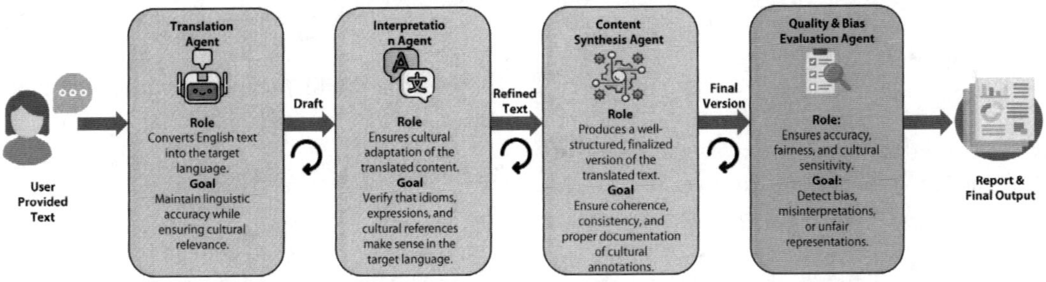

Figure 2: Our Workflow of Context-Aware Translation ThroughMulti-Agent AI Systems

learning tools, including bilingual storybooks and VR simulations, that not only support language acquisition but also promote cultural appreciation and ethical practices in the preservation process.

2.2 AI and Computational Techniques for Language Preservation

With the rapid advancements in AI and deep learning, researchers have increasingly explored machine learning, generative AI, and multimodal techniques for language revitalization. Bizan bin Ghowar (2023) applied AI to heritage analysis and NLP-driven historical text processing, aiming to preserve linguistic traditions through computational tools. Similarly, Liu et al. (2024) examined generative AI's potential in preserving ancient texts and facilitating multimodal research, highlighting its value in enhancing the accessibility of historical languages. However, Putri et al. (2024) pointed out that while LLMs can generate syntactically coherent text, they often fail to capture the cultural depth and contextual accuracy crucial for low-resource languages. This reveals a significant limitation in generative models, where AI systems lack the cultural nuances and real-world understanding necessary for effective language preservation. Further addressing this gap, Myung et al. (2024) introduced the BLEND benchmark to assess LLMs' cultural knowledge across multiple languages, revealing substantial performance discrepancies for underrepresented cultures. In response to these challenges, AJUZIEOGU (2024) proposed a multimodal generative AI framework for African language documentation, integrating neural architectures with community-driven approaches to mitigate the impact of data scarcity. While these studies highlight the potential of AI in language revitalization, they also underscore ongoing challenges in achieving true cultural adaptation and contextual accuracy, particularly in the face of limited and diverse datasets. This calls for more nuanced, culturally-aware AI frameworks that can bridge these gaps and offer robust solutions for underrepresented languages.

Existing AI models struggle with cultural depth, linguistic bias, and adaptability, often reinforcing English-centric hierarchies while failing to integrate underrepresented languages. Current LLM approaches lack collaborative, multi-agent frameworks, limiting contextual adaptation and ethical oversight. Our work distinguishes itself from existing research by introducing a multi-agent AI framework that specifically addresses the cultural and contextual shortcomings of traditional AI-driven translation models. While previous efforts, such as those by Nekoto et al. and Louadi (2024), have focused on improving language preservation through community-driven or single-agent AI approaches, our framework incorporates specialized agents—Translation, Interpretation, Content Synthesis, and Quality and Bias Evaluation. Our multi-agent framework enhances linguistic accuracy and cultural relevance, addressing the complexities of low-resource languages and idiomatic expressions. By using iterative cross-validation with external sources like DuckDuckGo, we mitigate biases and ensure cultural fidelity, outperforming traditional LLMs. This approach offers a novel, inclusive solution for language revitalization and preservation, overcoming the limitations of prior models.

3 Methodology

This section presents the design and implementation of our Multi-Agent AI Framework for Cross-Language Adaptation, focusing on system architecture, agent roles, and the translation refinement process.

3.1 System Overview

Our framework operates on a multi-agent architecture, leveraging `CrewAI` (Duan and Wang, 2024) for task delegation and collaboration. We employ Aya

Expanse 8B, an open-weight multilingual LLM from Cohere for AI, optimized through data arbitrage, multilingual preference training, safety tuning, and model merging (Dang et al., 2024). Aya Expanse 8B excels in 23 languages, ensuring robust cross-language performance. We integrate the `LiteLLM` proxy for optimized inference and use DuckDuckGo search for real-time external validation, allowing for cultural and contextual verification (Saravanos et al., 2022; Agarwal et al., 2024). The model undergoes 3-5 training epochs for general adaptation tasks and 10 epochs for fine-tuning on low-resource languages [1]. Our agents operate sequentially, with each module processing the text iteratively to refine grammatical accuracy, cultural fidelity, and bias mitigation. The system follows a task delegation structure, where each agent contributes to refining the output until it meets contextual and ethical standards. Our full experimental codebase is publicly available at: `github.com/ciol-researchlab/Context-Aware_Translation_MAS`.

3.2 Agent Crew for Linguistic Transformation

Our framework utilizes four autonomous agents, each designed to address specific aspects of the translation process. Each agent operates independently, contributing its specialized task to ensure a culturally adaptive and linguistically accurate translation. The agents are designed to work sequentially with possible back and forth if required, with each task building upon the previous one to refine and enhance the output. Below, we describe the purpose, goals, and design of each of these agents. Table 1 provides a brief description of the agents.

3.2.1 Translation Agent

The Translation Agent is responsible for converting the source text from English into the target language while ensuring syntactic correctness and linguistic precision. This agent utilizes Neural Machine Translation (NMT) techniques to generate a raw translation that preserves the meaning of the original content. The goal of this agent is to ensure that the translation remains grammatically accurate, following the rules and structure of the target language. To achieve this, the agent leverages large-scale pre-trained models and context-aware mechanisms to produce an initial, linguistically sound translation. By allowing delegation, the Translation Agent can also pass its output to other specialized agents for further refinement, ensuring that the translation process is adaptable and efficient.

3.2.2 Interpretation Agent

The Interpretation Agent's primary purpose is to ensure that the translated content is culturally relevant and meaningful in the target language. This agent focuses on adapting idioms, expressions, cultural references, and regional nuances to make the translation more natural and appropriate for the target audience. Its goal is not merely linguistic accuracy but the cultural adaptation of the text, ensuring that humor, traditions, and local contexts are accurately conveyed. The agent uses contextual understanding and cultural knowledge to evaluate the translation and make necessary changes. Allowing delegation here means the agent can pass its results to other agents for further analysis or validation, which is essential for complex linguistic tasks involving culture.

3.2.3 Content Synthesis Agent

The Content Synthesis Agent plays a pivotal role in structuring the translated text into its final, polished form. Its responsibility is to ensure that the translation reads coherently and fluently while preserving both linguistic accuracy and cultural authenticity. This agent organizes the text logically, ensuring that sentences and paragraphs flow smoothly and that the structure aligns with the conventions of the target language. Additionally, the Content Synthesis Agent integrates cultural annotations and decisions made by the Interpretation Agent, making the translated content not only readable but also reflective of the cultural and linguistic choices made throughout the process. This agent's design does not allow delegation, ensuring it holds the final responsibility for the presentation of the output.

3.2.4 Quality and Bias Evaluation Agent

The Quality and Bias Evaluation Agent is tasked with performing a thorough review of the translated text to detect any issues related to fairness, accuracy, or cultural sensitivity. This agent's role is to ensure that the translation upholds ethical standards by checking for bias or misrepresentation of cultural elements. It cross-references the translated content with external sources, such as DuckDuckGo, to validate the factual accuracy of cultural references and check the translation against real-

[1] Upon acceptance, we will release the full working code as an open-source project, ensuring transparency, reproducibility, and broader accessibility for researchers and developers.

Table 1: Roles and Capabilities of Different Agents in Our System

Agent	Goal	Task Delegation	Back story	Tool Capability
Translation Agent	Translate English text into another language while maintaining cultural essence.	Can delegate task	You are a linguistic expert. Your job is to translate English text into the target language while ensuring cultural relevance and accuracy	None
Interpretation Agent	Ensure that cultural references in the translation are correctly adapted to the target language.	Can delegate task	You specialize in cultural adaptation. Your task is to ensure that idioms, expressions, and references in the translated text are meaningful and accurate in the target culture.	None
Content Synthesis Agent	Create a well-structured, final version of the translated text with cultural annotations.	Can not delegate task	You produce a final, structured version of the translated text. This includes annotations on cultural adaptations and linguistic decisions.	None
Quality & Bias Evaluation Agent	Ensure the translation is accurate, fair, and culturally sensitive.	Can not delegate task	You are a quality assurance expert. Your job is to check for accuracy, fairness, and cultural sensitivity in the translated text.	Web Search Tool

world contexts. This agent helps identify potential errors or distortions that might arise during the translation process, ensuring the final output is both accurate and free of harmful bias. By not allowing delegation, this agent ensures that no oversight occurs in the final evaluation phase.

In summary, the four agents in our framework work collaboratively to ensure that translations are linguistically accurate, culturally relevant, and contextually sensitive. Each agent brings a specialized skill set to the process, allowing for a seamless and adaptive translation workflow. By incorporating autonomous agents for each phase of translation, we ensure high-quality, culturally rich, and unbiased results. This workflow follows a sequential but dynamic structure, ensuring maximum accuracy and cultural fidelity. The Translation Agent first generates the raw translation, which is then refined by the Interpretation Agent to ensure cultural alignment. Once adapted, the Content Synthesis Agent organizes the text into a structured, reader-friendly format. Finally, the Quality and Bias Evaluation Agent verifies the correctness, fairness, and relevance of the translation using external sources. If any issue is detected, the translation is sent back to the responsible agent for revision. This iterative back-and-forth process ensures that the final output is not just a linguistically correct translation but also a culturally accurate and fair representation of the original text.

3.3 Iterative Translation Processing and Output Refinement

Our system follows a well-defined execution pipeline to ensure high-quality translations. First, users input a text, which is processed by the Translation Agent to ensure linguistic accuracy. The Interpretation Agent then steps in to adapt cultural references, idioms, and regional expressions, refining the translation for context. Next, the Content Synthesis Agent polishes the text, improving clarity and readability while maintaining coherence. The final step involves the Quality and Bias Evaluation Agent, which cross-validates the translation for accuracy, detects potential biases, and verifies cultural elements against reliable external sources. If inconsistencies or discrepancies are found, the system revisits the Content Synthesis Agent for necessary revisions before generating the final output. This iterative process ensures that the translation preserves cultural nuances, maintains linguistic precision, and upholds contextual relevance. By combining context-aware refinement with continuous validation, the system produces translations that are accurate, culturally sensitive, and fair, offering a balanced approach to multilingual communication.

4 Results and Findings

As there is no benchmark or evaluation framework available for most cultural translation aspects of low-resource models, we adopt a simple qualitative evaluation to assess our model's capability. Table 2 discusses the output quality of the model by assessing the translations generated by our multi-agent AI framework across three cultural contexts—Festival, Religion, and History—for three languages: Hindi, Turkish, and Hebrew. Table 3 presents a comparative analysis between our multi-agent AI framework and GPT-4, highlighting key differences in cultural preservation and contextual depth.

4.1 Evaluation of Model Output Across Cultural Contexts

Table 2 presents the outputs generated by our multi-agent AI framework, demonstrating its effectiveness in translating content across three cultural contexts—Festival, Religion, and History—in Hindi, Turkish, and Hebrew while ensuring cul-

Table 2: Model Outputs on Different Linguistic and Cultural Setups

Languages	Cultural Context	Input (English Text)	Output (Final Translated Text with Cultural Adaption)
Hindi	Festival	Diwali, India's grand festival of lights, symbolizes the victory of good over evil as homes are adorned with diyas (oil lamps), families perform Lakshmi Puja, and fireworks light up the sky in joyous celebration	दिवाली भारत का महान प्रकाश उत्सव है, जो अच्छाई की जीत का प्रतीक है। घरों को दीयों (तेल के दीपक) से सजाया जाता है, परिवार लक्ष्मी पूजा करते हैं और फूलों के धुएं से आसमान खुशियों से भर जाता है।
	Religion	Every evening, the sacred banks of the Ganga River come alive with the mesmerizing Ganga Aarti, where priests chant Vedic hymns, waving golden-lit lamps, and devotees offer floating diyas to seek divine blessings.	हर शाम, गंगा नदी के तट **मनमोहक** गंगा आर्ती से जीवंत हो उठते हैं, जहां पुजारी वेदिक मंत्रों का उच्चारण करते हुए सुनहरी लौ वाले दीपक लहराते हैं और भक्त अपनी मनोकामनाओं के लिए प्रतिष्ठित दीया (दिया) नदी में उतारते हैं।
	History	The Revolt of 1857, India's first war of independence, saw brave warriors like Rani Lakshmibai, Mangal Pandey, and Bahadur Shah Zafar rise against British rule, igniting the spirit of freedom across the nation	१८५७ का संघर्ष भारत के स्वतंत्रता संग्राम की शुरुआत थी। इस युद्ध में रानी लक्ष्मीबाई, मंगल पांडेय और बहादुर शाह ज़फ़र जैसे वीर स्वतंत्रता सेनानियों ने ब्रिटिश शासन के ख़िलाफ़ विद्रोह करके देश को आज़ादी की ओर अग्रसर करने में महत्वपूर्ण भूमिका निभाई। उनकी बहादुरी और बलिदान ने लाखों भारतीयों को प्रेरित किया और एक नई राष्ट्रीय पहचान का निर्माण किया।
Turkish	Festival	Nevruz, the ancient Turkish and Central Asian New Year, marks the arrival of spring with bonfire jumping, folk dances, and feasts featuring traditional dishes like Baklava and Pilav, symbolizing renewal and unity.	Nevruz, Türk ve Orta Asya'nın köklü Yeni Yılı, baharın gelişini ateşin üzerinde zıplayarak, halk danslarıyla ve geleneksel lezzetlerle dolu şölenlerle karşılıyor. Baklava ve Pilav gibi yemekler, yenilenme ve birlik sembolü olarak masalarımızı süslüyor.
	Religion	The mystical Sema Ceremony of the Whirling Dervishes, rooted in Sufi traditions, is a spiritual dance where dervishes spin in rhythmic meditation, symbolizing a connection between earth and the divine	Sufi geleneklerine dayanan ve dervişlerin ritmik meditasyonda döndükleri mistik Sema Töreni, bir ruhani dans şeklidir. Bu dans, dünyayı ve ilahi arasında bir bağın sembolüdür.
	History	The Fall of Constantinople in 1453, led by Sultan Mehmed II (Fatih Sultan Mehmet), marked the rise of the Ottoman Empire, blending Eastern and Western cultures and transforming Istanbul into a global center of trade, art, and religion	İstanbul'un 1453'te düşüşü, Sultan II. Mehmed (Fatih) tarafından başlatılan Osmanlı İmparatorluğu'nun yükselişine yol açtı. Doğu ve Batı kültürlerinin bir araya gelmesi, İstanbul'u ticaret, sanat ve din açısından küresel bir merkez haline getirdi.
Hebrew	Festival	Passover (Pesach) is a sacred Jewish festival celebrating the Exodus from Egypt, where families gather for the Seder meal, retelling the story of liberation, eating matzah (unleavened bread), and reciting traditional blessings.	במשפחות מתכנסות .הוא חג יהודי קדוש המציין את היציאה ממצרים (פסחא)פסוח ומקיימות (לחם לא מותסס)אוכלות מצה ,מספרות סיפור השחרור ,לסעודה מסורתית .ברכות מסורתיות
	Religion	Shabbat, the weekly day of rest, begins at sunset on Friday with the lighting of Shabbat candles, the recitation of Kiddush (blessing over wine), and the sharing of Challah bread, as families come together in spiritual reflection.	שבת, יום המנוחה השבועי, מתחילה בשקיעה ביום שישי עם הדלקת נרות שבת, אמירת קדושה (ברכה על .היין), ואכילת לחם השבת, כשמשפחות מתאחדות ברפלקציה רוחנית
	History	in 70 CE, the Roman destruction of the Second Temple in Jerusalem marked a turning point in Jewish history, leading to the diaspora, the preservation of Jewish identity through Torah study, and the hope of one day returning to Zion.	ב-70 לספירה, חורבן המקדש השני בירושלים על ידי הרומאים סימן נקודת מפנה בהיסטוריה היהודית.שהובילה לגלות, שימור הזהות היהודית דרך לימוד התורה, .ותקווה לשוב יום אחד לציון

tural authenticity and contextual relevance. Unlike conventional translation models that prioritize direct linguistic conversion, our approach integrates cultural adaptation, refining grammatical precision, idiomatic expressions, and contextual depth. The Translation Agent ensures structural accuracy, while the Interpretation Agent adapts idiomatic phrases, religious references, and culturally significant expressions to enhance natural fluency and cultural immersion.

For instance, in the Hindi translation of Diwali, "grand festival of lights" becomes "mahaan prakaash utsav", emphasizing brilliance and festivity, while "victory of good over evil" is rendered as "acchai ki jeet", reinforcing the moral essence of the celebration. Cultural markers such as "Lakshmi Puja" remain unchanged, while "diyas" are translated as "deepak" to preserve their traditional significance. Similarly, in Turkish translations of Nevruz, "Bonfire jumping" is translated as "atesin uzerinde ziplamak", retaining its ritualistic importance, and "halk danslariyla" ensures the centrality of folk dances. Traditional foods such as Baklava and Pilav are adapted with idiomatic clarity, reinforcing their symbolic and cultural relevance. In the Sema Ceremony of the Whirling Dervishes, words like "mistik" and "ilahi" effectively capture its spiritual nature, ensuring linguistic and cultural accuracy. For Hebrew religious texts, "weekly day of rest" is translated as "yom hanukha shavu'i", emphasizing Shabbat's sacred nature, while "begins at sunset" becomes "matchila beshkia" to maintain traditional timing. Ritual elements such as "Shabbat candles", "Kiddush", and "Challah bread" are explicitly included, ensuring theological precision. The translation also preserves Shabbat's communal and reflective aspects, reinforcing its deeper spiritual meaning.

Beyond translation, the Content Synthesis Agent refines coherence and readability, while the Quality & Bias Evaluation Agent prevents cultural distortions and ensures historical accuracy. This is particularly crucial in historical translations, such as the 1857 Revolt and the Fall of Constantinople, where contextual and geopolitical precision is essential. The results confirm that multi-agent collaboration enhances cross-language understanding, producing translations that go beyond literal meaning to retain cultural significance. By integrating context-aware adaptation, idiomatic refinement, and external validation, the framework ensures culturally immersive and linguistically accurate translations. Table 2 validates the effectiveness of this approach, reinforcing its potential for AI-driven cultural preservation and cross-linguistic communication.

Table 3: Model Outputs Comparison with ChatGPT (GPT-4o)

English Text	Agent Translation	GPT Translation
Diwali, India's grand festival of lights, symbolizes the victory of good over evil as homes are adorned with diyas (oil lamps), families perform Lakshmi Puja, and fireworks light up the sky in joyous celebration.	दिवाली भारत का महान प्रकाश उत्सव है, जो अच्छाई की जीत का प्रतीक है। घरों को दीयों (तेल के दीपक) से सजाया जाता है, परिवार लक्ष्मी पूजा करते हैं और फूलों के धुएं से आसमान खुशियों से भर जाता है।	दीवाली, भारत का भव्य प्रकाश पर्व, बुराई पर अच्छाई की विजय का प्रतीक है, जब घर दीपों (तेल के दीयों) से सजाए जाते हैं, परिवार लक्ष्मी पूजा करते हैं, और आतिशबाज़ी आकाश में खुशियों की रोशनी बिखेरती है।
Every evening, the sacred banks of the Ganga River come alive with the mesmerizing Ganga Aarti, where priests chant Vedic hymns, waving golden-lit lamps, and devotees offer floating diyas to seek divine blessings.	हर शाम, गंगा नदी के तट **मनमोहक** गंगा आर्ती से जीवंत हो उठते हैं, जहां पुजारी वेदिक मंत्रों का उच्चारण करते हुए सुनहरी लौ वाले दीपक लहराते हैं और भक्त अपनी मनोकामनाओं के लिए प्रतिष्ठित दीया (दियों) नदी में उतारते हैं।	हर शाम, पवित्र गंगा नदी के तट गंगा आरती की मंत्रमुग्ध कर देने वाली छटा से जीवंत हो उठते हैं, जहाँ पुरोहित वेद मंत्रों का उच्चारण करते हुए स्वर्णिम दीप लहराते हैं, और भक्त दिव्य आशीर्वाद प्राप्त करने के लिए जल में तैरते दीप अर्पित करते हैं।
The Revolt of 1857, India's first war of independence, saw brave warriors like Rani Lakshmibai, Mangal Pandey, and Bahadur Shah Zafar rise against British rule, igniting the spirit of freedom across the nation.	१८५७ का संघर्ष भारत के स्वतंत्रता संग्राम की शुरुआत थी। इस युद्ध में रानी लक्ष्मीबाई, मंगल पांडेय और बहादुर शाह ज़फर जैसे वीर स्वतंत्रता सेनानियों ने ब्रिटिश शासन के ख़िलाफ़ विद्रोह करके देश को आज़ादी की ओर अग्रसर करने में महत्वपूर्ण भूमिका निभाई। उनकी बहादुरी और बलिदान ने लाखों भारतीयों को प्रेरित किया और एक नई राष्ट्रीय पहचान का निर्माण किया।	1857 का विद्रोह, भारत का पहला स्वतंत्रता संग्राम, बहादुर योद्धाओं जैसे रानी लक्ष्मीबाई, मंगल पांडे और बहादुर शाह ज़फर को ब्रिटिश शासन के खिलाफ उठते हुए देखा, जिसने पूरे राष्ट्र में स्वतंत्रता की भावना को प्रज्वलित किया।
Nevruz, the ancient Turkish and Central Asian New Year, marks the arrival of spring with bonfire jumping, folk dances, and feasts featuring traditional dishes like Baklava and Pilav, symbolizing renewal and unity.	Nevruz, Türk ve Orta Asya'nın köklü Yeni Yılı, baharın gelişini ateşin üzerinde zıplayarak, halk danslarıyla ve geleneksel lezzetlerle dolu şölenlerle karşılıyor. Baklava ve Pilav gibi yemekler, yenilenme ve birlik sembolü olarak masalarımızı süslüyor.	Nevruz, kadim Türk ve Orta Asya Yeni Yılı, baharın gelişini ateş üzerinden atlama, halk dansları ve Baklava ile Pilav gibi geleneksel yemeklerin yer aldığı şölenlerle kutlar, yenilenmeyi ve birliği simgeler.
The mystical Sema Ceremony of the Whirling Dervishes, rooted in Sufi traditions, is a spiritual dance where dervishes spin in rhythmic meditation, symbolizing a connection between earth and the divine.	Sufi geleneklerine dayanan ve dervişlerin ritmik meditasyonda döndükleri mistik Sema Töreni, bir ruhani dans şeklidir. Bu dans, dünyayı ve ilahi arasında bir bağın sembolüdür.	Mevlevi Dervişlerinin mistik Sema Töreni, Sufi geleneklerine dayanan ruhani bir danstır; dervişler ritmik bir meditasyon içinde dönerken, yeryüzü ile ilahi olan arasındaki bağı simgeler.
The Fall of Constantinople in 1453, led by Sultan Mehmed II (Fatih Sultan Mehmet), marked the rise of the Ottoman Empire, blending Eastern and Western cultures and transforming Istanbul into a global center of trade, art, and religion.	İstanbul'un 1453'te düşüşü, Sultan II. Mehmed (Fatih) tarafından başlatılan Osmanlı İmparatorluğu'nun yükselişine yol açtı. Doğu ve Batı kültürlerinin bir araya gelmesi, İstanbul'u ticaret, sanat ve din açısından küresel bir merkez haline getirdi.	1453 yılında Sultan II. Mehmed (Fatih Sultan Mehmet) liderliğinde gerçekleşen İstanbul'un Fethi, Osmanlı İmparatorluğu'nun yükselişini simgelerken, Doğu ve Batı kültürlerini bir araya getirmiş ve İstanbul'u ticaret, sanat ve dinin küresel bir merkezi haline getirmiştir.
Passover (Pesach) is a sacred Jewish festival celebrating the Exodus from Egypt, where families gather for the Seder meal, retelling the story of liberation, eating matzah (unleavened bread), and reciting traditional blessings.	במשפחות מתכנסות לסעודה .הוא חג יהודי קדוש המציין את היציאה ממצרים (פסחא) ומקיימות ברכות (לחם לא מותסס)אוכלות מצה ,מספרות סיפור השחרור ,מסורתית מסורתיות.	חג הפסח הוא חג יהודי קדוש החוגג את יציאת מצרים, שבו משפחות מתאספות לסעודת הסדר, מספרות מחדש את סיפור הגאולה, אוכלות מצה ומברכות ברכות מסורתיות.
Shabbat, the weekly day of rest, begins at sunset on Friday with the lighting of Shabbat candles, the recitation of Kiddush (blessing over wine), and the sharing of Challah bread, as families come together in spiritual reflection.	שבת, יום המנוחה השבועי, מתחילה בשקיעה ביום שישי עם הדלקת נרות שבת, אמירת קדושה (ברכה על .היין), ואכילת לחם השבת, כשמשפחות מתאחדות ברפלקציה רוחנית	שבת, יום המנוחה השבועי, מתחילה בשקיעת השמש ביום שישי עם הדלקת נרות שבת, אמירת קידוש (ברכה על היין) ושיתוף חלת שבת, כאשר משפחות מתכנסות יחד להרהור רוחני.
in 70 CE, the Roman destruction of the Second Temple in Jerusalem marked a turning point in Jewish history, leading to the diaspora, the preservation of Jewish identity through Torah study, and the hope of one day returning to Zion.	ב-70 לספירה, חורבן המקדש השני בירושלים על ידי הרומאים סימן נקודת מפנה בהיסטוריה היהודית.שהובילה לגלות, שימור הזהות היהודית דרך לימוד התורה, ותקווה לשוב יום אחד לציון.	בשנת 70 לספירה, חורבן בית המקדש השני בירושלים בידי הרומאים ציין נקודת מפנה בהיסטוריה היהודית, שהובילה לתפוצות, לשימור הזהות היהודית דרך לימוד התורה, ולטיפוח התקווה לשוב יום אחד לציון.

4.2 Comparative Analysis

Table 3 compares our multi-agent AI framework with GPT-4o, highlighting key differences in cultural preservation, contextual depth, and linguistic expressiveness. Our system outperforms GPT-4o in two major aspects: evocative language and contextualization. The Translation and Interpretation Agents incorporate figurative expressions, idiomatic phrases, and poetic descriptions, making the translations more immersive and culturally resonant.

For instance, in the Hindi translation of Ganga Aarti, our model renders the phrase as "mohak chhata chha jati hai" ("a mesmerizing aura"), effectively capturing the spiritual and visual grandeur of the event, whereas GPT-4o's simpler rendering of "bhavya Ganga Aarti" lacks emotional depth. Similarly, in the translation of the 1857 Revolt, our system uses "jwalant udaharan" ("a blazing example") to emphasize the passion and heroism of freedom fighters, while GPT-4o remains more neutral in its phrasing. In Turkish translations, our model adapts "Bonfire jumping" in Nevruz celebrations as "atesin uzerinde ziplamak", effectively reflecting the ritualistic importance, while GPT-4o's version remains technically correct but lacks cultural vibrancy. Additionally, our Whirling Dervishes translation integrates "mistik" (mystical) and "ilahi" (divine) to reinforce the spiritual and meditative essence of the dance, whereas GPT-4o provides a more standard description that does not fully capture its Sufi traditions. For Hebrew religious texts, our framework ensures spiritual authenticity by explicitly incorporating key observances such as Shabbat candles, Kiddush, and Challah bread, while GPT-4o omits or generalizes some religious details. In the Passover translation, our model maintains the ritualistic depth by carefully referencing traditional elements like unleavened bread and storytelling, ensuring greater alignment with Jewish traditions.

Additionally, our agents expand on traditions by linking events to their historical and cultural roots, whereas GPT-4o tends to remain neutral and lacks explanatory richness. Our framework also enhances transliterated cultural terms by adding brief clarifiers, making the text more accessible to native speakers. While GPT-4o ensures grammatical correctness, it often lacks cultural resonance and emotional warmth, reinforcing the need for a specialized multi-agent system in cross-language understanding and preservation.

5 Discussion

Our study presents a multi-agent AI framework designed to enhance cross-language translation by integrating linguistic accuracy, cultural adaptation, and bias mitigation. Unlike conventional LLM models, our approach distributes tasks across specialized agents—Translation, Interpretation, Content Synthesis, and Quality and Bias Evaluation—ensuring contextually enriched and culturally aligned translations. The Translation Agent guarantees grammatical correctness, while the Interpretation Agent adapts idiomatic expressions and cultural nuances. The Content Synthesis Agent refines readability, and the Quality and Bias Evaluation Agent validates fairness and authenticity using external sources. To evaluate our system's performance, we tested translations across multiple cultural domains, including historical narratives, religious traditions, and festival descriptions. Comparative evaluation with GPT-4o (Table 2) reveals that our framework consistently produces more evocative, idiomatic, and culturally grounded translations, demonstrating its ability to capture deeper contextual meaning across various content types rather than excelling in a single category. The agent-based approach effectively addresses limitations in conventional translation models, particularly in ensuring cultural depth and contextual relevance (Ogie et al., 2022). By incorporating external validation mechanisms, our system minimizes linguistic distortions and biases, making it more suitable for real-world multilingual applications. The results indicate that multi-agent collaboration enhances cross-language understanding, providing a scalable and adaptable solution for preserving linguistic heritage and reducing biases in AI-generated translations. This framework presents a significant step forward in AI-driven language processing, offering a context-aware, culturally sensitive, and ethically responsible approach to translation.

5.1 Limitations

Despite its effectiveness, our framework has several limitations. The multi-agent collaboration improves fairness and transparency but increases processing time compared to single-agent models, reducing efficiency for real-time applications. Although the system supports multiple languages, challenges persist with low-resource languages due to limited training data and digital resources, affecting translation quality and adaptability (Gong et al., 2024). External validation via DuckDuckGo enhances accuracy but may introduce inconsistencies if sources lack credibility or cultural specificity (Ootani and Yamana, 2018). Lastly, cultural subjectivity remains a challenge, as idioms and expressions often lack direct equivalents, requiring interpretative adjustments across contexts.

5.2 Future Work

Future research will focus on refining our multi-agent AI framework to address its current limitations. One area for improvement is optimizing the processing time for multi-agent collaboration, making the system more efficient for real-time applications without compromising translation quality. Expanding the framework's capabilities to better support low-resource languages through data augmentation and community-driven input is essential for improving translation adaptability and reducing biases in underrepresented languages. Additionally, enhancing the external validation mechanisms to incorporate more reliable and region-specific sources will further reduce inconsistencies in the system. Future work will also explore integrating more advanced cultural adaptation algorithms to handle nuanced expressions and idioms more effectively across diverse contexts. Moreover, we plan to expand the system's scope to include specialized domains such as legal and medical translations, where accuracy and cultural sensitivity are crucial. Collaborative research with cross-regional teams will be key to ensuring that the framework remains inclusive and adaptable to global linguistic and cultural needs.

6 Conclusion

Our study introduces a multi-agent AI framework that significantly enhances culturally adaptive cross-language translation, overcoming key limitations of traditional AI models. By employing specialized agents for translation, interpretation, content synthesis, and bias evaluation, our system ensures greater linguistic accuracy, cultural sensitivity, and contextual depth in translations. Although challenges such as computational efficiency and coverage for low-resource languages persist, our approach offers a promising pathway for more inclusive and context-aware AI-driven translation systems. The comparative analysis with GPT-4o further demonstrates the effectiveness of our framework in producing translations that are more culturally embedded and nuanced. As we look ahead, future work should focus on optimizing real-time processing capabilities, expanding language support, and refining external validation techniques to further enhance the scalability and reliability of cross-language communication. Ultimately, this research paves the way for a more equitable, culturally informed, and accurate AI translation landscape, contributing to the preservation and revitalization of diverse languages and cultures.

Acknowledgements

We express our sincere gratitude to Computational Intelligence and Operations Laboratory (CIOL) for their invaluable guidance, unwavering support, and continuous assistance throughout this journey. We are deeply appreciative of their efforts in organizing the CIOL Winter ML Bootcamp (Wasi et al., 2024), which provided an enriching learning environment and a strong foundation for collaborative research.

Author Contributions

M. A. Anik and A. T. Wasi conceptualized the idea and developed the methodology. M. A. Anik implemented the agents, conducted the literature review, carried out the experiments and analysis, and wrote the core sections of the work. A. Rahman contributed to visualization, literature analysis, and writing. A. T. Wasi supervised the project, provided overall guidance, and edited the manuscript. M. M. Ahsan also offered valuable support and guidance throughout various phases of the project.

References

Shubham Agarwal, Issam H Laradji, Laurent Charlin, and Christopher Pal. 2024. Litllm: A toolkit for scientific literature review. *arXiv preprint arXiv:2402.01788*.

UCHECHUKWU C AJUZIEOGU. 2024. Multimodal generative ai for african language preservation: A framework for language documentation and revitalization.

Gábor Bella, Paula Helm, Gertraud Koch, and Fausto Giunchiglia. 2023. Towards bridging the digital language divide. *arXiv preprint arXiv:2307.13405*.

Samy Bizan bin Ghowar. 2023. Recent trends in the use of artificial intelligence in the field of heritage. *International Journal of Artificial Intelligence and Emerging Technology*, 6(2):66–82.

John Dang, Shivalika Singh, Daniel D'souza, Arash Ahmadian, Alejandro Salamanca, Madeline Smith, Aidan Peppin, Sungjin Hong, Manoj Govindassamy, Terrence Zhao, Sandra Kublik, Meor Amer, Viraat Aryabumi, Jon Ander Campos, Yi-Chern Tan, Tom Kocmi, Florian Strub, Nathan Grinsztajn, Yannis Flet-Berliac, Acyr Locatelli, Hangyu Lin, Dwarak Talupuru, Bharat Venkitesh, David Cairuz, Bowen Yang, Tim Chung, Wei-Yin Ko, Sylvie Shang Shi, Amir Shukayev, Sammie Bae, Aleksandra Piktus, Roman Castagné, Felipe Cruz-Salinas, Eddie Kim, Lucas Crawhall-Stein, Adrien Morisot, Sudip Roy, Phil Blunsom, Ivan Zhang, Aidan Gomez, Nick Frosst, Marzieh Fadaee, Beyza Ermis, Ahmet Üstün, and Sara Hooker. 2024. Aya expanse: Combining research breakthroughs for a new multilingual frontier. *Preprint*, arXiv:2412.04261.

Zhihua Duan and Jialin Wang. 2024. Exploration of llm multi-agent application implementation based on langgraph+ crewai. *arXiv preprint arXiv:2411.18241*.

Neha Garg. 2024. Linguistic landscape of gen z: The impact of english dominance on endangered languages. *Journal of Research Scholars and Professionals of English Language Teaching*, 8(43):1–7.

Adiva Goel. Preserving south asian tribal legacies: Exploring oral traditions, traditional spoken narratives and folk tales.

Cheng Gong, Erica Cooper, Xin Wang, Chunyu Qiang, Mengzhe Geng, Dan Wells, Longbiao Wang, Jianwu Dang, Marc Tessier, Aidan Pine, et al. 2024. An initial investigation of language adaptation for tts systems under low-resource scenarios. *arXiv preprint arXiv:2406.08911*.

James Hutson, Pace Ellsworth, and Matt Ellsworth. 2024. Preserving linguistic diversity in the digital age: a scalable model for cultural heritage continuity. *Journal of Contemporary Language Research*, 3(1).

Graham M Jones, Shai Satran, and Arvind Satyanarayan. 2025. Toward cultural interpretability: A linguistic anthropological framework for describing and evaluating large language models. *Big Data & Society*, 12(1):20539517241303118.

Anne Kandler and Roman Unger. 2023. Modeling language shift. In *Diffusive spreading in nature, technology and society*, pages 365–387. Springer.

Nir Kshetri. 2024. Linguistic challenges in generative artificial intelligence: Implications for low-resource languages in the developing world.

Haley Lepp and Parth Sarin. 2024. A global ai community requires language-diverse publishing. *arXiv preprint arXiv:2408.14772*.

Jiangfeng Liu, Ziyi Wang, Jing Xie, and Lei Pei. 2024. From chatgpt, dall-e 3 to sora: How has generative ai changed digital humanities research and services? *arXiv preprint arXiv:2404.18518*.

Mohamed El Louadi. 2024. On the preservation of africa's cultural heritage in the age of artificial intelligence. *arXiv preprint arXiv:2403.06865*.

So Miyagawa. 2024. Ainu–japanese bi-directional neural machine translation: A step towards linguistic preservation of ainu, an under-resourced indigenous language in japan. *Journal of Data Mining & Digital Humanities*, (Digital humanities in languages).

Salikoko S Mufwene. 2005. Globalization and the myth of killer languages: What's really going on. *Perspectives on endangerment*, 5(21):19–48.

Junho Myung, Nayeon Lee, Yi Zhou, Jiho Jin, Rifki Afina Putri, Dimosthenis Antypas, Hsuvas Borkakoty, Eunsu Kim, Carla Perez-Almendros, Abinew Ali Ayele, et al. 2024. Blend: A benchmark for llms on everyday knowledge in diverse cultures and languages. *arXiv preprint arXiv:2406.09948*.

Dinesh Kumar Nanduri and Elizabeth M Bonsignore. 2023. Revitalizing endangered languages: Ai-powered language learning as a catalyst for language appreciation. *arXiv preprint arXiv:2304.09394*.

Wilhelmina Onyothi Nekoto, Julia Kreutzer, Jenalea Rajab, Millicent Ochieng, and Jade Abbott. Participatory translations of oshiwambo: Towards culture preservation with language technology.

Robert I Ogie, Sharon O'Brien, and Federico M Federici. 2022. Towards using agent-based modelling for collaborative translation of crisis information: A systematic literature review to identify the underlying attributes, behaviours, interactions, and environment of agents. *International Journal of Disaster Risk Reduction*, 68:102717.

Kazuyoshi Ootani and Hayato Yamana. 2018. External content-dependent features for web credibility evaluation. In *2018 IEEE International Conference on Big Data (Big Data)*, pages 5414–5416. IEEE.

Rifki Afina Putri, Faiz Ghifari Haznitrama, Dea Adhista, and Alice Oh. 2024. Can llm generate culturally relevant commonsense qa data? case study in indonesian and sundanese. *arXiv preprint arXiv:2402.17302*.

Angelika Romanou, Negar Foroutan, Anna Sotnikova, Zeming Chen, Sree Harsha Nelaturu, Shivalika Singh, Rishabh Maheshwary, Micol Altomare, Mohamed A Haggag, Alfonso Amayuelas, et al. 2024. Include: Evaluating multilingual language understanding with regional knowledge. *arXiv preprint arXiv:2411.19799*.

Antonios Saravanos, Stavros Zervoudakis, Dongnanzi Zheng, Amarpreet Nanda, Georgios Shaheen, Charles Hornat, Jeremiah Konde Chaettle, Alassane Yoda, Hyeree Park, and Will Ang. 2022. Reputation, risk, and trust on user adoption of internet search engines: The case of duckduckgo. In *International Conference on Human-Computer Interaction*, pages 683–691. Springer.

Chuanmao Tian, Xu Wang, and Mingwu Xu. 2022. Historico-cultural recontextualization in translating ancient classics: a case study of gopal sukhu's the songs of chu. *Perspectives*, 30(2):181–194.

Azmine Toushik Wasi, MD Shakiqul Islam, Sheikh Ayatur Rahman, and Md Manjurul Ahsan. 2024. Ciol presnts winter ml bootcamp. 6 December, 2024 to 6 February, 2025.

Enhancing Small Language Models for Cross-Lingual Generalized Zero-Shot Classification with Soft Prompt Tuning

Fred Philippy[1,2], Siwen Guo[1], Cedric Lothritz[3], Jacques Klein[2], Tegawendé F. Bissyandé[2]

[1] Zortify Labs, Zortify S.A., Luxembourg
[2] SnT, University of Luxembourg, Luxembourg
[3] Luxembourg Institute of Science and Technology (LIST), Luxembourg
{fred, siwen}@zortify.com cedric.lothritz@list.lu
{tegawende.bissyande, jacques.klein}@uni.lu

Abstract

In NLP, Zero-Shot Classification (ZSC) has become essential for enabling models to classify text into categories unseen during training, particularly in low-resource languages and domains where labeled data is scarce. While pretrained language models (PLMs) have shown promise in ZSC, they often rely on large training datasets or external knowledge, limiting their applicability in multilingual and low-resource scenarios. Recent approaches leveraging natural language prompts reduce the dependence on large training datasets but struggle to effectively incorporate available labeled data from related classification tasks, especially when these datasets originate from different languages or distributions. Moreover, existing prompt-based methods typically rely on manually crafted prompts in a specific language, limiting their adaptability and effectiveness in cross-lingual settings. To address these challenges, we introduce RoSPrompt, a lightweight and data-efficient approach for training soft prompts that enhance cross-lingual ZSC while ensuring robust generalization across data distribution shifts. RoSPrompt is designed for small multilingual PLMs, enabling them to leverage high-resource languages to improve performance in low-resource settings without requiring extensive fine-tuning or high computational costs. We evaluate our approach on multiple multilingual PLMs across datasets covering 106 languages, demonstrating strong cross-lingual transfer performance and robust generalization capabilities over unseen classes.

1 Introduction

Zero-Shot Classification (ZSC) is a task in NLP where a model classifies inputs into classes that it has not seen during training. This task is crucial in real-world scenarios where some classes are underrepresented with little or no labeled data. Traditionally, two approaches have dominated the landscape: entailment-based and similarity-based approaches. Entailment-based approaches (Yin et al., 2019) focus on understanding relationships between sentences, particularly determining the level of entailment between the document and the potential class labels. This method requires the model to have a deep understanding of language structure and logic. On the other hand, similarity-based approaches focus on computing the similarity between the input and labels of each class, even if the model has never encountered them during training. This method often relies on embeddings or vector representations of text, allowing the model to make inferences based on how closely the input aligns with class descriptors (Schopf et al., 2023).

However, these methods face inherent drawbacks, as they depend on Natural Language Inference or Semantic Text Similarity datasets that require considerable effort to develop and are susceptible to potential biases (Pavlick and Kwiatkowski, 2019; Kalouli et al., 2023). In light of this, and with the acknowledgment of the extensive knowledge embedded in general pre-trained language models (PLMs) and the potential to extract it, a novel paradigm has arisen: prompting. Prompting reformulates a task as a cloze-style task using a natural language prompt, retrieves the model's masked or next token prediction, and maps it to the right class via a verbalizer, while requiring little to no training data. Nevertheless, traditional prompting methods are hindered not only by manual effort and inherent biases of the individuals creating the prompts and verbalizers, but also by other factors such as the order of examples in the prompt during in-context learning (Zhao et al., 2021; Lu et al., 2022).

To address this, Shin et al. (2020) developed an automated system for generating prompts and verbalizers using a limited number of training samples. Furthermore, Hu et al. (2022) introduced a technique that eliminates the need for training data by automatically creating a verbalizer using an external knowledge base. Motivated by the goal of elim-

Proceedings of the 1st Workshop on Language Models for Underserved Communities (LM4UC 2025), pages 61–75
May 4, 2025 ©2025 Association for Computational Linguistics

inating the need for any additional data, Zhao et al. (2023) proposed a method that forms a verbalizer using only the PLM's embedding space, without requiring any training data or external knowledge base. This approach, while efficient and effective in various ZSC tasks, shares a limitation with the methods of Shin et al. (2020) and Hu et al. (2022): it relies on language-specific prompts which introduce a language bias, making the method less effective in multilingual scenarios. Moreover, despite the high efficiency and appeal of methods that operate without existing data, their inability to leverage even a minimal amount of available data from a similar classification task in a high-resource language, can be seen as a significant limitation in our data-abundant world.

To address these shortcomings, we suggest to transform the language-specific hard prompts into trainable soft prompts (Lester et al., 2021), which can then be fine-tuned. However, directly adopting the conventional soft prompt tuning (SPT) setup leads to overfitting on the seen classes (§7), therefore, does not generalize under data distribution shifts. In response to this constraint, we introduce ***Robust Soft Prompts*** (**`RoSPrompt`**), a novel method for cross-lingual zero-shot topic classification through few-shot SPT, which exhibits robust out-of-distribution generalization and strong cross-lingual transfer performance. `RoSPrompt` not only retains the efficiency and effectiveness of leveraging the knowledge of PLMs but also enhances it by incorporating small sets of existing data. By doing so, we aim to broaden the applicability of ZSC in a multilingual context, ensuring more accurate topic classification across diverse languages and datasets.

Specifically, our approach

(a) enables the training of soft prompts, which are better suited for ZSC tasks compared to hand-crafted, natural language hard prompts.

(b) shows strong cross-lingual transfer performance after few-shot fine-tuning in English, with soft prompts significantly improving accuracy compared to hard prompts.

(c) displays significant robustness against data distribution shifts, enabling the fine-tuning of the prompt on any available topic classification data for subsequent use in diverse topic classification tasks.

(d) exhibits computational efficiency, as fewer than 1% of parameters are fine-tuned in comparison to full-model fine-tuning.

To showcase the efficacy of our proposed approach, we conduct a comprehensive evaluation using three distinct types of multilingual language models (encoder-only, decoder-only, and encoder-decoder) and three diverse datasets, encompassing 106 languages, thereby highlighting the versatility and applicability of our method in cross-lingual scenarios.

2 Background

Soft Prompt Tuning (SPT) Our approach is based on SPT (Lester et al., 2021), extending it specifically for cross-lingual zero-shot topic classification. SPT appends tunable vectors (soft prompts) to the input of a PLM, training only the soft prompts while keeping the original model weights frozen. This method demonstrates efficacy in various downstream tasks, providing a balance between model performance and resource efficiency, and is particularly effective for cross-lingual transfer (Philippy et al., 2024).

Given an input sequence $\mathbf{x}$ and the set of C potential classes $\mathcal{C}$, we define the two main components of SPT:

- A **soft prompt** $\mathbf{p}$ that is appended to $\mathbf{x}$ in order to obtain $\mathbf{x}' = [\mathbf{x}; \mathbf{p}]$, where $[\cdot; \cdot]$ is the concatenation function.
- A **verbalizer** $v : \mathcal{T} \to \mathcal{C}$ which maps the token predicted by the model to the respective class. $\mathcal{T} = \{t_1, \ldots, t_C\}$ is a subset of the model's vocabulary $\mathcal{V}$ and the token t_c "describes" the class c.

If we denote the function performed by the model as f, with its parameters θ (which are frozen during SPT), the logits over the vocabulary $\mathcal{V}$ for the next token in the sequence are given by:

$$f_\theta(\mathbf{x}') = \{z_1, \ldots, z_{|\mathcal{V}|}\}$$

The predicted class will then be

$$\hat{y} = \arg\max_{c \in \mathcal{C}} z_{t_c}$$

Nonparametric Prompting (NPPrompt) Zhao et al. (2023) demonstrated that PLMs possess significant innate capabilities for ZSC, even without task-specific fine-tuning. Their technique,

NPPrompt, involves adding a natural language prompt to the input example, prompting the model to fill in the [MASK] for BERT-based models, or predict the next token for autoregressive and Seq2Seq models, which are then used for the final classification of the sample. Nevertheless, their strategy is primarily designed for English, as the prompts employed are in English. Applying their method to additional languages would necessitate the engineering of new prompts specific to those languages. Furthermore, despite the appeal of their zero-shot framework, particularly when there is a lack of fine-tuning data, it falls short by not accommodating the use of existing labeled data when it is available. Therefore, we suggest to extend their method by transforming the natural language prompt into a trainable soft prompt (Lester et al., 2021), enabling its training through any available topic classification data in the source language for subsequent zero-shot topic classification in any target language.

3 RoSPrompt

We describe our technique as a hybrid of SPT (Lester et al., 2021) and NPPrompt (Zhao et al., 2023). SPT excels in data efficiency but is sensitive to data distribution shifts, needing unique prompts for each topic classification dataset. On the other hand, NPPrompt uses one prompt for various data distributions but fails to leverage existing data. Our strategy combines their strengths, using a single, robust soft prompt for different data distributions and enhancing data utilization (Figure 1).

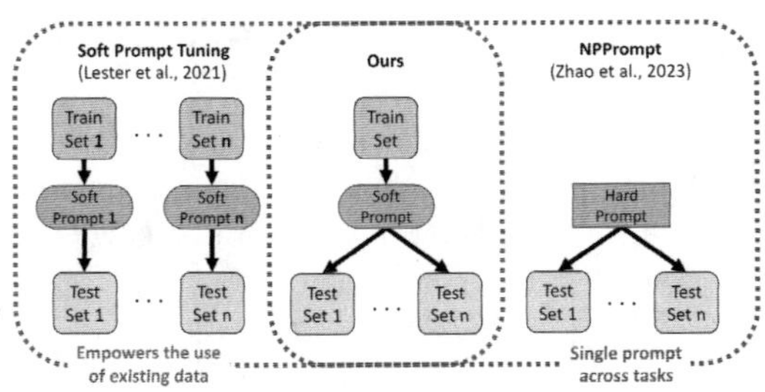

Figure 1: Conventional SPT (Lester et al., 2021), while effective in leveraging existing data, requires distinct training for each topic classification task. Conversely, NPPrompt (Zhao et al., 2023) offers versatility with a single natural language prompt for various tasks but lacks data leverage. Our method combines the strengths of both methods, enabling data utilization with a single soft prompt applicable across diverse topic classification tasks, while effectively overcoming the drawbacks of both methods.

Figure 2 provides a graphical illustration of our approach. The novelty of our method is most apparent in the training phase (§3.1), which involves three main components: **1)** the application of a multilingual verbalizer; **2)** the use of contrastive label smoothing; **3)** the adoption of a custom loss function penalty. For the inference phase of our method, we adopt the technique proposed by Zhao et al. (2023), aligning seamlessly with our goals.

3.1 Training

Below, we detail the three main components of our training approach.

1) Multilingual Class Description Tokens As mentioned before, in the standard methodology of SPT, a class c is characterized, via the verbalizer, by a single token t_c from the vocabulary $\mathcal{V}$. However, this single token might not fully capture the essence of the respective class. Moreover, it is confined to one language, leading to potential inconsistencies in multilingual settings, where the sample and the verbalizer token may be in different languages.

Therefore we propose, during training, to extend the single verbalizer token t_c to a multilingual set of verbalizer tokens $T_c = \{t_c^{(1)}, t_c^{(2)}, \ldots\}$. These augmented verbalizer tokens could be additional descriptive tokens, such as synonyms or translations of the original label token.

Our method does not mandate a uniform number of verbalizer tokens across different classes, and the manual labor involved in generating these labels is a one-time effort only required for fine-tuning the soft prompt.

2) Contrastive Label Smoothing Conventionally, when pre-training large language models, using self-supervised tasks such as the masked language modeling or next-token prediction objective, a single token from the vocabulary is considered to be the gold truth.

Mathematically, given a token vocabulary $\mathcal{V}$, $y = [y_1, \ldots, y_{|\mathcal{V}|}]$ represents the "true" masked or next token in one-hot encoded form. When using a "hard" probability distribution, if t^* is the "true" token, $\forall t \in \mathcal{V}$,

$$y_t = 1 \times \mathbb{1}_{\{t=t^*\}}$$

for the cross-entropy loss defined as

$$CE(\hat{y}, y) = -\sum_{t=1}^{|\mathcal{V}|} y_t \times \log(\hat{y}_t)$$

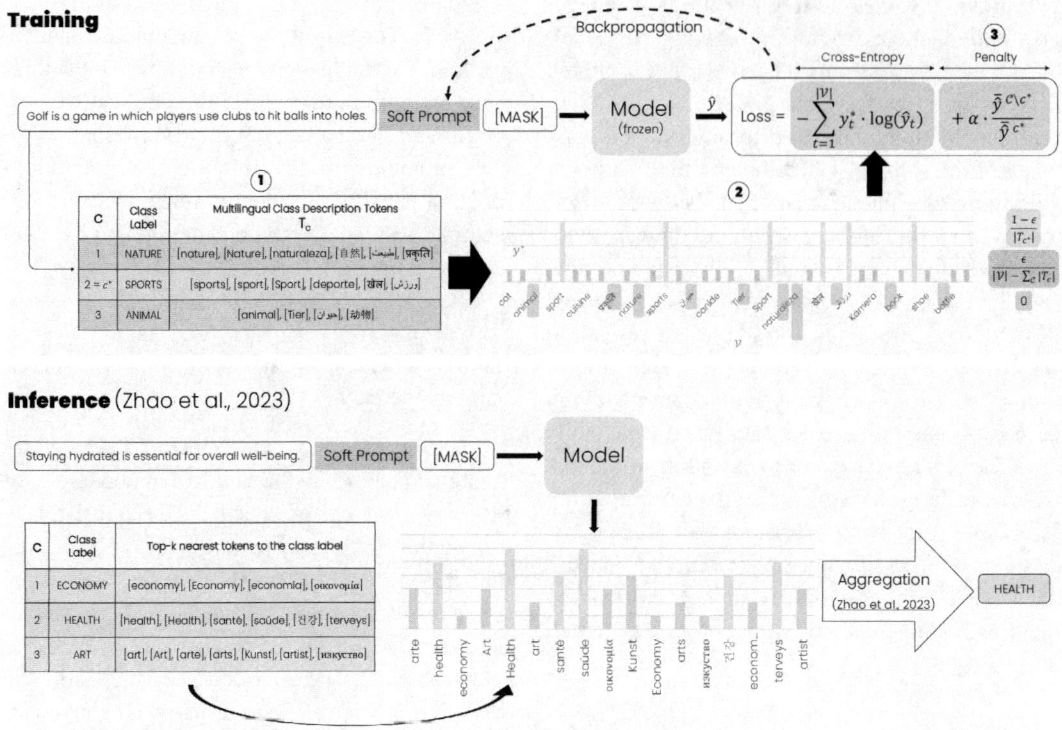

Figure 2: Visual representation of **RoSPrompt**. During training, each class is categorized by a **multilingual set of label tokens** (①). We apply **contrastive label smoothing** (②) to the probability distribution across the entire vocabulary. To further deter overfitting, we integrate a **custom penalty** (③) into the loss function. During inference, we retrieve the logits predicted by the model and use the aggregation technique proposed by Zhao et al. (2023) to make the final prediction.

where $\hat{y}$ represents the probabilities predicted by the model.

In other words, this standard method assigns a probability of 1 to the true token and 0 to the others, which might lead to overfitting as the model becomes overly confident in certain predictions. A strategy to resolve this is label smoothing (Szegedy et al., 2016), a regularization technique penalizing models for over-confident predictions and thereby mitigating overfitting. Label smoothing achieves this by shifting from a "hard" probability distribution, where only the true token gets a non-zero probability, to a "soft" distribution, where small probabilities are allocated to all or some vocabulary tokens, and the probability for the true token is reduced.

Our method employs a modified form of conventional label smoothing, which we refer to as *contrastive label smoothing*. This variation is designed to handle multiple "true" tokens for each class. Additionally, it not only prevents overconfident predictions by the model but also penalizes it for consistently favoring class label tokens over those without a class assignment. We argue that this approach leads to improved generalization over unseen classes in ZSC setups.

If $\mathcal{C}$ represents the potential classes of the training data, we denote $(T_c)_{c\in\mathcal{C}}$ as the label class token collections for each class, where T_c is the collection of verbalizer tokens of class c. If a sample belongs to class c^* we distribute the probabilities across the vocabulary, $\forall t \in \mathcal{V}$, as follows:

$$y_t = \begin{cases} \frac{1-\epsilon}{|T_{c^*}|} & \text{if } t \in T_{c^*} \\ \frac{\epsilon}{|\mathcal{V}|-\sum_{c\in\mathcal{C}}|T_c|} & \text{if } t \notin \bigcup\limits_{c\in\mathcal{C}} T_c \\ 0 & \text{otherwise} \end{cases}$$

In other words we uniformly distribute a collective probability of $1-\epsilon$ over the label tokens of the true class, i.e. T_{c^*}, and the remaining probability ϵ over all other tokens in the vocabulary **except** the label tokens of other classes.

3) Penalty In order to further penalize the soft prompt for overfitting on the seen classes during training, we additionally add a penalty to the cross-entropy loss function. We define

$$\bar{\hat{y}}^{\mathcal{C}\setminus c^*} = \frac{\sum_{c \in \mathcal{C}\setminus c^*} \sum_{t \in T_c} \hat{y}_t}{\sum_{c \in \mathcal{C}\setminus c^*} |T_c|} \quad \textbf{and} \quad \bar{\hat{y}}^{c^*} = \frac{\sum_{t \in T_{c^*}} \hat{y}_t}{|T_{c^*}|}$$

as the average predicted probabilities for all verbalizer tokens across all classes except the true class c^*, and for all verbalizer tokens within the class c^*, respectively.

With these definitions, we express the penalty Ω as:

$$\Omega\left(\hat{y}\right) = \frac{\bar{\hat{y}}^{\mathcal{C}\setminus c^*}}{\bar{\hat{y}}^{c^*}}$$

This penalty simply expresses the ratio of the average predicted probabilities for the true class tokens and the class tokens for all other potential classes.

Hence, the final loss function used in our approach becomes

$$L(\hat{y}, y) = CE(\hat{y}, y) + \alpha \times \Omega\left(\hat{y}\right)$$

where α is the coefficient that controls the influence of the penalty.

3.2 Inference

During inference we use the methodology proposed by Zhao et al. (2023).

The verbalizer tokens get automatically chosen by selecting the the top-k nearest tokens in the embedding space to each original English class label t_c. More specifically, for a given class c, its verbalizer tokens are given by

$$T_c = \underset{t \in \mathcal{V}}{\text{Top-k}} \left\{ S(\text{emb}(t), \text{emb}(t_c)) \right\}$$

where $S(\cdot)$ is the cosine similarity function.

For a given input document x, the aggregated prediction score for class c, based on the model's output logits for the next or MASK token, $\hat{y}$, is given by

$$Q(c|x) = \sum_{t \in T_c} w(t, t_c) \cdot \hat{y}_t$$

where the weight of each token in the verbalizer for a given class c is given by

$$w(t, t_c) = \frac{\exp(S(\text{emb}(t), \text{emb}(t_c)))}{\sum_{j \in T_c} \exp(S(\text{emb}(j), \text{emb}(t_c)))}$$

The final predicted class is then given by

$$\hat{c} = \underset{c \in \mathcal{C}}{\arg\max}\, Q(c|x)$$

This selects the class with the highest aggregated prediction probability.

4 Experimental Setup

We provide a general description of the datasets for training and evaluation, along with the models used in our experiments. Further specific details about the experimental setup can be found in Appendix A.

4.1 Datasets

For our experiments, a general English document classification dataset serves as the source data for training the soft prompts. We then evaluate these prompts on three diverse multilingual datasets, each with its own set of classes.

4.1.1 Training

As training data we use the English `DBPedia14` dataset, an ontology classification dataset, compiled from Wikipedia's most frequently used infoboxes and containing 14 distinct classes. Every class includes 40.000 samples for training and 5.000 samples for testing.

4.1.2 Evaluation

For evaluation we use 3 distinct multilingual topic classification datasets. Further details being provided in Appendix A.3.

`MLSUM` (Scialom et al., 2020), a multilingual news summarization dataset. We classify articles based on their summaries, using six main categories per language, although the exact categories differ slightly across languages.

`MTOP` (Li et al., 2021), a multilingual utterance classification dataset, featuring 11 different domains and covering 6 languages.

`SIB-200` (Adelani et al., 2024), a multilingual topic classification dataset featuring 7 categories and covering more than 200 languages.

We focus on using MTOP and MLSUM to test the robustness of our method under distribution shifts, but since they are limited to high-resource languages, we leverage SIB-200 to assess cross-lingual transfer to low-resource languages, thanks to its broader language coverage

4.2 Models

We evaluate our method on three distinct models, each one based on a different architecture:

`XGLM` (Lin et al., 2022), a *decoder-only* model supporting 30 different languages.

`mT0` (Muennighoff et al., 2023), an *encoder-decoder* model supporting 101 languages, which is a multi-task fine-tuned version of the mT5 model (Xue et al., 2021).

`XLM-R` (Conneau et al., 2020), an *encoder-only* model, supporting 100 languages.

More specifically, we use the `XGLM-564M`, `mT0-base` and `XLM-RoBERTa-large` variants. We describe them in more detail in Appendix A.4.

4.3 Baselines

We evaluate RoSPrompt against different baselines:

NPPrompt (Zhao et al., 2023), previously described in Section 2, using the English hard prompt "In this sentence, the topic is about [MASK]".

NPPrompt-t, a variant of NPPrompt where the English prompt is translated into the target language for inference.[1]

SPT (Lester et al., 2021), previously described in Section 2, where a soft prompt is fine-tuned on English samples using standard SPT practices and then used with NPPrompt during inference.

Zero-Shot Prompting, where we evaluate generative LLMs prompted in a zero-shot manner using a natural language instruction. Specifically, we use the 8-bit quantized variants of *Llama3.1-8B* (Dubey et al., 2024) and *Phi3.5-mini* (Abdin et al., 2024). We focus on SIB-200 for this baseline, as RoSPrompt is not designed for high-resource languages where smaller models cannot compete with large LLMs trained on extensive data. For transparency, results on MTOP and MLSUM are included in Appendix B, along with further details on this baseline.

4.4 Technical Details

Our experimental setup includes freezing all model parameters and appending a soft prompt to the initial input, as detailed in Section 2. We start by initializing the soft prompt with the embeddings of the natural language prompt from Zhao et al. (2023): "In this sentence, the topic is about". We then fine-tune this prompt using 8 randomly selected English samples from each class in DBPedia. Our methodology includes using translations of the original English label tokens into a diverse range of languages[2], and selecting words that tokenize as a single token for our multilingual label tokens. We then assess the model's performance using the trained soft prompt on all three evaluation datasets across all supported languages. During evaluation, only the original English class names are needed, with no need for further translation efforts.

To account for variability in few-shot experiments, we repeat each experiment four times using different random seeds and report the average results.

5 Results

For each of the three models, our experimental findings are presented in Table 1 for `MLSUM` and `MTOP`, across all languages. Given the extensive range of languages in SIB-200, we present average results for each major language family in Table 2, while detailed results for individual languages are shown in Appendix C (see Table 10). Overall, our methodology shows a significant advantage over NPPrompt in nearly all cases. In particular, our training method, which leverages a mere 8 samples per class from an existing topic classification dataset, generates a soft prompt that is more effective for ZSC than a natural language prompt, demonstrating robust generalization capabilities for unseen classes.

Additionally, we observe that while larger generative LLMs slightly outperform the smaller RoSprompt-enhanced LLMs on high-resource languages, they significantly underperform, often worse than the random baseline, on low-resource languages, highlighting the effectiveness of our method in such scenarios.

6 Ablation Study

To illustrate the individual contributions of each component in our training method, we carry out an ablation study. We assess the efficacy of our original method against variants lacking the loss penalty, contrastive label smoothing, and/or multilingual labels.

[1] Languages unsupported by Google Translate or with syntax that does not place the [MASK] token at the end are excluded. In Table 2, English prompt performance is used for reporting.

[2] We used the following languages as they are spoken by at least one member of our team: de, en, es, fa, fr, hi, ro, sv, uk, zh.

Model		MTOP						MLSUM			
		de	en	es	fr	hi	th	de	es	fr	ru
XGLM	**RoSPrompt**	**54.99**	**64.31**	**58.95**	**55.38**	**56.47**	47.59	**79.47**	**70.77**	**71.60**	**62.66**
	NPPrompt	48.72	55.02	47.77	47.57	52.49	**49.26**	56.30	48.83	43.92	42.97
	NPPrompt-t	26.63	55.02	42.03	19.14	-	33.27	61.22	21.68	31.97	38.24
	SPT	30.52	31.98	32.51	30.98	28.69	29.46	63.12	53.26	54.00	53.68
mT0	**RoSPrompt**	**47.65**	**53.23**	**51.48**	**48.21**	**49.42**	**46.28**	**65.24**	50.58	**48.00**	45.22
	NPPrompt	43.14	46.35	48.57	43.60	46.04	38.37	65.07	48.10	43.23	43.14
	NPPrompt-t	33.14	46.35	33.36	7.02	-	39.89	59.51	43.36	31.33	26.80
	SPT	46.22	52.31	47.87	44.19	44.42	42.98	64.64	**52.81**	47.32	**45.92**
XLM-R	**RoSPrompt**	**55.64**	**63.93**	**54.79**	**52.91**	**62.25**	**53.28**	**81.77**	**65.46**	**60.66**	53.39
	NPPrompt	36.38	46.03	35.76	34.95	47.69	39.02	62.38	50.77	52.79	**58.17**
	NPPrompt-t	35.25	46.03	35.29	28.47	-	47.05	72.95	41.89	38.18	48.37
	SPT	39.10	43.75	35.29	36.35	40.04	37.55	69.00	57.83	50.40	49.59

Table 1: Comparison of accuracy scores on the **MTOP** and **MLSUM** datasets between RoSPrompt and baselines.

Model		Afro-Asiatic	Atlantic-Congo	Austro-nesian	Dravi-dian	Indo-European	Sino-Tibetan	Turkic	Uralic
XGLM	**RoSPrompt**	**69.12**	**65.32**	**73.04**	**64.95**	**70.80**	**72.92**	**72.55**	**71.51**
	NPPrompt	60.78	61.76	59.31	58.09	61.48	58.83	62.25	62.26
	NPPrompt-t	53.92	58.82	63.73	58.09	54.41	53.68	62.25	40.69
	SPT	59.19	55.51	66.05	58.15	60.94	54.05	60.42	66.54
mT0	**RoSPrompt**	**71.69**	**71.69**	**75.61**	**75.61**	**75.75**	**74.27**	**74.39**	**73.10**
	NPPrompt	57.11	59.13	59.95	61.64	61.52	62.42	61.03	63.40
	NPPrompt-t	46.41	51.16	51.84	61.64	54.84	59.47	61.03	53.27
	SPT	65.05	66.42	67.37	70.07	69.91	72.18	68.28	69.40
XLM-R	**RoSPrompt**	**72.67**	**65.69**	**71.69**	**66.91**	**68.65**	**68.63**	**67.89**	**70.59**
	NPPrompt	57.43	56.62	63.14	64.83	64.20	63.73	65.13	65.69
	NPPrompt-t	45.26	38.24	57.25	64.83	52.05	57.84	65.13	57.03
	SPT	56.78	52.33	61.96	64.49	61.65	65.28	61.40	57.31
Llama3.1-8B		25.42	18.44	26.42	8.58	39.84	35.29	26.82	44.61
Phi-3.5-mini		42.30	38.11	57.95	7.72	55.17	54.09	46.08	65.03

Table 2: Comparison of accuracy scores on the **SIB-200** dataset between RoSPrompt and baselines.

The outcomes of this study, presented in Table 3 for MTOP across three models, indicate that all three elements are integral to our method's success. Notably, the removal of the loss penalty leads to the most significant decline in performance for XGLM and mT0, while the lack of multilingual labels has the greatest negative impact on XLM-R.

	XGLM	mT0	XLM-R
RoSPrompt	**56.28**	49.38	**57.13**
w/o penalty	30.22	31.91	51.59
w/o LS	50.05	49.71	48.18
w/o penalty & LS	29.38	41.53	51.26
w/o ML labels	50.05	**50.37**	47.40

Table 3: Ablation study results for MTOP.

This could potentially be attributed to XLM-R's enhanced code-switching capabilities (Winata et al., 2021; Zhang et al., 2023), making it more efficient at using multilingual label tokens during training compared to XGLM and mT0.

7 Generalized Zero-Shot Learning

In our initial experiments, training (*seen*) and evaluation (*unseen*) classes were distinct with merely minimal overlap. In contrast, the *Generalized Zero-Shot Learning* (GZSL) settings, which mirror real-world situations more closely, involve evaluating on a mix of both seen and unseen classes. Models in this setting often struggle with overfitting to seen classes and fail to perform well on unseen classes

(Xian et al., 2019).

Therefore, we aim to investigate whether our method is also efficient under GZSL settings. For this, we fine-tune the soft prompt on a subset of classes from a dataset, then test it on the entire set of classes. Considering the potential variability resulting from the specific choice of seen and unseen classes, we repeat this process four times for each dataset and model, each time with a different subset of seen classes. We then average the F1 scores for seen and unseen classes and present them in Table 4. These experiments are conducted with all three models, but only for the SIB-200[3] and MTOP datasets, as MLSUM does not support English, and has varying categories across languages.

		SIB-200		**MTOP**	
		Unseen	*Seen*	*Unseen*	*Seen*
XGLM	SPT	20.02	48.56	28.04	49.04
	RoSPrompt	48.68	49.60	62.41	61.50
mT0	SPT	31.32	39.44	32.26	23.49
	RoSPrompt	67.11	65.44	39.33	52.98
XLM-R	SPT	26.88	53.78	17.63	43.88
	RoSPrompt	56.64	55.68	62.54	57.96

Table 4: Comparison of average F1 scores for seen and unseen classes using standard SPT versus RoSPrompt.

For conventional SPT, there is a notable imbalance in performance between seen and unseen classes, with seen classes showing higher performance, suggesting overfitting to seen classes and poor generalization to unseen classes. However, when training the soft prompts using our method, the performance is more balanced, indicating improved generalization to unseen classes.

8 Contextualizing Our Approach

In this study, we acknowledge that comparing our approach with NPPrompt may not constitute an entirely fair comparison. RoSPrompt uses a small dataset for training, while NPPrompt directly leverages a PLM without additional fine-tuning. However, it is important to emphasize that the intent of our research is not to demonstrate RoSPrompt's performance superiority over NPPrompt. Instead, our objective is to illustrate how RoSPrompt's methodology can effectively improve cross-lingual transfer capabilities of natural language prompts. This aspect is vital as our findings indicate that merely converting hard prompts to soft prompts and then fine-tuning them using the standard SPT approach results in non-robust prompts which are ineffective for Generalized ZSC.

Additionally, while our paper focuses on topic classification, we believe that our approach could be equally effective for other types of classification tasks as well. Nonetheless, we emphasize the significance of zero-shot learning in topic classification, where classes often change more frequently over time or across domains, unlike in more stable tasks like sentiment analysis, where classes show less variation.

Furthermore, we want to emphasize the threefold efficiency of our approach: **1)** it is data efficient, requiring only a small number of labeled training samples from any comparable classification task; **2)** it is computationally efficient as fewer than 0.1% of parameters are fine-tuned compared to full-model fine-tuning, reducing training time by approximately 50% in our experiments; **3)** it is memory-efficient, as for n training processes, besides the resulting n prompts that take up a few hundred KBs at most, only one model copy is stored, in contrast to full-model fine-tuning where each model occupies several GBs of storage.

Moreover, while our method is theoretically applicable to larger models with billions of parameters, our primary target is smaller LLMs, which are often sufficient for tasks like zero-shot classification but need more focused guidance. These smaller multilingual models also excel in low-resource languages, where larger English-centric models, as we demonstrate, are less effective.

9 Conclusion

In this paper, we introduced `RoSPrompt`, a novel approach for cross-lingual zero-shot topic classification. It combines the advantages of few-shot SPT with the extensive knowledge acquired by language models in their pre-training phase. Our training method is designed for computational efficiency and incorporates three key components to enhance the standard SPT methodology, contributing to RoSPrompt's cross-lingual abilities and resilience to data distribution shifts.

[3]For computational efficiency during this experiment, we limited our evaluation to a subset of ten linguistically diverse languages (en, ru, zh, de, ar, bn, ta, ko, my, sw) instead of all supported ones.

Limitations

Our research was conducted on datasets encompassing a variety of classes and data distributions. However, the absence of multilingual datasets across entirely distinct domains limits our ability to test the method's effectiveness in distant or niche domains. Therefore, while our results are promising within the domains we studied, they may not fully represent the model's capabilities across all specific domains.

In addressing the few-shot learning nature of our approach, varied the training samples across 4 iterations for each experiment to reduce potential biases. Nonetheless, the specific selection of these samples can still influence the outcomes due to the inherent characteristics of few-shot learning. This limitation suggests that our findings could be partially influenced by the particular datasets used, and might not entirely reflect the model's performance with different or broader data samples.

Ethics Statement

In our work, we prioritized two key ethical aspects, through which we strive to contribute to the inclusive and responsible advancement of NLP technology.

Language Diversity and Equity. Our method aims to balance performance across various languages, addressing the common disparity in model effectiveness between high- and low-resource languages. By enhancing multilingual capabilities, `RoSPrompt` contributes towards more balanced performance across languages, ensuring fair and inclusive technology across diverse linguistic groups.

Environmental Responsibility. Our method is designed for computational efficiency, requiring fine-tuning of fewer than 1% of parameters compared to traditional methods. This approach not only conserves computational resources but also aligns with environmental sustainability goals by reducing the energy consumption and carbon footprint associated with training and deploying NLP models.

Acknowledgment

The author Cedric Lothritz is supported by the Luxembourg National Research Fund (FNR) PEARL program, grant agreement 16544475.

References

Marah Abdin, Sam Ade Jacobs, Ammar Ahmad Awan, Jyoti Aneja, Ahmed Awadallah, Hany Awadalla, Nguyen Bach, Amit Bahree, Arash Bakhtiari, Harkirat Behl, et al. 2024. Phi-3 technical report: A highly capable language model locally on your phone. *arXiv preprint arXiv:2404.14219*.

David Adelani, Hannah Liu, Xiaoyu Shen, Nikita Vassilyev, Jesujoba Alabi, Yanke Mao, Haonan Gao, and En-Shiun Lee. 2024. SIB-200: A Simple, Inclusive, and Big Evaluation Dataset for Topic Classification in 200+ Languages and Dialects. In *Proceedings of the 18th Conference of the European Chapter of the Association for Computational Linguistics (Volume 1: Long Papers)*, pages 226–245, St. Julian's, Malta. Association for Computational Linguistics.

Alexis Conneau, Kartikay Khandelwal, Naman Goyal, Vishrav Chaudhary, Guillaume Wenzek, Francisco Guzmán, Edouard Grave, Myle Ott, Luke Zettlemoyer, and Veselin Stoyanov. 2020. Unsupervised Cross-lingual Representation Learning at Scale. In *Proceedings of the 58th Annual Meeting of the Association for Computational Linguistics*, pages 8440–8451, Online. Association for Computational Linguistics.

Abhimanyu Dubey, Abhinav Jauhri, Abhinav Pandey, Abhishek Kadian, Ahmad Al-Dahle, Aiesha Letman, Akhil Mathur, Alan Schelten, Amy Yang, Angela Fan, et al. 2024. The llama 3 herd of models. *arXiv preprint arXiv:2407.21783*.

Shengding Hu, Ning Ding, Huadong Wang, Zhiyuan Liu, Jingang Wang, Juanzi Li, Wei Wu, and Maosong Sun. 2022. Knowledgeable Prompt-tuning: Incorporating Knowledge into Prompt Verbalizer for Text Classification. In *Proceedings of the 60th Annual Meeting of the Association for Computational Linguistics (Volume 1: Long Papers)*, pages 2225–2240, Dublin, Ireland. Association for Computational Linguistics.

Aikaterini-Lida Kalouli, Hai Hu, Alexander F. Webb, Lawrence S. Moss, and Valeria De Paiva. 2023. Curing the SICK and Other NLI Maladies. *Computational Linguistics*, 49(1):199–243.

Jens Lehmann, Robert Isele, Max Jakob, Anja Jentzsch, Dimitris Kontokostas, Pablo N. Mendes, Sebastian Hellmann, Mohamed Morsey, Patrick Van Kleef, Sören Auer, and Christian Bizer. 2015. DBpedia – A large-scale, multilingual knowledge base extracted from Wikipedia. *Semantic Web*, 6(2):167–195.

Brian Lester, Rami Al-Rfou, and Noah Constant. 2021. The Power of Scale for Parameter-Efficient Prompt Tuning. In *Proceedings of the 2021 Conference on Empirical Methods in Natural Language Processing*, pages 3045–3059, Online and Punta Cana, Dominican Republic. Association for Computational Linguistics.

Haoran Li, Abhinav Arora, Shuohui Chen, Anchit Gupta, Sonal Gupta, and Yashar Mehdad. 2021. MTOP: A Comprehensive Multilingual Task-Oriented Semantic Parsing Benchmark. In *Proceedings of the 16th Conference of the European Chapter of the Association for Computational Linguistics: Main Volume*, pages 2950–2962, Online. Association for Computational Linguistics.

Xi Victoria Lin, Todor Mihaylov, Mikel Artetxe, Tianlu Wang, Shuohui Chen, Daniel Simig, Myle Ott, Naman Goyal, Shruti Bhosale, Jingfei Du, Ramakanth Pasunuru, Sam Shleifer, Punit Singh Koura, Vishrav Chaudhary, Brian O'Horo, Jeff Wang, Luke Zettlemoyer, Zornitsa Kozareva, Mona Diab, Veselin Stoyanov, and Xian Li. 2022. Few-shot Learning with Multilingual Generative Language Models. In *Proceedings of the 2022 Conference on Empirical Methods in Natural Language Processing*, pages 9019–9052, Abu Dhabi, United Arab Emirates. Association for Computational Linguistics.

Yinhan Liu, Myle Ott, Naman Goyal, Jingfei Du, Mandar Joshi, Danqi Chen, Omer Levy, Mike Lewis, Luke Zettlemoyer, and Veselin Stoyanov. 2019. RoBERTa: A Robustly Optimized BERT Pretraining Approach. ArXiv:1907.11692 [cs].

Ilya Loshchilov and Frank Hutter. 2019. Decoupled Weight Decay Regularization.

Yao Lu, Max Bartolo, Alastair Moore, Sebastian Riedel, and Pontus Stenetorp. 2022. Fantastically Ordered Prompts and Where to Find Them: Overcoming Few-Shot Prompt Order Sensitivity. In *Proceedings of the 60th Annual Meeting of the Association for Computational Linguistics (Volume 1: Long Papers)*, pages 8086–8098, Dublin, Ireland. Association for Computational Linguistics.

Niklas Muennighoff, Thomas Wang, Lintang Sutawika, Adam Roberts, Stella Biderman, Teven Le Scao, M Saiful Bari, Sheng Shen, Zheng Xin Yong, Hailey Schoelkopf, Xiangru Tang, Dragomir Radev, Alham Fikri Aji, Khalid Almubarak, Samuel Albanie, Zaid Alyafeai, Albert Webson, Edward Raff, and Colin Raffel. 2023. Crosslingual Generalization through Multitask Finetuning. In *Proceedings of the 61st Annual Meeting of the Association for Computational Linguistics (Volume 1: Long Papers)*, pages 15991–16111, Toronto, Canada. Association for Computational Linguistics.

NLLB Team, Marta R. Costa-jussà, James Cross, Onur Çelebi, Maha Elbayad, Kenneth Heafield, Kevin Heffernan, Elahe Kalbassi, Janice Lam, Daniel Licht, Jean Maillard, Anna Sun, Skyler Wang, Guillaume Wenzek, Al Youngblood, Bapi Akula, Loic Barrault, Gabriel Mejia Gonzalez, Prangthip Hansanti, John Hoffman, Semarley Jarrett, Kaushik Ram Sadagopan, Dirk Rowe, Shannon Spruit, Chau Tran, Pierre Andrews, Necip Fazil Ayan, Shruti Bhosale, Sergey Edunov, Angela Fan, Cynthia Gao, Vedanuj Goswami, Francisco Guzmán, Philipp Koehn, Alexandre Mourachko, Christophe Ropers, Safiyyah Saleem, Holger Schwenk, and Jeff Wang. 2022. No Language Left Behind: Scaling Human-Centered Machine Translation. ArXiv:2207.04672 [cs].

Ellie Pavlick and Tom Kwiatkowski. 2019. Inherent Disagreements in Human Textual Inferences. *Transactions of the Association for Computational Linguistics*, 7:677–694.

Fred Philippy, Siwen Guo, Shohreh Haddadan, Cedric Lothritz, Jacques Klein, and Tegawendé F. Bissyandé. 2024. Soft Prompt Tuning for Cross-Lingual Transfer: When Less is More. In *Proceedings of the 1st Workshop on Modular and Open Multilingual NLP (MOOMIN 2024)*, pages 7–15, St Julians, Malta. Association for Computational Linguistics.

Tim Schopf, Daniel Braun, and Florian Matthes. 2023. Evaluating Unsupervised Text Classification: Zero-shot and Similarity-based Approaches. In *Proceedings of the 2022 6th International Conference on Natural Language Processing and Information Retrieval*, NLPIR '22, pages 6–15, New York, NY, USA. Association for Computing Machinery.

Thomas Scialom, Paul-Alexis Dray, Sylvain Lamprier, Benjamin Piwowarski, and Jacopo Staiano. 2020. MLSUM: The Multilingual Summarization Corpus. In *Proceedings of the 2020 Conference on Empirical Methods in Natural Language Processing (EMNLP)*, pages 8051–8067, Online. Association for Computational Linguistics.

Taylor Shin, Yasaman Razeghi, Robert L. Logan IV, Eric Wallace, and Sameer Singh. 2020. AutoPrompt: Eliciting Knowledge from Language Models with Automatically Generated Prompts. In *Proceedings of the 2020 Conference on Empirical Methods in Natural Language Processing (EMNLP)*, pages 4222–4235, Online. Association for Computational Linguistics.

Christian Szegedy, Vincent Vanhoucke, Sergey Ioffe, Jon Shlens, and Zbigniew Wojna. 2016. Rethinking the Inception Architecture for Computer Vision. In *2016 IEEE Conference on Computer Vision and Pattern Recognition (CVPR)*, pages 2818–2826, Las Vegas, NV, USA. IEEE.

Guillaume Wenzek, Marie-Anne Lachaux, Alexis Conneau, Vishrav Chaudhary, Francisco Guzmán, Armand Joulin, and Edouard Grave. 2020. CCNet: Extracting High Quality Monolingual Datasets from Web Crawl Data. In *Proceedings of the Twelfth Language Resources and Evaluation Conference*, pages 4003–4012, Marseille, France. European Language Resources Association.

Genta Indra Winata, Samuel Cahyawijaya, Zihan Liu, Zhaojiang Lin, Andrea Madotto, and Pascale Fung. 2021. Are Multilingual Models Effective in Code-Switching? In *Proceedings of the Fifth Workshop on Computational Approaches to Linguistic Code-Switching*, pages 142–153, Online. Association for Computational Linguistics.

Thomas Wolf, Lysandre Debut, Victor Sanh, Julien Chaumond, Clement Delangue, Anthony Moi, Pierric Cistac, Tim Rault, Remi Louf, Morgan Funtowicz, Joe Davison, Sam Shleifer, Patrick von Platen, Clara Ma, Yacine Jernite, Julien Plu, Canwen Xu, Teven Le Scao, Sylvain Gugger, Mariama Drame, Quentin Lhoest, and Alexander Rush. 2020. Transformers: State-of-the-Art Natural Language Processing. In *Proceedings of the 2020 Conference on Empirical Methods in Natural Language Processing: System Demonstrations*, pages 38–45, Online. Association for Computational Linguistics.

Yongqin Xian, Christoph H. Lampert, Bernt Schiele, and Zeynep Akata. 2019. Zero-Shot Learning—A Comprehensive Evaluation of the Good, the Bad and the Ugly. *IEEE Transactions on Pattern Analysis and Machine Intelligence*, 41(9):2251–2265.

Linting Xue, Noah Constant, Adam Roberts, Mihir Kale, Rami Al-Rfou, Aditya Siddhant, Aditya Barua, and Colin Raffel. 2021. mT5: A Massively Multilingual Pre-trained Text-to-Text Transformer. In *Proceedings of the 2021 Conference of the North American Chapter of the Association for Computational Linguistics: Human Language Technologies*, pages 483–498, Online. Association for Computational Linguistics.

Wenpeng Yin, Jamaal Hay, and Dan Roth. 2019. Benchmarking Zero-shot Text Classification: Datasets, Evaluation and Entailment Approach. In *Proceedings of the 2019 Conference on Empirical Methods in Natural Language Processing and the 9th International Joint Conference on Natural Language Processing (EMNLP-IJCNLP)*, pages 3914–3923, Hong Kong, China. Association for Computational Linguistics.

Ruochen Zhang, Samuel Cahyawijaya, Jan Christian Blaise Cruz, Genta Winata, and Alham Fikri Aji. 2023. Multilingual Large Language Models Are Not (Yet) Code-Switchers. In *Proceedings of the 2023 Conference on Empirical Methods in Natural Language Processing*, pages 12567–12582, Singapore. Association for Computational Linguistics.

Xuandong Zhao, Siqi Ouyang, Zhiguo Yu, Ming Wu, and Lei Li. 2023. Pre-trained Language Models Can be Fully Zero-Shot Learners. In *Proceedings of the 61st Annual Meeting of the Association for Computational Linguistics (Volume 1: Long Papers)*, pages 15590–15606, Toronto, Canada. Association for Computational Linguistics.

Zihao Zhao, Eric Wallace, Shi Feng, Dan Klein, and Sameer Singh. 2021. Calibrate Before Use: Improving Few-shot Performance of Language Models. In *Proceedings of the 38th International Conference on Machine Learning*, pages 12697–12706. PMLR.

A Technical Details

Access to the code used in our research will provided in the camer-ready version.

A.1 Training

We conducted all of our experiments using the Transformers library (Wolf et al., 2020) and ran them on 4 A100 Nvidia GPUs within a few hours. We used AdamW (Loshchilov and Hutter, 2019) as an optimizer. We provide the hyperparameters used during our experiments in Table 5. Due to computational constraints, we did not perform exhaustive hyper-parameter optimization, but instead selected hyper-parameters that demonstrated satisfactory performance in preliminary experiments.

	XGLM	XLM-R	mT0
Batch size	8	8	8
Learning rate	0.01	0.01	0.3
Epochs	10	10	10
α	100	10	200
ϵ	0.2	0.1	0.8
Prompt length	8	8	9

Table 5: Hyperparameters

A.2 Evaluation

During evaluation, NPPrompt (Zhao et al., 2023) requires a parameter k, which is referred to as the *neighborhood number*. In our experimental setup, for each model and dataset type, we selected the value of k that achieved the highest average performance across the development sets of all supported languages. The specific values selected for k in the evaluation of RoSPrompt, NPPrompt (including NPPrompt-t) and SPT are presented in Tables 6, 7 and 8 respectively.

	XGLM	XLM-R	mT0
SIB-200	3	4	14
MTOP	4	2	8
MLSUM	300	5	7

Table 6: Chosen *neighborhood number* k values for **RoSPrompt**.

	XGLM	XLM-R	mT0
SIB-200	4	3	6
MTOP	3	2	5
MLSUM	5	4	6

Table 7: Chosen *neighborhood number* k values for **NPPrompt** Zhao et al. (2023) and **NPPrompt-t** (Zhao et al. (2023) with translated hard prompt).

	XGLM	XLM-R	mT0
SIB-200	2	17	5
MTOP	100	7	12
MLSUM	200	16	7

Table 8: Chosen *neighborhood number k* values for **SPT**.

Impact of Hyperparameters RoSPrompt's training methodology primarily relies on two numerical hyperparameters: the contrastive label smoothing factor, denoted as ϵ, and the penalty strength, represented by α.

In Figure 3, we illustrate RoSPrompt's performance using XGLM and mT0 on the SIB-200 dataset, using a diverse subset of languages[4], across various values for α and ϵ, while maintaining the other hyperparameter at zero each time. Generally, we find that both excessively low and high values for α and ϵ do not lead to optimal outcomes.

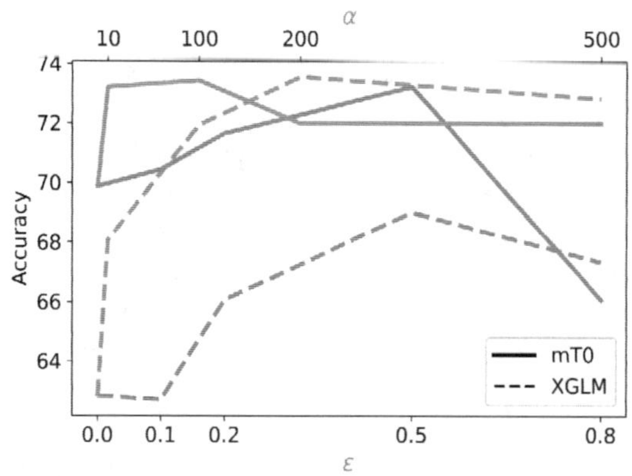

Figure 3: Average performance (accuracy) of RoSPrompt across 10 languages on SIB-200 for different values of ϵ and α.

A.3 Datasets

As source data to train the soft prompts, we use the `DBPedia14` ontology classification dataset[5] (Lehmann et al., 2015). It is a subset of the English version of DBpedia 2014[6], consisting of randomly chosen 560 000 training and 70 000 test samples equally distributed across 14 distinct classes. These classes represent the most common infobox categories on Wikipedia, including categories like `Company`, `Artist`, `Athlete`, `Village`, `Animal`, among others.

[4]en, ru, zh, de, ar, bn, ta, ko, my, sw

[5]https://huggingface.co/datasets/dbpedia_14

[6]https://downloads.dbpedia.org/wiki-archive/data-set-2014.html

For evaluation we use three different multilingual datasets:

`MLSUM` (Scialom et al., 2020), a multilingual news summarization dataset. However, each article-summary pair is also labeled with its respective news category. Therefore, in our experiments, we use, for each article, the summary for its classification. Given the differing data sources for different languages, the categories across languages slightly differ. More specifically we use articles on `society`, `politics`, `culture`, `sports`, `economy` and `science` for Spanish, Russian and French and articles on `politics`, `sports`, `economy`, `travel`, `car` and `education` for German. This selection amounts to 8935, 612, 5950, 5315 test samples for German, Russian, French and Spanish respectively. MLSUM is licensed under the MIT License[7].

`MTOP`[8] (Li et al., 2021), a multilingual utterance classification dataset, featuring 11 different domains, such as `alarm`, `reminder`, `recipes` or `weather`. The dataset covers 6 languages: English, German, Spanish, French, Hindi and Thai, with respective test sample counts of 4386, 3549, 2998, 3193, 2789, and 2765. `MTOP` is licensed under the Creative Commons Attribution-ShareAlike 4.0 International License[9].

`SIB-200`[10] (Adelani et al., 2024), a multilingual topic classification dataset covering 203 languages. The dataset is derived from the FLORES-200 benchmark (NLLB Team et al., 2022) and consists of 701 training, 99 validation and 204 test samples in each language. It features 7 distinct classes: `geography`, `politics`, `science/technology`, `travel`, `sports`, `health` and `entertainment`. `SIB-200` is licensed under the Apache License 2.0[11].

A.4 Models

In our work, we use the following models:

`XGLM`$_{564M}$[12] (Lin et al., 2022) is a decoder-only multilingual model supporting a diverse selection of 30 languages. Pre-trained on the CC100-XL dataset,

[7]https://opensource.org/license/mit/

[8]https://huggingface.co/datasets/mteb/mtop_domain

[9]https://creativecommons.org/licenses/by-sa/4.0/

[10]https://github.com/dadelani/sib-200

[11]https://www.apache.org/licenses/LICENSE-2.0.txt

[12]https://huggingface.co/facebook/xglm-564M

	MTOP						MLSUM			
Model	**de**	**en**	**es**	**fr**	**hi**	**th**	**de**	**es**	**fr**	**ru**
Llama3.1-8B	83.26	93.50	85.32	83.15	84.69	75.26	78.13	70.21	68.27	53.92
Phi-3.5-mini	79.57	86.34	78.62	78.52	70.49	66.22	77.08	71.17	66.91	59.64

Table 9: Accuracy scores on the **MTOP** and **MLSUM** obtained through zero-shot prompting.

an expansion of CC100 (Conneau et al., 2020; Wenzek et al., 2020), it features 564 million parameters, 24 layers, a hidden dimension size of 1024, and 16 attention heads.

XLM-R$_{Large}$ [13] (Conneau et al., 2020) is an encoder-only multilingual RoBERTa-based (Liu et al., 2019) model supporting 100 languages, pre-trained on CC100 (Conneau et al., 2020; Wenzek et al., 2020) using the MLM objective. It consists of 550 million parameters, 24 hidden layers, a dimension of 1024, and 16 attention heads.

mT0$_{Base}$ [14] (Muennighoff et al., 2023) is an encoder-decoder model supporting 101 languages. It is an mT5 model (Xue et al., 2021) that has been multi-task fine-tuned on the xP3 dataset[15] (Muennighoff et al., 2023). It features 584 million parameters, 12 encoder and decoder layers, 12 attention heads, and a hidden dimension size of 768.

B Additional Details on "Zero-Shot Prompting" Baseline

For this baseline, we used the 8-bit quantized versions of *Llama3.1-8B*[16] (Dubey et al., 2024) and *Phi-3.5-mini*[17] (Abdin et al., 2024), which have been designed with robust multilingual capabilities. *Llama3.1-8B* is a transformer-based language model with 8.03 billion parameters, designed for efficient text generation tasks. *Phi-3.5-mini*, a smaller variant, has 3.82 billion parameters and shares a similar transformer architecture optimized for lightweight inference. Both models were prompted using the prompt shown in Figure 4 and used with 8-bit quantization.

The results on MTOP and MLSUM are provided in Table 9.

[13] https://huggingface.co/xlm-roberta-large

[14] https://huggingface.co/bigscience/mt0-base

[15] https://huggingface.co/datasets/bigscience/xP3

[16] https://huggingface.co/meta-llama/Llama-3.1-8B-Instruct

[17] https://huggingface.co/microsoft/Phi-3.5-mini-instruct

```
I will provide text and potential
categories, and I would like you
to classify the text into one
of the given categories based on
its content. Please ensure the
classification is accurate and
consistent.

Categories:
- Label 1
- Label 2
- ...

Text: "{Document}"

Only return the category name.
```

Figure 4: The prompt used for the **Zero-Shot LLMs** baseline with *Llama3.1-8B* and *Phi-3.5-mini*.

C Full Results for SIB-200

Table 10 presents the experimental results for each language on SIB-200, with average values per language family reported in Table 2 in Section 5.

	XGLM				mT0				XLM-R					
	RoSPrompt	*NPPrompt*	*NPPrompt-t*	*SPT*	*RoSPrompt*	*NPPrompt*	*NPPrompt-t*	*SPT*	*RoSPrompt*	*NPPrompt*	*NPPrompt-t*	*SPT*	*Llama3.1-8B*	*Phi-3.5-mini*
afr_Latn					74.02	63.24	62.75	**74.39**	**69.85**	62.75	38.73	59.07	44.12	**74.51**
als_Latn					**75.37**	62.75	56.86	70.47	**69.24**	65.69	24.02	61.15	30.88	**58.82**
amh_Ethi					**64.71**	55.39	-	63.11	**65.56**	59.80	-	62.38	2.45	**3.92**
arb_Arab	**69.12**	60.78	53.92	59.19	**71.69**	62.25	64.71	71.08	**72.67**	69.61	55.39	71.69	48.53	**72.06**
asm_Beng									**72.30**	62.75	-	59.31	**15.20**	11.76
azb_Arab					**65.07**	54.41	-	58.58	**59.80**	57.35	-	49.02	23.04	**37.25**
azj_Latn					**75.37**	63.24	-	69.73	67.52	**69.61**	-	67.16	33.33	**52.94**
bel_Cyrl					**74.02**	62.75	60.29	69.36	**67.89**	64.71	44.61	66.67	44.61	**51.47**
ben_Beng	**69.36**	61.27	61.27	59.44	**72.30**	57.35	-	69.85	**67.28**	64.22	-	59.07	**31.86**	25.00
bos_Latn									**68.14**	64.71	60.29	58.70	48.53	**60.29**
bul_Cyrl	**69.49**	63.73	57.35	63.73	**77.45**	63.24	55.88	74.02	**68.26**	66.18	59.80	67.77	51.96	**67.65**
cat_Latn	**71.81**	65.69	59.80	59.19	**79.90**	65.20	51.47	71.32	**69.61**	64.71	59.31	67.77	53.43	**75.98**
ceb_Latn					**69.12**	61.27	54.41	**69.12**					29.90	**65.20**
ces_Latn					**75.25**	62.25	50.98	71.81	**65.93**	64.71	53.92	64.83	55.88	**72.06**
cym_Latn					**63.97**	55.88	32.84	63.48	**65.69**	59.80	46.57	59.19	28.92	**49.51**
dan_Latn					**73.77**	64.22	61.76	72.06	**69.00**	67.16	38.24	64.22	52.94	**74.51**
deu_Latn	**70.22**	62.25	48.04	66.91	**75.12**	66.18	62.25	72.55	**69.36**	68.14	50.49	64.34	66.67	**80.39**
ell_Grek	**69.36**	57.84	52.45	62.75	**73.65**	58.82	65.20	69.49	69.12	**70.10**	47.06	64.83	**51.47**	43.63
eng_Latn	**73.53**	63.73	63.73	69.00	**79.41**	65.20	65.20	73.53	**68.01**	61.76	61.76	52.33	75.98	**83.33**
epo_Latn					**77.08**	67.16	40.20	73.04	**67.65**	67.16	20.59	59.44	43.14	**62.25**
est_Latn	**69.36**	61.76	22.55	65.56	**73.28**	66.18	45.59	72.30	**69.73**	66.18	47.06	58.21	36.76	**55.88**
eus_Latn	**71.20**	63.73	-	60.17	**74.51**	63.73	-	74.02	**65.81**	58.82	-	58.33	31.37	**52.45**
fin_Latn	**73.65**	62.75	58.82	67.52	**72.92**	62.25	52.45	67.28	**71.45**	66.18	59.31	60.17	47.06	**69.12**
fra_Latn	**71.08**	58.33	36.76	60.05	**77.70**	64.22	58.33	70.71	**66.18**	65.20	31.86	60.17	65.20	**78.92**
gaz_Latn									**44.24**	35.29	29.41	38.48	9.31	**25.98**
gla_Latn					**60.42**	48.53	38.24	56.13	**59.19**	54.90	41.67	53.19	13.24	**30.88**
gle_Latn					69.00	60.78	29.90	**69.24**	**63.60**	57.84	44.61	56.86	19.61	**42.16**
glg_Latn					**76.47**	67.65	47.55	**76.47**	**68.75**	64.71	52.45	68.50	52.94	**77.94**
guj_Gujr					**74.02**	65.20	-	69.24	**68.26**	60.29	-	64.09	**6.86**	2.94
hat_Latn	**65.81**	59.80	62.25	48.41	**69.73**	55.39	40.69	67.40					18.63	**54.41**
hau_Latn					60.91	51.47	42.65	**61.64**	**60.54**	59.31	45.59	51.10	23.53	**33.33**
heb_Hebr					**73.41**	59.80	51.47	68.26	**67.28**	65.20	41.67	64.83	52.45	**58.33**
hin_Deva	**67.89**	62.25	-	58.09	**72.43**	62.25	-	71.45	**71.20**	65.69	-	65.56	50.00	**55.39**
hrv_Latn									**68.26**	66.67	62.75	58.09	48.04	**64.22**
hun_Latn					**72.92**	61.76	-	68.63	**69.98**	64.71	-	53.55	50.00	**70.10**
hye_Armn					**71.69**	61.27	65.69	66.54	**70.10**	66.67	68.14	63.60	11.27	**25.00**
ibo_Latn					**71.45**	62.25	55.88	68.75					24.51	**34.80**
ind_Latn	**73.04**	59.31	63.73	66.05	**75.61**	67.16	57.84	72.92	**71.69**	67.16	63.73	67.28	52.94	**79.41**
isl_Latn					**70.96**	61.27	53.92	69.61	**67.77**	67.65	39.22	58.82	24.51	**48.53**
ita_Latn	**72.43**	63.24	48.53	63.24	**75.00**	63.24	53.43	73.16	**66.79**	65.69	44.61	63.73	64.22	**79.41**
jav_Latn									66.54	60.78	51.96	**66.67**	19.12	**61.76**
jpn_Jpan	**72.30**	62.25	-	59.68	**75.49**	62.75	-	72.18	**69.12**	64.22	-	64.22	49.51	**72.55**
kan_Knda					**72.92**	62.25	-	68.75	65.20	**66.18**	-	66.05	**8.82**	2.45
kat_Geor					**74.14**	62.25	58.33	72.30	**70.47**	66.18	55.88	65.93	5.39	**18.63**
kaz_Cyrl					**76.96**	63.24	-	71.20	**73.04**	70.10	-	69.24	28.92	**56.86**
khk_Cyrl					69.73	58.33	-	**69.85**	**65.69**	60.29	-	53.92	20.10	**34.80**
khm_Khmr					**71.57**	65.69	61.27	70.71	66.54	**66.67**	52.45	64.71	3.43	**4.90**
kir_Cyrl					**70.83**	60.78	-	69.00	**69.49**	66.67	-	61.76	22.55	**50.00**
kmr_Latn					57.35	52.94	-	**57.84**	**64.09**	59.31	-	61.40	20.10	**43.14**
kor_Hang	**68.38**	60.78	-	62.99	**71.57**	59.31	-	68.87	**69.00**	63.24	-	62.62	45.59	**73.53**
lao_Laoo					**74.39**	65.69	61.76	74.02	**68.63**	61.27	60.78	65.44	**3.92**	2.94
lit_Latn					**74.02**	64.71	64.71	69.98	66.05	**67.65**	25.98	57.35	36.76	**59.31**
ltz_Latn					66.42	55.88	44.61	**66.54**					23.53	**65.69**
lvs_Latn					**74.26**	61.76	47.55	70.22	**69.12**	62.75	24.51	48.53	38.24	**56.37**
mal_Mlym					**72.06**	58.33	-	68.26	**70.10**	66.18	-	64.83	8.33	**10.78**
mar_Deva					**71.45**	61.27	-	67.52	**67.03**	61.27	-	57.60	**35.29**	33.33
mkd_Cyrl					**76.47**	60.78	63.73	72.06	**70.83**	61.27	59.80	62.38	40.20	**63.24**
mlt_Latn					**68.26**	58.82	27.45	66.18					28.92	**65.69**
mri_Latn					56.13	47.06	26.47	**58.09**					11.76	**32.35**
mya_Mymr	**72.30**	62.75	-	61.40	**71.32**	58.33	-	70.71	**68.38**	61.76	-	**68.38**	2.45	**3.92**
nld_Latn					**76.35**	63.73	66.18	74.63	**70.34**	68.14	51.96	60.29	58.82	**79.41**
nno_Latn					**74.14**	63.73	-	69.24	**69.98**	62.75	-	66.30	40.69	**75.00**

	XGLM				mT0				XLM-R					
	RoSPrompt	*NPPrompt*	*NPPrompt-t*	*SPT*	*RoSPrompt*	*NPPrompt*	*NPPrompt-t*	*SPT*	*RoSPrompt*	*NPPrompt*	*NPPrompt-t*	*SPT*	*Llama3.1-8B*	*Phi-3.5-mini*
nob_Latn					**75.25**	62.75	58.82	70.59	**70.96**	64.71	38.73	62.62	51.47	**73.53**
npi_Deva					**73.04**	62.25	-	70.34	**69.85**	66.18	-	65.44	25.98	**45.10**
nya_Latn					**70.59**	61.76	-	69.24					15.69	**38.24**
pan_Guru					**72.30**	61.76	-	71.94					**9.31**	2.94
pbt_Arab					66.91	55.88	-	**67.65**	**65.07**	62.75	-	62.62	23.04	**38.24**
pes_Arab					**75.00**	60.29	-	68.75	**68.75**	65.69	-	61.03	45.10	**52.94**
plt_Latn					**67.28**	55.88	-	66.54	**62.99**	54.90	-	48.04	13.24	**42.65**
pol_Latn					**75.98**	62.75	54.41	74.14	**66.42**	64.71	47.55	64.95	57.84	**78.43**
por_Latn	**72.92**	64.71	50.49	66.18	**76.35**	67.16	37.25	74.02	**70.34**	66.67	57.35	68.63	60.78	**77.45**
quy_Latn	**45.71**	44.12	-	32.48									14.71	**41.18**
ron_Latn					72.43	64.22	37.25	**75.86**	**71.32**	68.63	56.86	62.01	50.00	**72.55**
rus_Cyrl	**70.22**	60.78	57.84	64.95	**75.49**	63.73	61.27	72.55	68.75	**69.12**	65.69	67.28	59.80	**75.98**
san_Deva									**64.34**	62.25	-	59.93	18.63	**41.18**
sin_Sinh					**72.18**	60.29	-	69.12	**68.14**	62.25	-	60.05	**4.41**	3.92
slk_Latn					**70.96**	62.25	31.86	69.61	67.77	**69.12**	65.20	63.85	44.61	**71.57**
slv_Latn					72.43	62.25	52.94	**73.53**	**65.93**	64.71	61.27	62.62	40.20	**67.65**
smo_Latn					60.91	50.49	49.51	**63.48**					13.24	**33.33**
sna_Latn					**67.03**	59.31	48.53	64.71					15.20	**39.71**
snd_Arab					**65.32**	58.33	43.63	63.85	**67.40**	58.82	16.67	55.15	26.47	**32.84**
som_Latn					59.44	54.90	36.76	**60.05**	**59.19**	55.39	39.71	52.21	12.75	**36.76**
sot_Latn					**70.34**	58.33	46.57	67.40					14.71	**34.80**
spa_Latn	**74.39**	60.29	44.12	55.88	**78.19**	67.65	56.86	74.02	**66.67**	65.69	46.57	68.50	68.63	**80.39**
srp_Cyrl					**76.84**	64.22	64.71	71.08	**69.36**	62.75	57.35	59.56	46.08	**60.78**
sun_Latn					**73.04**	60.29	54.90	70.83	**68.14**	67.16	57.35	67.40	17.16	**62.25**
swe_Latn					**72.92**	62.25	55.88	70.96	**71.81**	67.16	57.35	66.67	54.90	**75.49**
swh_Latn	**65.32**	61.76	58.82	55.51	**71.69**	61.76	49.51	68.87	**65.69**	62.75	50.00	55.27	28.43	**44.12**
tam_Taml	**67.65**	60.78	-	61.40	**76.10**	62.75	-	71.32	**66.05**	63.24	-	63.48	10.29	**15.20**
tel_Telu	**62.25**	55.39	-	54.90	**75.12**	63.24	-	71.94	**67.77**	63.73	-	63.60	**6.86**	2.45
tgk_Cyrl					**70.47**	60.29	57.84	66.79					23.04	**35.78**
tgl_Latn					**71.94**	63.73	59.80	68.63					41.67	**70.10**
tha_Thai	**67.65**	58.82	53.92	59.31	**73.28**	62.25	63.73	70.96	**69.12**	65.69	54.90	68.87	52.45	**54.90**
tur_Latn	**72.55**	62.25	-	60.42	**74.39**	61.27	-	71.69	**67.89**	65.20	-	63.11	42.16	**70.10**
uig_Arab									**67.16**	62.25	-	59.93	**15.20**	9.31
ukr_Cyrl					**73.65**	62.75	63.24	71.32	67.89	**69.61**	51.96	66.79	50.00	**69.61**
urd_Arab	**67.65**	56.86	-	55.27	**71.81**	59.80	-	69.00	**70.83**	61.76	-	65.69	**53.92**	40.69
uzn_Latn					**74.63**	63.24	-	69.49	**69.00**	64.71	-	59.56	22.55	**46.08**
vie_Latn	**69.61**	66.18	58.33	59.31	**72.79**	62.25	62.75	70.34	66.79	**68.14**	54.90	62.50	44.12	**69.61**
xho_Latn					**69.36**	61.27	50.49	67.89	**52.82**	50.49	26.47	49.39	16.18	**42.16**
ydd_Hebr					**60.66**	53.43	43.14	59.80	**62.25**	51.47	30.39	43.14	16.67	**18.14**
yor_Latn					55.88	49.51	40.69	**59.07**					14.22	**30.88**
zho_Hans	**73.53**	54.90	44.61	46.69	**77.21**	63.24	58.33	74.88	**68.87**	63.24	56.86	65.56	54.90	**78.92**
zho_Hant					**74.14**	65.69	61.76	70.96	**70.22**	66.18	54.90	61.89	48.53	**79.41**
zsm_Latn					**73.16**	65.69	55.88	69.36	**69.61**	65.69	58.33	60.42	38.73	**74.51**
zul_Latn					**67.77**	58.82	55.88	65.44					18.63	**40.20**

Table 10: Comparison of accuracy scores on the SIB-200 dataset between RoSPrompt and different baselines across all supported languages. For each language, the best overall result is underlined, and the best result within each column group is highlighted in **bold**.

Cognate and Contact-Induced Transfer Learning for Hamshentsnag: A Low-Resource and Endangered Language

Onur Keleş
Boğaziçi University
Department of Linguistics
onur.keles1@bogazici.edu.tr

Baran Günay
Boğaziçi University
İstanbul Aydın University
baran.gunay@std.bogazici.edu.tr

Berat Doğan
Boğaziçi University
berat.dogan@std.bogazici.edu.tr

Abstract

This study investigates zero-shot and few-shot cross-lingual transfer effects in Part-of-Speech (POS) tagging and Named Entity Recognition (NER) for Hamshentsnag, an endangered Western Armenian dialect. We examine how different source languages, Western Armenian (contact cognate), Eastern Armenian (ancestral cognate), Turkish (substrate or contact-induced), and English (non-cognate), affect the task performance using multilingual BERT and BERTurk. Results show that cognate varieties improved POS tagging by 8% F1, while the substrate source enhanced NER by 15% F1. BERTurk outperformed mBERT on NER but not on POS. We attribute this to task-specific advantages of different source languages. We also used script conversion and phonetic alignment with the target for non-Latin scripts, which alleviated transfer.

Introduction

This study examines cross-lingual transfer from contact and cognate variety languages in Part-of-Speech (POS) and Named Entity Recognition (NER) tagging for a truly low-resource and endangered language Hamshentsnag[1] (hyh). While supervised sequence tagging is a solved problem for high-resource languages (Bohnet et al., 2018), it is indeed difficult for truly low-resource settings with mean accuracies below 50% (Sonkar et al., 2023; Cho et al., 2018; Kann et al., 2020; Malmasi et al., 2022; Choenni et al., 2023), especially in the dearth of available annotated data.

NLP technologies remain limited for underserved communities, and model accuracies in various NLP tasks are significantly lower for languages and cultures that are less represented (Myung et al., 2024). Many available solutions include either continual mixed language pre-training (Liu et al., 2021), using parallel corpora (Ramesh et al., 2022), or employing cross-lingual transfer methods from a higher-resource to a lower-resource language by fine-tuning pre-trained models to increase performance in downstream NLP tasks (Eronen et al., 2023; Cotterell and Duh, 2017). To this end, we have curated a small Hamshentsnag dataset with online resources and working together with the Hemshin community (data elicitation) and employed zero-shot and few-shot cross-lingual transfer by testing two models (i) multilingual BERT (mBERT) (Devlin et al., 2019) and BERT model for Turkish (BERTurk) (Schweter, 2020) for sequence tagging. The source languages were Western Armenian - hyw, Eastern or Standard Armenian - hy; and Standard Modern Turkish - tr), and English (en) that have more resources available (Figure 1). We use the terminology in Table 1 to refer to these languages in the present study. Among the source languages, tr is a substrate to the target; hyw and hy are cognates that share structural similarity with the target, and English (as a reference level for our comparisons) has no contact and little typological similarity.

From a typological background, hy and hyw are distinct dialects of Armenian, but to some degree they are mutually intelligible. hyw has phonological and syntactic differences from hy. hyw retains most of the features of Classical Armenian (Dum-Tragut, 2009), whereas hyw underwent relatively more morpho-phonological and morpho-syntactic simplifications. hyh (the target language) is closest to hyw, while being highly influenced by tr due to prolonged contact. Moreover, the interaction

[1] https://glottolog.org/resource/languoid/id/hams1239

Proceedings of the 1st Workshop on Language Models for Underserved Communities (LM4UC 2025), pages 76–85
May 4, 2025 ©2025 Association for Computational Linguistics

between the historical hyw and hyh speakers led to potential linguistic exchange or shared features (Khanjian, 2013).

The Hamshentsnag[2] Language

Hamshentsnag (hyh) is considered a dialect of Western Armenian (hyw) (Vaux, 2001), which belongs to the Armenic branch of the Indo-European family. Following the claims (Vaux, 2007) about hyh's typological status, its syntax (Günay et al.) and lexicon, we selected typologically similar languages to transfer knowledge from, which are: hyw, hy, and tr. Our decision behind choosing these three source languages comes from the following features of hyh: the typological landscape of hyh resembles hyw, hy, and tr, in terms of its syntax and morphology. The shared similarities between these three languages are listed below (1), (2). The similarities between the Armenic languages are evident. All of the words in (1-a) to (1-e) in bold are *postpositions*, which are commonly attested in the languages in question (Stevick, 1955). The importance that this carries comes from the ordering in the nominal domain w.r.t. each language, (1) is just one example.

(1)	a. dun-e medan **hedev**	hyh
	b. dun ertale **jedk**	hyw
	c. tun-e mat'neluc **het'o**	hy
	d. ev-e girdikten **sonra**	tr
	e. 'after entering the home'	en

Furthermore, the boldfaced morphemes in (2-a) (2-b) (2-c) are the definite (DEF) markers, which are obligatory with proper names. (2-e) is the translation. The boldfaced morpheme in (2-d) is not a definite marker but a genitive (GEN) suffix, it resembles the Hamshentsnag morphology *-i-n* (-GEN-DEF) in terms of its form.

(2)	a. Hasan-i-**n** *u* Ahmed-i-**n**...	hyh
	b. Hasmig-**n** *u* Aram-**e**...	hyw
	c. Hasmig-**n** *u* Aram-**n**...	hy
	d. Hasan-**ın** ve Ahmet-**in**...	tr
	e. 'Hasan and Ahmet...'	en

In all three Armenic languages, even the definite marker is subject to the same phonological (3) and morphological (4) constraints (Sigler, 1997):

(3) /-DEF/ $\rightarrow$ [*e*] / [CONSONANT]__
(4) /-DEF/ $\rightarrow$ [*n*] / __[CLITIC$_{\text{al, u, ...}}$]

Ultimately, the aforementioned observations veered us in selecting these three languages as sources, in addition to English as a reference level.

Related Work

To our knowledge, there is no computational work specifically on hyh. However, there are studies that investigate mBERT's performance on a variety of low-resource languages. Among them, Lauscher et al. (2020) examined languages from 8 different language families on different NLP tasks and found that transfer performance was strongly aligned with the linguistic similarity of the target and source languages. Pires et al. (2019) also showed that mBERT performed surprisingly well in zero-shot transfer for the POS and NER tasks across many languages and even scripts.

Rahimi et al. (2019) proposed two models (one with an unsupervised transfer and another with a supervised transfer setting by using a small set of 100 target sentences) and evaluated them in a NER task. Using only English as a source language in an unsupervised setting often did not transfer well as opposed to the oracle choice of the source language. Furthermore, in their experiments, script mismatch decreased direct transfer.

Similar to the present study, Şaziye Betül Özateş et al. (2025) and Karagöz et al. (2024) evaluated cross-lingual transfer in both mBERT and BERTurk. The authors introduced *OTA-BOUN*, a Universal Dependencies (UD) treebank for historical Turkish, and fine-evaluated mBERT and BERTurk on POS and NER. They reported improvements when combined with Standard Modern Turkish in the training data, alluding to cross-lingual transfer from a higher-source but out-of-domain variety.

However, languages may not be represented equally in multilingual models. Wu and Dredze (2020) tested mBERT on 153 languages in total for POS and NER, and found improvements in the performance when paired with similar languages to the target, although mBERT is claimed to still learn even in the absence of a shared lexicon or domain across languages (Conneau et al., 2020b), with the caveat that models like mBERT should not be employed alone for low-resource languages.

[2]Hamshentsnag has other names as well: *Homshetsi*, *Homshetsma*. We have been advised by the native speakers to use *Hamshentsnag* when referring to it.

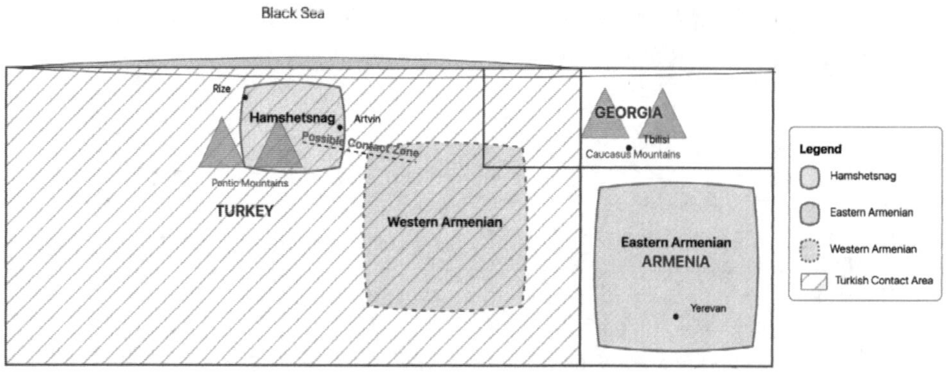

Figure 1: Geographical distribution of Armenian languages in the Caucasus region. The map shows three varieties: Hamshentsnag in northeastern Turkey, Western Armenian's historical speaking area, and Eastern Armenian in modern Armenia. The hatched pattern indicates Turkish linguistic contact areas, while the dotted line between Hamshentsnag and Western Armenian represents a possible historical contact zone.

Term	**Definition**
Target	The language of interest for which NLP tools are being developed (Hamshentsnag in this study)
Substrate Source (SS)	Language that historically influenced the target language through language contact (e.g., Turkish)
Ancestral Cognate Source (ACS)	Ancestral language that shares a common ancestor with the target language with no contact (e.g., Eastern Armenian)
Contact Cognate Source (CCS)	Language that both influenced the target through contact and shares ancestry with it (e.g., Western Armenian)
Non-Cognate Source (NCS)	Language with no historical contact or a close genetic relationship to the target language (e.g., English)

Table 1: Our Definitions of Language Types

Otherwise, as the authors showed, mBERT performed worse than monolingual models for lower-resource languages. Furthermore, as Artetxe et al. (2020) report, it is not only multilingual models that can learn to generalize to unseen languages, but monolingual models may also transfer at a lexical level and become compatible with mBERT or even perform better. As far as we know, there remains a paucity of research specifically looking at the effects of contact and cognate source languages on the target performance in the context of zero-shot and few-shot cross-lingual transfer from a typological perspective. Also, working together with the community is essential when developing NLP technologies for endangered languages (Liu et al., 2022; Zhang et al., 2022). Therefore, we aim to bridge this gap by investigating how leveraging contact and cognate source languages affects the performance of NLP models specifically for Hamshentsnag and also by collaborating with the Hemshin community and curating relevant linguistic data for few-shot transfer.

Data Resources for Hamshentsnag

Endangered languages come with the cost of the scarcity of data. We alleviated this problem by collecting primary data from four native speakers of the language, who agreed to participate in the data collection process, and written informed consent was obtained from all consultants.[3] Our data collection process was mostly in the form of a Q&A, where the consultants were asked to translate the prepared sentences. Additionally, the consultants were asked to produce sentences about a specific topic. As a second resource, we also utilized a voluntary and nonprofit journal titled *GOR*[4], that aims to preserve the culture, the language, and the history of the Hamshen people. We have benefited from the open-source Hamshen stories that can be found online, which were written in the target language. Lastly, we have benefited from the work of Yenigül (2021), which included in-depth interviews

[3]Data elicitation experiments received ethical approval.
[4]https://gordergi.blogspot.com

with the Hamshen and personal narratives in the target language.

Ultimately, these three approaches increased the number of tokens in our dataset in the following ways: the first approach was tailored towards giving us detailed and crucially more directed naturally produced data, while the second and third approaches were aimed at being efficient with regards to time management in augmenting our dataset, as well as representing the Hamshentsnag language as intended.

Text Normalization and Challenges in Transliteration

The curated data (stored in a text document) were normalized and standardized. The sentences collected for the POS task were further reformatted according to the CoNLL-U format. Because there is no standardized spelling system for the target language, we detected some orthographic inconsistencies (due to speaker variation) and fixed them using Regular Expressions (Regex) together with a researcher who is a native speaker of Hamshentsnag. Since it is spelled using the Latin alphabet, no transliteration was needed.

Additionally, to test multilingual transfer effects, we used Western Armenian (`hyw`) and Eastern Armenian (`hy`) datasets. Using transliteration (i.e., the process of converting text from one writing system to another based on phonetic correspondences) and phonetic transcriptions are known to alleviate cross-lingual transfer (Murikinati et al., 2020; Bharadwaj et al., 2016). For this reason, since these dialects use the Armenian script, we also prepared versions of these datasets which were transliterated into Latin using the `transliterate`[5] package in Python. However, the transliteration outputted by the program significantly differed from the spelling of Hamshentsnag in our corpus given the phonological and orthographic differences between the dialects. Key issues included historical orthographic discrepancies, phonemic variations across dialects, positional allophones, and individual speaker idiosyncrasies. To address these and align the transliteration of `hyw` and `hy` with the target `hyh`, we developed dynamic context-sensitive rules using Regex (see Table 2) by relying on the linguistic judgments and having community validation from our native speaker consultants.

[5]https://pypi.org/project/transliterate

Experimentation

Models The sequence labeling experiments (POS and NER) were implemented using the Flair framework (Akbik et al., 2019). For this task, Google's multilingual BERT (mBERT) (Devlin et al., 2019) and BERTurk (Schweter, 2020) (both of which are cased) were fine-tuned with different training sets, resulting in 9 experiments for POS, and 7 experiments for NER (16 in total) for each model (mmBERT and BERTurk).

mBERT is a multilingual encoder-only model that shares the same architecture with BERT (Devlin et al., 2019) and was trained on 104 different languages. Since `hyh` has close contact with `tr` as illustrated in Figure 1, we also decided to test BERTurk (Schweter, 2020), which is another BERT model trained on a large corpus of Turkish. We also considered XLM-R (Conneau et al., 2020a) but our preliminary experiments showed it underperformed, so we focused on mBERT and BERTurk.

For the fine-tuning, we used the AdamW optimizer with 0.01 weight decay, a learning rate of 5e-5, and a batch size of 32 for a maximum of 15 epochs with early stopping (patience = 5). All experiments were conducted on Google Colab using a Tesla T4 GPU.

POS Data For the POS task, the training datasets include four different languages, as can be seen in Table 3. Our own Hamshentsnag (`hyh`) dataset for POS, described in detail in Section 1, has 373 sentences for the train set, 153 sentences for the development set, and 153 sentences for the test set, all of which were annotated for UPOS by the authors along with native speaker consultants. While the train and development sets come from the same resources (speaker elicitation and open-source Hemshin stories), the test set contains sentences from a different domain (personal experience narratives and dialogues).

The UPOS training data for other higher-resource languages were obtained from Universal Dependency (UD) Treebank datasets. These include Western Armenian (`hyw`), Eastern or Standard Armenian (`hy`), and Turkish (`tr`) to investigate how language contact and cognateness (i.e., typological similarity) contribute to possible multilingual transfer effects. We also trained the model with English (`en`) to test the effect of a high-resource language with no contact and little typological similarity. All testing was conducted only

Armenian Ch.	transliterate	Our Transliteration	IPA Transcription
է, ե†	ē, e†	e, ye†	/ɛ/, /je/†
ու	ow	u	/u/
ը	ë	ğ	/ə/
շ	š	ş	/ʃ/
չ	č	ç	/tʃ/
ժ	ž	j	/ʒ/
ղ	ġ	ğ	/ʁ/
ռ	ṙ	r	/r/ or /ɾ/‡
ջ	ǰ	c/ç	/dʒ/ or /tʃ/‡
ո	ò	vo† or o	/vo/† or /ɔ/
և	ew	yev† or ev	/jev/† or /ev/
ձ	j	c or ts	/d͡z/ or /t͡s/‡
ւ	w	v	/v/

Table 2: Transliteration of the Armenian Script

† only word-initially

‡ in HYW

on the target language (Hamshentsnag or hyh).

Dataset	# Sents.	# Tokens
hyh (ours)	373	2,394
hyw (Yavrumyan et al., 2017)	~5,000	~73,000
hy (Yavrumyan et al., 2017)	~2,000	~34,000
tr (Türk et al., 2022)	~10,000	~120,000
en (Silveira et al., 2014)	~13,000	~216,000

Table 3: POS Datasets Used for Training

NER Data We report three languages for the NER task (Table 4). Our own hyh developing NER corpus includes a small set of 143 sentences for the training set (all annotated for PERSON (N = 88) and LOCATION (N = 93) entities by the authors under native speaker consultation, consistent with the BIO annotation scheme. Due to the scarcity of open-source data and limitations in linguistic elicitation in Hamshentsnag, other entity types (such as ORGANIZATION) occurred very sparsely and thus were not annotated. Other 46 sentences were curated for the development set, and 115 sentences for the test set (with 109 PER and 58 LOC entities). Like the POS experiment, while the training and development sets in NER came from similar domains and sources (sentences elicited through native speakers and open-source online stories), the test set exclusively included sentences from a different domain and source (personal narrative and dialogues). The NER training set included three higher-resource languages: hy, tr and en, all of which had more than 150K tokens, compared to our own hyh corpus with 2K tokens. hyw dialect was excluded from NER experiments due to the non-availability of data for this task. Like the previous task, all the testing was done only on the target Hamshentsnag.

Dataset	# Sents.	# Tokens
hyh (ours)	143	1785
hy (Yavrumyan, 2024)	~1,000	~150,000
tr (Tür et al., 2003)	~20,000	~450,000
en (Sang and Meulder, 2003)	~15,000	~200,000

Table 4: NER Datasets Used for Training

The descriptions of the model and source combinations for both POS and NER tasks can be found in Table 5.

Experiment Results

POS Each of the 18 models (9 mBERT, 9 BERTurk) were fine-tuned and tested on the target UPOS tags in the test set three times and we report the mean macro-averaged precision, recall, and F1 scores obtained from these experiments. Table 6 illustrates the results for the mBERT models. Zero-shot models (with only hyw, hy, tr, and en), we can see that English as a non-contact and non-cognate language performed worse, followed by Turkish (as a substrate or contact-only source). The cognate varieties Eastern and Western Armenian had the best performance. The baseline F1 achieved by the model trained only on our low-resource corpus ($\text{mBERT}_{\text{hyh}}$) was 0.63, which could be improved when other contact or cognate languages were added to the training data up to 0.68. The combination of hyh and hyw resulted in the highest recall (0.70). However, the model trained with both the target and English did not show transfer effects.

The BERTurk models exhibited similar trends in

Model	Description	Train Language
mBERT/BERTURK$_{HYH}$	mBERT/BERTURK fine-tuned only with our own small corpus reported in this study	Target
mBERT/BERTURK$_{HYW}$ †	mBERT/BERTURK fine-tuned only with the UD_Western_Armenian-ArmTDP Treebank for POS	CCS
mBERT/BERTURK$_{TR}$	mBERT/BERTURK fine-tuned only with the UD_Turkish-BOUN Treebank for POS and MilliyetNER dataset for NER	SS
mBERT/BERTURK$_{HY}$	mBERT/BERTURK fine-tuned only with the UD_Armenian-ArmTDP Treebank for POS and ArmTDP-NER dataset for NER	ACS
mBERT/BERTURK$_{EN}$	mBERT/BERTURK fine-tuned only with the UD_English-EWT for POS and English CoNLL-2003 dataset for NER	NCS
mBERT/BERTURK$_{hyh+HYW}$ †	mBERT/BERTURK fine-tuned with both our hyh corpus and hyw dataset only for POS	Target + CCS
mBERT/BERTURK$_{hyh+TR}$	mBERT/BERTURK fine-tuned with both our hyh corpus and tr datasets for POS and NER	Target + SS
mBERT/BERTURK$_{hyh+HY}$	mBERT/BERTURK fine-tuned with both our hyh corpus and hy datasets for POS and NER	Target + ACS
mBERT/BERTURK$_{hyh+EN}$	mBERT/BERTURK fine-tuned with both our hyh corpus and en datasets for POS and NER	Target + NCS

Table 5: Model Descriptions and Dataset Types Used in the Training Set. CCS: Contact Cognate Source, SS: Substrate Source, ACS: Ancestral Cognate Source, and NCS:Non-Cognate Source.

† These models are only for the POS task since there is no available NER data for hyw.

Model	Precision	Recall	F1
mBERT$_{HYH}$	0.64	0.65	0.63
mBERT$_{HYW}$	0.45	0.37	0.38
mBERT$_{TR}$	0.34	0.27	0.27
mBERT$_{HY}$	0.47	0.35	0.38
mBERT$_{EN}$	0.22	0.22	0.19
mBERT$_{HYH+HYW}$	0.67	**0.70**	0.67
mBERT$_{HYH+TR}$	0.67	0.66	0.66
mBERT$_{HYH+HY}$	**0.69**	0.69	**0.68**
mBERT$_{HYH+EN}$	0.67	0.61	0.63

Table 6: mBERT Results on hyh Test Set for POS

Model	Precision	Recall	F1
BERTURK$_{HYH}$	0.67	0.66	0.64
BERTURK$_{HYW}$	0.43	0.38	0.38
BERTURK$_{TR}$	0.30	0.28	0.26
BERTURK$_{HY}$	0.45	0.34	0.36
BERTURK$_{EN}$	0.21	0.22	0.18
BERTURK$_{hyh+HYW}$	0.67	**0.70**	**0.68**
BERTURK$_{hyh+TR}$	**0.70**	0.69	**0.68**
BERTURK$_{hyh+HY}$	0.67	0.67	0.65
BERTURK$_{hyh+EN}$	0.63	0.59	0.60

Table 7: BERTurk Results on hyh Test Set for POS

POS tagging to the mBERT models, with cognate languages demonstrating superior performance compared to non-cognate languages (Table 7). The baseline model, BERTURK$_{HYH}$, achieved an F1 score of 0.64, which is comparable to the mBERT baseline. When combined with other languages, the BERTurk models showed improvements, with BERTURK$_{hyh+HYW}$ and BERTURK$_{hyh+TR}$ achieving the highest F1 scores of 0.68. Notably, BERTURK$_{hyh+TR}$ also attained the highest precision (0.70), while BERTURK$_{hyh+HYW}$ achieved the highest recall (0.70). However, similar to the mBERT results, the model trained with English (BERTURK$_{hyh+EN}$) showed the least improvement, with an F1 score of 0.60.

NER As in the first experiment, each of the 16 models (8 mBERT, 8 BERTurk) were tested on target NER annotations. The baseline model, mBERT$_{hyh}$, achieved an F1 score of 0.52 (Table 8). Among the zero-shot models, Turkish (mBERT$_{TR}$) achieved the highest precision (0.67) but suffered from low recall (0.31), resulting in a F1 score of 0.35. The model trained on English (mBERT$_{EN}$) performed the worst, with an F1 score of 0.31. When combined with other languages, the mBERT models showed notable improvements: Specifically, mBERT$_{hyh+TR}$ achieved the best performance, with an F1 score of 0.60. In contrast, the model trained with English (mBERT$_{hyh+EN}$) showed limited improvement, achieving an F1 score of 0.47, which is lower than the baseline.

The BERTurk models, on the other hand, demonstrated stronger performance for NER, with the baseline model (BERTURK$_{hyh}$) achieving an F1 score of 0.57, outperforming its mBERT counter-

Model	Precision	Recall	F1
$\text{mBERT}_{\text{hyh}}$	0.57	0.48	0.52
mBERT_{TR}	0.67	0.31	0.35
mBERT_{HY}	0.54	0.33	0.41
mBERT_{EN}	0.46	0.25	0.31
$\text{mBERT}_{\text{hyh+TR}}$	**0.79**	**0.51**	**0.60**
$\text{mBERT}_{\text{hyh+HY}}$	0.65	0.45	0.52
$\text{mBERT}_{\text{hyh+EN}}$	0.58	0.41	0.47

Table 8: mBERT Results on hyh Test Set for NER

part (Table 9). Among zero-shot models, Turkish ($\text{BERTURK}_{\text{TR}}$) performed better than English, though both fell short of the baseline. Combining the target language with other languages yielded improvements, with $\text{BERTURK}_{\text{hyh+TR}}$ achieving the highest F1 score of 0.64. Adding Armenian ($\text{BERTURK}_{\text{hyh+HY}}$) also showed competitive results, while English ($\text{BERTURK}_{\text{hyh+EN}}$) did not improve the baseline scores.

Taken together, our findings show that leveraging typologically related or contact languages enhanced model performance in sequence tagging for hyh. Cognate varieties (hyw, hy) improved POS tagging by 8% F1, while substrate language (tr) boosted NER by 15% F1. We also observed that BERTurk consistently outperformed mBERT on NER but not in POS. This result perhaps could be attributed to the substrate influence of tr, which shares lexical and cultural overlap with the target. In contrast, POS tagging might depend more on structural cues, where cognate varieties like hy and hyw (more so possibly due to an additional historical contact with the target) perform better due to their syntactic and morphological convergence with the target language. Overall, both experiments highlight the importance of task-specific language selection for cross-lingual transfer in truly low-resource NLP.

Model	Precision	Recall	F1
$\text{BERTURK}_{\text{hyh}}$	0.74	0.49	0.57
$\text{BERTURK}_{\text{TR}}$	0.49	0.43	0.46
$\text{BERTURK}_{\text{HY}}$	0.61	0.38	0.48
$\text{BERTURK}_{\text{EN}}$	0.57	0.33	0.40
$\text{BERTURK}_{\text{hyh+TR}}$	**0.77**	**0.54**	**0.64**
$\text{BERTURK}_{\text{hyh+HY}}$	0.74	0.53	0.62
$\text{BERTURK}_{\text{hyh+EN}}$	0.60	0.55	0.57

Table 9: BERTurk Results on hyh Test Set for NER

Effects of Script and Transliteration We also experimented with the impact of script and phonetic transliteration on model performance, focusing specifically on BERTurk. For POS tagging, Eastern (Standard) Armenian using the Armenian script achieved a macro-averaged F1 score of 0.31. When transliterated to Latin using the `transliterate` package in Python, the F1 score improved to 0.33. Further improvement was observed with our custom transliteration alignment method, which achieved an F1 score of 0.36, as reported earlier. Similarly, for NER, the Armenian script yielded an F1 score of 0.41, while Latin transliteration using the `transliterate` package improved the score to 0.46. Our transliteration alignment method achieved the highest F1 score of 0.48. These results demonstrate that script conversion and phonetic alignment enhance model performance, particularly for languages with non-Latin scripts, aligning well with Muller et al. (2021).

Conclusion

This study explored zero-shot and few-shot cross-lingual transfer for part-of-speech (POS) and named entity recognition (NER) tagging in Hamshentsnag, a truly low-resource and endangered language. By leveraging contact and cognate source languages (Western Armenian, Eastern Armenian, and Turkish), we demonstrated that typologically similar languages significantly improve model performance in sequence tagging tasks. Our experiments revealed that cognate languages, particularly Western Armenian, enhanced POS tagging performance, while Turkish, as a substrate language, transferred most in NER. Additionally, BERTurk outperformed mBERT in NER tasks, likely due to the lexical and cultural overlap between Turkish and Hamshentsnag. Overall, these findings underscore the importance of selecting task-specific source languages for cross-lingual transfer, especially in low-resource settings. Furthermore, our work highlights the value of community collaboration and phonetic transliteration in improving model performance for endangered languages, offering a pathway for future research in under-resourced NLP.

Acknowledgments

We thank Metin Bağrıaçık, Ümit Atlamaz, Tunga Güngör, and Şaziye Betül Özateş for their insightful feedback and comments. Furthermore, our heartfelt thanks go to Cengiz Gülcihan, Ayşegül Gülcihan and our other anonymous Hamshentsnag consultants for their support with their language.

Limitations

This study has several limitations that warrant consideration: (i) the dataset for Hamshentsnag remains small due to the lack of open-source online resources and due to working with a relatively small number of language consultants, which inevitably leads to a rather restricted amount of data collection process. This may limit the generalizability of our findings. In addition, (ii) our preliminary hyh dataset at this stage includes sentences from similar domains (mostly stories, personal experiences, and dialogues) and lacks other domains, which might reduce transferability. Furthermore, (iii) the reliance on transliteration for Armenian scripts introduced potential inconsistencies, despite our efforts to align transliterations with native speaker input. Finally, (iv) while BERTurk showed promise, its performance may not extend to other low-resource languages without similar substrate influences since it is a monolingual model.

References

Alan Akbik, Tanja Bergmann, Duncan Blythe, Kashif Rasul, Stefan Schweter, and Roland Vollgraf. 2019. FLAIR: An easy-to-use framework for state-of-the-art NLP. In *Proceedings of the 2019 conference of the North American chapter of the association for computational linguistics (demonstrations)*, pages 54–59.

Mikel Artetxe, Sebastian Ruder, and Dani Yogatama. 2020. On the cross-lingual transferability of monolingual representations. In *Proceedings of the 58th Annual Meeting of the Association for Computational Linguistics*. Association for Computational Linguistics.

Akash Bharadwaj, David Mortensen, Chris Dyer, and Jaime Carbonell. 2016. Phonologically aware neural model for named entity recognition in low resource transfer settings. In *Proceedings of the 2016 Conference on Empirical Methods in Natural Language Processing*, pages 1462–1472, Austin, Texas. Association for Computational Linguistics.

Bernd Bohnet, Ryan McDonald, Gonçalo Simões, Daniel Andor, Emily Pitler, and Joshua Maynez. 2018. Morphosyntactic tagging with a meta-BiLSTM model over context sensitive token encodings. In *Proceedings of the 56th Annual Meeting of the Association for Computational Linguistics (Volume 1: Long Papers)*, pages 2642–2652, Melbourne, Australia. Association for Computational Linguistics.

Jaejin Cho, Murali Karthick Baskar, Ruizhi Li, Matthew Wiesner, Sri Harish Mallidi, Nelson Yalta, Martin Karafiát, Shinji Watanabe, and Takaaki Hori. 2018. Multilingual Sequence-to-Sequence Speech Recognition: Architecture, Transfer Learning, and Language Modeling. In *2018 IEEE Spoken Language Technology Workshop (SLT)*, pages 521–527.

Rochelle Choenni, Dan Garrette, and Ekaterina Shutova. 2023. How do languages influence each other? studying cross-lingual data sharing during LM fine-tuning. In *Proceedings of the 2023 Conference on Empirical Methods in Natural Language Processing*, pages 13244–13257, Singapore. Association for Computational Linguistics.

Alexis Conneau, Kartikay Khandelwal, Naman Goyal, Vishrav Chaudhary, Guillaume Wenzek, Francisco Guzmán, Edouard Grave, Myle Ott, Luke Zettlemoyer, and Veselin Stoyanov. 2020a. Unsupervised cross-lingual representation learning at scale. In *Proceedings of the 58th Annual Meeting of the Association for Computational Linguistics*, pages 8440–8451, Online. Association for Computational Linguistics.

Alexis Conneau, Shijie Wu, Haoran Li, Luke Zettlemoyer, and Veselin Stoyanov. 2020b. Emerging cross-lingual structure in pretrained language models. In *Proceedings of the 58th Annual Meeting of the Association for Computational Linguistics*, pages 6022–6034, Online. Association for Computational Linguistics.

Ryan Cotterell and Kevin Duh. 2017. Low-resource named entity recognition with cross-lingual, character-level neural conditional random fields. In *Proceedings of the Eighth International Joint Conference on Natural Language Processing (Volume 2: Short Papers)*, pages 91–96, Taipei, Taiwan. Asian Federation of Natural Language Processing.

Şaziye Betül Özateş, Tarık Emre Tıraş, Ece Elif Adak, Berat Doğan, Fatih Burak Karagöz, Efe Eren Genç, and Esma F. Bilgin Taşdemir. 2025. Building foundations for natural language processing of historical Turkish: Resources and models. *Preprint*, arXiv:2501.04828.

Jacob Devlin, Ming-Wei Chang, Kenton Lee, and Kristina Toutanova. 2019. BERT: Pre-training of deep bidirectional transformers for language understanding. In *Proceedings of the 2019 Conference of the North American Chapter of the Association for Computational Linguistics: Human Language Technologies, Volume 1 (Long and Short Papers)*, pages 4171–4186, Minneapolis, Minnesota. Association for Computational Linguistics.

Jasmine Dum-Tragut. 2009. *Armenian: Modern Eastern Armenian*, volume 14 of *London Oriental and African Language Library*. John Benjamins Publishing Company, Amsterdam/Philadelphia.

Juuso Eronen, Michal Ptaszynski, and Fumito Masui. 2023. Zero-shot cross-lingual transfer language selection using linguistic similarity. *Information Processing Management*, 60(3):103250.

Baran Günay, Ümit Atlamaz, and Ömer Demirok. Single conjunct agreement in homshetsma. In *Proceedings of the 55th Annual Meeting of the North East Linguistic Society (NELS 55)*. To appear.

Katharina Kann, Ophélie Lacroix, and Anders Søgaard. 2020. Weakly supervised pos taggers perform poorly on truly low-resource languages. In *Proceedings of the AAAI Conference on Artificial Intelligence*, volume 34, pages 8066–8073. Issue: 05.

Fatih Karagöz, Berat Doğan, and Şaziye Betül Özateş. 2024. Towards a clean text corpus for Ottoman Turkish. In *Proceedings of the First Workshop on Natural Language Processing for Turkic Languages (SIGTURK 2024)*, pages 62–70, Bangkok, Thailand and Online. Association for Computational Linguistics.

Hrayr Khanjian. 2013. *(Negative) concord and head directionality in Western Armenian*. Ph.D. thesis, Massachusetts Institute of Technology.

Anne Lauscher, Vinit Ravishankar, Ivan Vulić, and Goran Glavaš. 2020. From zero to hero: On the limitations of zero-shot language transfer with multilingual Transformers. In *Proceedings of the 2020 Conference on Empirical Methods in Natural Language Processing (EMNLP)*, pages 4483–4499, Online. Association for Computational Linguistics.

Zihan Liu, Genta Indra Winata, and Pascale Fung. 2021. Continual mixed-language pre-training for extremely low-resource neural machine translation. In *Findings of the Association for Computational Linguistics: ACL-IJCNLP 2021*, pages 2706–2718, Online. Association for Computational Linguistics.

Zoey Liu, Crystal Richardson, Richard Hatcher, and Emily Prud'hommeaux. 2022. Not always about you: Prioritizing community needs when developing endangered language technology. In *Proceedings of the 60th Annual Meeting of the Association for Computational Linguistics (Volume 1: Long Papers)*, pages 3933–3944, Dublin, Ireland. Association for Computational Linguistics.

Shervin Malmasi, Anjie Fang, Besnik Fetahu, Sudipta Kar, and Oleg Rokhlenko. 2022. MultiCoNER: A Large-scale Multilingual Dataset for Complex Named Entity Recognition. In *Proceedings of the 29th International Conference on Computational Linguistics*, pages 3798–3809, Gyeongju, Republic of Korea. International Committee on Computational Linguistics.

Benjamin Muller, Antonios Anastasopoulos, Benoît Sagot, and Djamé Seddah. 2021. When being unseen from mBERT is just the beginning: Handling new languages with multilingual language models. In *Proceedings of the 2021 Conference of the North American Chapter of the Association for Computational Linguistics: Human Language Technologies*, pages 448–462, Online. Association for Computational Linguistics.

Nikitha Murikinati, Antonios Anastasopoulos, and Graham Neubig. 2020. Transliteration for cross-lingual morphological inflection. In *Proceedings of the 17th SIGMORPHON Workshop on Computational Research in Phonetics, Phonology, and Morphology*, pages 189–197, Online. Association for Computational Linguistics.

Junho Myung, Nayeon Lee, Yi Zhou, Jiho Jin, Rifki Afina Putri, Dimosthenis Antypas, Hsuvas Borkakoty, Eunsu Kim, Carla Perez-Almendros, Abinew Ali Ayele, Víctor Gutiérrez-Basulto, Yazmín Ibáñez García, Hwaran Lee, Shamsuddeen Hassan Muhammad, Kiwoong Park, Anar Sabuhi Rzayev, Nina White, Seid Muhie Yimam, Mohammad Taher Pilehvar, Nedjma Ousidhoum, Jose Camacho-Collados, and Alice Oh. 2024. Blend: A benchmark for llms on everyday knowledge in diverse cultures and languages. In *Advances in Neural Information Processing Systems*, volume 37, pages 78104–78146. Curran Associates, Inc.

Telmo Pires, Eva Schlinger, and Dan Garrette. 2019. How multilingual is multilingual BERT? In *Proceedings of the 57th Annual Meeting of the Association for Computational Linguistics*, pages 4996–5001, Florence, Italy. Association for Computational Linguistics.

Afshin Rahimi, Yuan Li, and Trevor Cohn. 2019. Massively multilingual transfer for NER. In *Proceedings of the 57th Annual Meeting of the Association for Computational Linguistics*, pages 151–164, Florence, Italy. Association for Computational Linguistics.

Gowtham Ramesh, Sumanth Doddapaneni, Aravinth Bheemaraj, Mayank Jobanputra, Raghavan AK, Ajitesh Sharma, Sujit Sahoo, Harshita Diddee, Mahalakshmi J, Divyanshu Kakwani, Navneet Kumar, Aswin Pradeep, Srihari Nagaraj, Kumar Deepak, Vivek Raghavan, Anoop Kunchukuttan, Pratyush Kumar, and Mitesh Shantadevi Khapra. 2022. Samanantar: The largest publicly available parallel corpora collection for 11 Indic languages. *Transactions of the Association for Computational Linguistics*, 10:145–162.

Erik F. Tjong Kim Sang and Fien De Meulder. 2003. Introduction to the CoNLL-2003 shared task: Language-independent named entity recognition. In *Proceedings of the Seventh Conference on Natural Language Learning at HLT-NAACL 2003*, pages 142–147.

Stefan Schweter. 2020. BERTurk-BERT models for Turkish. *Zenodo*, 2020:3770924.

Michele Sigler. 1997. *Specificity and agreement in standard Western Armenian*. Ph.D. thesis, Massachusetts Institute of Technology.

Natalia Silveira, Timothy Dozat, Marie-Catherine de Marneffe, Samuel Bowman, Miriam Connor, John Bauer, and Chris Manning. 2014. A Gold Standard Dependency Corpus for English. In *Proceedings of the Ninth International Conference on Language Resources and Evaluation (LREC'14)*, pages 2897–2904, Reykjavik, Iceland. European Language Resources Association (ELRA).

Shashank Sonkar, Zichao Wang, and Richard Baraniuk. 2023. MANER: Mask augmented named entity recognition for extreme low-resource languages. In *Proceedings of The Fourth Workshop on Simple and Efficient Natural Language Processing (SustaiNLP)*, pages 219–226, Toronto, Canada (Hybrid). Association for Computational Linguistics.

Earl Wilson Stevick. 1955. *Syntax of Colloquial East Armenian*. Cornell University.

Gökhan Tür, Dilek Hakkani-Tür, and Kemal Oflazer. 2003. A statistical information extraction system for turkish. *Natural Language Engineering*, 9(2):181–210.

Utku Türk, Furkan Atmaca, Şaziye Betül Özateş, Gözde Berk, Seyyit Talha Bedir, Abdullatif Köksal, Balkız Öztürk Başaran, Tunga Güngör, and Arzucan Özgür. 2022. Resources for Turkish dependency parsing: Introducing the BOUN treebank and the BoAT annotation tool. *Language Resources and Evaluation*, pages 1–49. Publisher: Springer.

Bert Vaux. 2001. Hemshinli: The forgotten black sea Armenians. *Journal of Armenian studies*, 6(2):47–71.

Bert Vaux. 2007. Homshetsma: The language of the armenians of Hamshen. In *The Hemshin*, pages 257–278. Routledge.

Shijie Wu and Mark Dredze. 2020. Are all languages created equal in multilingual BERT? In *Proceedings of the 5th Workshop on Representation Learning for NLP*, pages 120–130, Online. Association for Computational Linguistics.

Marat M. Yavrumyan. 2024. ArmTDP-NER: Named Entity Corpus of Modern Eastern Armenian.

Marat M. Yavrumyan, Hrant Khachatrian, Anna Danielyan, and Gor Arakelyan. 2017. ArmTDP: Eastern Armenian treebank and dependency parser. In *XI International Conference on Armenian Linguistics, Abstracts. Yerevan.*

Anıl Yenigül. 2021. *The role of translation in the efforts for the survival of disappearing languages in a globalized world: The case of hemshin*. Ph.D. thesis, Yıldız Technical University.

Shiyue Zhang, Ben Frey, and Mohit Bansal. 2022. How can NLP help revitalize endangered languages? a case study and roadmap for the Cherokee language. In *Proceedings of the 60th Annual Meeting of the Association for Computational Linguistics (Volume 1: Long Papers)*, pages 1529–1541, Dublin, Ireland. Association for Computational Linguistics.

Nayana OCR: A Scalable Framework for Document OCR in Low-Resource Languages

Adithya S Kolavi[1], Samarth P[1], Vyoman Jain[1]

[1]CognitiveLab

Correspondence: adithyaskolavi@gmail.com, samarthprakash8@gmail.com, vyomanjain@gmail.com

Abstract

We introduce Nayana, a scalable and efficient framework for adapting Vision-Language Models (VLMs) to low-resource languages. Despite significant advances, modern VLMs remain constrained by the scarcity of training data in non-English languages, limiting their global applicability. Our framework addresses this fundamental challenge through a novel layout-aware synthetic data generation pipeline combined with parameter-efficient adaptation techniques. Instead of requiring extensive manually annotated datasets, Nayana enables existing models to learn new languages effectively using purely synthetic data. Using Low-Rank Adaptation (LoRA), we demonstrate this capability across ten Indic languages: Bengali, Gujarati, Hindi, Kannada, Malayalam, Marathi, Odia, Punjabi, Tamil, and Telugu. Through extensive experiments in OCR tasks, we show that models can achieve strong performance in new languages without the traditional requirements of large-scale annotated datasets or extensive model modifications. Nayana's success in adapting VLMs to new languages with synthetic data establishes a practical pathway for extending AI capabilities to underserved language communities, particularly in scenarios where annotated data is scarce or unavailable.

1 Introduction

Vision-Language Models (Wang et al. (2024); Wu et al. (2024); Abdin et al. (2024); Chen et al. (2024); Liu et al. (2024a); Wei et al. (2024a)) have demonstrated remarkable success in high-resource languages like English. However, these advancements have not translated across all languages due to a fundamental challenge: the scarcity of high-quality training data. This limitation is particularly evident in languages with complex scripts, where creating large-scale manually annotated datasets is both time-consuming and prohibitively expensive. This has limited the adoption of VLMs for document understanding tasks across diverse languages.

Nayana is an adaptive framework designed to bridge this gap by enabling existing VLMs to learn new languages effectively without requiring extensive annotated datasets. While this paper demonstrates Nayana's capabilities through OCR tasks across ten Indic languages, the framework's approach is inherently flexible and can extend to other tasks and language families. Our methodology eliminates the traditional requirement of annotation by combining synthetic data generation with efficient model adaptation techniques.

The main contributions of this paper are:

1. **Novel Synthetic Data Generation Pipelines:** A layout-aware synthetic data generation pipeline that automates the creation of training datasets while preserving visual and structural relationships in documents. This approach significantly reduces the dependency on manually annotated data for low-resource languages.

2. **Systematic Analysis of LoRA-based Adaptation:** We conduct a comprehensive evaluation of different LoRA techniques and configurations to determine their effectiveness in multilingual adaptation. Our analysis explores whether supervised fine-tuning can enhance language transfer and identifies the optimal configurations for adapting VLMs to new languages with minimal computational overhead.

3. **Comprehensive Empirical Validation:** Through extensive experimentation and evaluation across ten Indic languages, we provide strong evidence that our synthetic data approach matches the performance of traditional OCR Models, establishing a scalable path forward for language adaptation in VLMs.

Proceedings of the 1st Workshop on Language Models for Underserved Communities (LM4UC 2025), pages 86–103
May 4, 2025 ©2025 Association for Computational Linguistics

2 Related Work

Recent Vision Language Models like Qwen 2.5 VL (Wang et al., 2024), Deepseek-VL2 (Wu et al., 2024), InternVL 2.5 (Chen et al., 2024), Llava-NeXT (Liu et al., 2024a), Phi 3.5 Vision (Abdin et al., 2024) have advanced significantly in OCR, captioning, and visual question answering (Antol et al., 2015). These developments stem from parameter-efficient fine-tuning, synthetic data generation, and improved multimodal architectures.

Parameter-efficient fine-tuning methods are crucial for adapting VLMs to specific tasks and languages. Low-Rank Adaptation (Hu et al., 2021) enables efficient parameter updates through low-rank matrix injection in transformer layers.

Multilingual OCR and document understanding have progressed substantially, with systems like Tesseract (Smith, 2007) and PaddleOCR (Du et al., 2020) establishing foundations for multilingual text recognition. Transformer-based approaches like ViLanOCR (Cheema et al., 2024) leverage synthetic data for improved performance on underrepresented languages, while LLaVA-NeXT (Liu et al., 2024a) advances OCR through high-resolution processing and improved visual instruction tuning for training.

Synthetic data generation addresses data scarcity in low-resource settings. SynthVLM (Liu et al., 2024b) uses diffusion models to create image-text pairs, while DocSynth300K (Zhao et al., 2024) demonstrates the effectiveness of generated data for document understanding tasks.

OCR-free approaches offer alternatives to traditional pipelines. DocPedia (Feng et al., 2024) processes documents in the frequency domain, while TextHawk2 (Yu et al., 2024) employs decoder-only architecture with efficient tokenization. Solutions like DocLayout-YOLO (Zhao et al., 2024), Donut (Kim et al., 2021) and Nougat (Blecher et al., 2023) have also explored document understanding without traditional OCR models.

Despite advances in parameter-efficient fine-tuning, synthetic data generation, and OCR-free approaches, challenges persist in adapting VLMs to low-resource languages. Our work introduces language-agnostic synthetic pipelines, combines parameter-efficient tuning with high-resolution vision encoders, and extends OCR-free paradigms to low-resource languages.

3 Synthetic Data Generation: A Scalable Cross-Lingual Framework

The cornerstone of our work lies in developing a sophisticated pipeline for generating high-fidelity synthetic training data that preserves the intricate relationships between document layout, visual elements, and textual content across languages. Our framework addresses the fundamental challenge of data scarcity in low-resource languages through a novel approach that combines advanced document understanding, a state-of-the-art English OCR model, and context-aware translation mechanisms. This section details the architectural components and methodological innovations that enable scalable, high-quality dataset generation for multilingual document understanding tasks.

The pipeline's design emphasizes three critical aspects: preservation of document structure and visual hierarchy, accurate text recognition across diverse scripts, and contextually appropriate translation that maintains semantic integrity. Through careful orchestration of these elements, we achieve a system capable of generating training data that closely mirrors the complexity and nuance of naturally occurring documents while scaling efficiently across multiple languages and document types.

3.1 Seed Dataset Collection

The foundation of our synthetic data generation pipeline rests upon a meticulously curated corpus of English-language documents, encompassing approximately 14,000 distinct samples. Our primary source materials comprise research papers from arXiv (2,000 documents), medical literature from PubMed (1,000 documents), newspaper articles (1,000 pages), and marketing materials (10,000 samples). This collection represents a strategic balance across multiple domains and document types, carefully selected to capture the diverse spectrum of real-world document layouts, content structures and ensures comprehensive coverage of various typographical elements, structural patterns, and domain-specific formatting conventions that characterize modern document ecosystems.

The academic papers, drawn from arXiv's extensive repository, provide exemplars of complex multi-column layouts, mathematical notation, and intricate figure-text relationships. Medical literature from PubMed introduces specialized terminology and standardized reporting formats, while newspaper pages contribute examples of dynamic

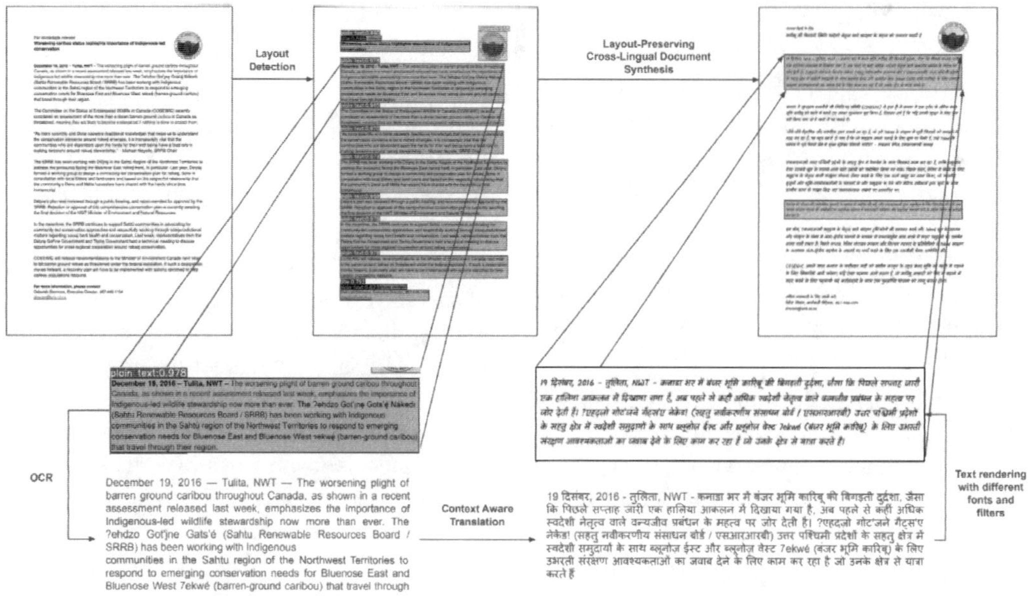

Figure 1: Nayana's end-to-end synthetic data generation pipeline. Starting from English document images, our pipeline generates multilingual datasets for OCR and Document level OCR tasks while preserving layout integrity and visual characteristics. The pipeline processes approximately one image every 3-5 seconds, enabling rapid dataset generation at scale.

layout patterns and diverse content organization. Marketing materials round out the collection with their rich variety of creative layouts, typographical treatments, and visual design elements.

3.2 Multi-stage Processing Pipeline

Our processing methodology employs a sophisticated multi-stage approach that preserves document integrity while enabling efficient multilingual adaptation. The pipeline initiates with high-resolution document preprocessing, converting all inputs to standardized 300 DPI images to ensure consistent quality and feature preservation across source formats. This standardization step establishes a robust foundation for subsequent processing stages.

The layout analysis phase employs an optimized implementation of DocLayout-YOLO (Zhao et al. (2024)), which systematically identifies and classifies document regions including text blocks, titles, figure captions, tables, and visual elements. While our initial research explored ensemble-based approaches using multiple layout detection models, empirical evaluation demonstrated that our optimized single-model implementation achieves comparable accuracy with significantly reduced computational overhead.

Text extraction and visual analysis proceed through a carefully orchestrated sequence of operations. Each identified text region undergoes precise optical character recognition to extract English text from our diverse document collection. We selected Tesseract (Smith (2007)) as the pipeline's OCR model amongst state-of-the-art candidates including PaddleOCR (Du et al. (2020)) and EasyOCR due to its high accuracy at low compute expenditure. The extracted text then undergoes comprehensive visual attribute analysis. This includes background and text color detection, font size estimation, and preservation of critical styling metadata. Our implementation maintains strict fidelity to the original document's visual hierarchy and structural relationships throughout this process.

The translation phase employs a sophisticated multi-engine approach, leveraging several state-of-the-art translation services: Google Translate API, Microsoft Azure Translate, IndicTrans2 (Gala et al. (2023)), and advanced language models such as Llama3.1 405B (Dubey et al. (2024)). This diverse ensemble of translation engines enables robust context-aware translation, with each service contributing its unique strengths in handling different aspects of document context, technical terminology, and formatting conventions.

Our system dynamically selects the most appropriate translation based on context, domain, and

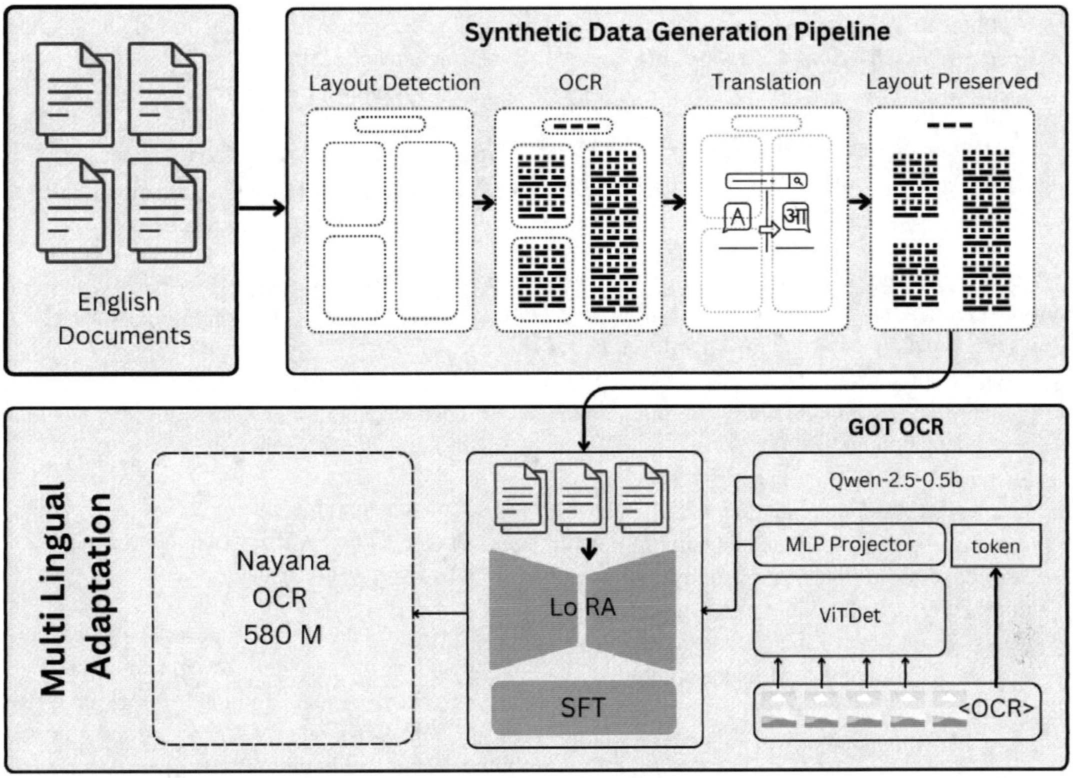

Figure 2: End-to-end Nayana system architecture: (1) A synthetic data generation pipeline transforming English documents into multilingual training data while preserving layout and visual fidelity, (2) OCR model with LoRA adapters for efficient multilingual adaptation, and (3) Training pipeline with Supervised Fine-Tuning (SFT). The modular architecture processes documents in 3-5 seconds while enabling rapid adaptation to new languages with high accuracy.

language pair, ensuring optimal translation quality across diverse document types. The final stage involves precise layout-preserving text replacement (Zhao et al. (2024)), incorporating dynamic font size adjustments and maintaining visual hierarchy while ensuring color contrast preservation.

3.3 Pipeline Performance Characteristics

Our pipeline achieves remarkable efficiency metrics, demonstrating both speed and accuracy at scale. Processing individual documents in approximately 3-5 seconds, the system maintains exceptional performance across all processing stages while enabling rapid dataset generation for new languages. The optimized DocLayout-YOLO (Zhao et al. (2024)) implementation consistently achieves 95.8% accuracy in structural analysis, while the OCR model and sophisticated translation architecture work in concert to ensure high-quality text extraction and translation.

The system's effectiveness is particularly evident in its data multiplication capabilities. Through our augmentation strategies and multi-task generation approach where we use the layout data to extract region-specific information, we achieve an output multiplication factor of 7-10× images per source document. This rich extraction process yields diverse training signals including layout structures, text content. The extracted multi-modal elements can be leveraged for training various downstream models such as VLMs for Visual Question Answering (Antol et al., 2015), Information Extraction systems, Multi-Modal Retrievers(Faysse et al., 2025).This multiplication effect significantly amplifies the utility of our seed dataset, enabling the creation of comprehensive training sets from a relatively modest collection of source documents. The combination of speed, multiplication factor, and rich multi-modal data extraction makes our pipeline particularly effective for rapidly bootstrapping vision-language capabilities in new languages and diverse document understanding applications.

4 Architectural Innovation: Parameter-Efficient Cross-Script Learning

The adaptation of vision-language models (VLMs) for multilingual document understanding presents a fundamental architectural challenge: How to effectively extend models trained primarily on Latin scripts to handle dramatically different writing systems while maintaining computational efficiency. This section details our systematic exploration of architectural approaches, empirically-driven design decisions, and the development of our parameter-efficient adaptation methodology.

Our initial investigation began with a comprehensive evaluation of contemporary VLM architectures, analyzing their fundamental capabilities in handling text-dense images. This exploration revealed a critical insight: while many models excel at general visual understanding, they often struggle with the precise geometric and spatial relationships inherent in document processing. Through extensive experimentation with architectures ranging from traditional CNN-based models to state-of-the-art transformer variants, we identified several key architectural requirements that would prove crucial for successful cross-script adaptation.

4.1 Foundation Model Selection and Analysis

The selection of an appropriate foundation model emerged from a rigorous empirical study evaluating multiple state-of-the-art architectures. Our investigation focused particularly on models' ability to handle the unique challenges presented by Indic scripts, including complex ligatures, overlapping characters, and varied writing directions. Initial experiments with popular vision-language models revealed significant limitations in handling dense textual content, despite their strong performance on general vision-language tasks.

The breakthrough came through our analysis of GOT OCR (580M parameters) (Wei et al. (2024b)), which demonstrated exceptional performance across key metrics. Based on published benchmarks, GOT OCR achieved superior results with an Edit Distance of 0.035/0.038 and F1-scores of 0.972/0.980 for English and Chinese respectively, significantly outperforming larger models like Qwen-VL-Max (>72B parameters) (Wang et al. (2024)) and Vary (7B parameters) (Wei et al. (2024a)). More importantly, its architecture demonstrated remarkable flexibility in handling non-Latin scripts, likely due to its original design for handling both English and Chinese characters – writing systems with significantly different visual characteristics.

Our choice of GOT OCR (Wei et al. (2024b)) was further validated through its optimal balance of performance and efficiency due to its:

- Superior vision transformer backbone architecture compared to contemporary VLM designs
- Specialized text detection heads optimized for dense textual content
- Efficient parameter count (580M) enabling practical deployment while maintaining state-of-the-art performance

The model's architecture, particularly its attention mechanisms and hierarchical feature processing, provided an ideal foundation for our cross-script adaptation strategy. Notably, its transformer-based design facilitated efficient parameter adaptation through Low-Rank Adaptation (Hu et al. (2021)), enabling us to preserve the model's fundamental visual understanding while extending its capabilities to new scripts.

During our initial exploration phase, we pursued several alternative approaches that, while ultimately unsuccessful, provided crucial insights. We conducted extensive experiments with vocabulary expansion techniques, hypothesizing that direct modification of the tokenization layer would enable better handling of Indic scripts. These experiments involved:

- Direct vocabulary expansion with script-specific tokens
- Hierarchical tokenization schemes for handling complex ligatures
- Script-aware embedding layer modifications

Despite systematic exploration of these approaches with various hyperparameter configurations, the results consistently plateaued at 50-60% accuracy for both training and evaluation. This empirical evidence led us to a crucial realization: the challenge lay not in the vocabulary representation but in the fundamental visual processing of different scripts.

4.2 Cross-Modal Alignment Learning

The Cross-Modal Alignment (CMA) phase extends GOT OCR's (Wei et al., 2024b) capabilities beyond its original English and Chinese training domain through a two-phase training approach. Built on GOT OCR's task-token architecture (e.g., <OCR>), our adaptation strategy systematically builds multilingual capabilities while preserving the model's core strengths.

The first phase focuses on section-level training 15, where we use layout-preserving translation to create training pairs from dense textual sections. By unfreezing all major components (ViTDet vision encoder, MLP projection layer, and Qwen 0.5B language model), we enable comprehensive adaptation to new language patterns. Ablation studies confirmed this phase's criticality - attempts to skip directly to document-level training resulted in stalled learning and hallucinations.

The second phase transitions to document-level OCR 10, training on complete document images while selectively freezing components. We maintain the trained visual features by freezing the ViTDet vision encoder while continuing to train the language model and projection layer. This approach successfully extends the model's capabilities to new languages while preserving its performance on English and Chinese texts.

Table 1: Training Phase Configuration Summary

Component	Phase 1	Phase 2
ViTDet Vision Encoder	Unfrozen	Frozen
MLP Projection Layer	Unfrozen	Unfrozen
Qwen 0.5B LLM	Unfrozen	Unfrozen
Training Data	Text-heavy Sections	Complete Documents

4.3 Single-Language Adaptation Results

4.3.1 Hindi Adaptation Performance

Our initial experiments with Hindi adaptation revealed several crucial insights about parameter-efficient adaptation strategies. The choice of 85,000 image-text pairs was determined through extensive preliminary testing, which showed that this dataset size provided optimal coverage of Hindi script variations while remaining computationally manageable.

The results in Table 2 demonstrate a clear progression in adaptation effectiveness across different configurations. The baseline LoRA configuration (r=32, α =64) established fundamental script adaptation but showed limitations in handling complex Hindi character combinations, as evidenced by its BLEU score of 0.29. The optimal configuration (r=64, α=128) achieved substantially better performance, with a BLEU score of 0.58, through improved capacity for modeling intricate script-specific features.

Particularly noteworthy is the preservation of English language capabilities. While the higher-rank LoRA configuration showed a slight decrease in English BLEU scores (from 0.84 to 0.79), it maintained strong overall performance (F1: 0.86, METEOR: 0.88), suggesting effective balance between adaptation and preservation of base capabilities.

Table 2: Hindi Adaptation Performance Comparison

Configuration	Lang	BLEU↑	ANLS↑	F1↑	METEOR↑
LoRA (r=32, α=64)	Hindi	0.29	0.71	0.56	0.57
	English	0.84	0.97	0.91	0.91
LoRA (r=64, α=128)	Hindi	**0.58**	**0.91**	**0.76**	**0.77**
	English	0.79	0.97	0.86	0.88
Full Fine-tune	Hindi	0.50	0.86	0.75	0.73
	English	0.74	0.95	0.85	0.85

4.3.2 Tamil Adaptation Performance

The Tamil adaptation experiments presented unique challenges due to the script's distinctive characteristics, including its cursive nature and complex grapheme structure. Table 3 reveals several important patterns in adaptation behavior. The LoRA configuration (r=64, α=128) demonstrated remarkable robustness in handling Tamil's unique script features, achieving a BLEU score of 0.37 despite the script's significant divergence from the model's original training domain. This performance is particularly impressive given Tamil's complex vowel modification system and the presence of compound characters that can span multiple positions. The comparison with full fine-tuning is especially illuminating. While full fine-tuning achieved reasonable performance (ANLS: 0.79), it showed significant degradation in English capabilities, suggesting potential catastrophic forgetting. In contrast, our LoRA approach maintained strong performance across both languages, with English metrics remaining notably stable (BLEU: 0.78, F1: 0.87).

4.4 Multi-Language Adaptation

We investigated three distinct approaches to handling multiple scripts simultaneously, each offering unique insights into cross-lingual transfer. The Single LoRA approach emerged as particularly effective, demonstrating strong performance across

Table 3: Tamil Adaptation Performance Comparison

Configuration	Lang	BLEU↑	ANLS↑	F1↑	METEOR↑
LoRA	Tamil	**0.37**	**0.87**	**0.66**	**0.64**
(r=64, α=128)	English	**0.78**	**0.96**	**0.87**	**0.88**
Full	Tamil	0.17	0.79	0.44	0.44
Fine-tune	English	0.69	0.96	0.76	0.80

multiple languages without requiring explicit language specification during inference. When language tags were provided both during training and inference, we observed further improvements in performance. A notable advantage of this approach was its ability to leverage cross-script learning - for instance, the model showed improved handling of Marathi text despite being primarily trained on Hindi, suggesting effective transfer between related Devanagari scripts. The Multi-LoRA approach, training separate LoRA modules for each language, achieved strong language-specific performance but sacrificed the beneficial cross-script transfer effects observed in the single LoRA strategy. Despite its strong per-language performance, this approach's inability to leverage script similarities represented a significant limitation in the multilingual context. Nayana We also explored a Merged LoRA strategy, where independently trained language-specific LoRAs were combined using model merging techniques. While this approach showed promising results for both languages, it did not outperform the single LoRA approach's ability to capture cross-script features.

Table 4: Multi-Language Adaptation Performance (Hindi + Kannada) in a single LoRA

Configuration	Lang	BLEU↑	ANLS↑	F1↑	METEOR↑
Single	Hindi	0.64	0.89	0.85	0.84
LoRA	Kannada	0.52	0.72	0.55	0.43
	English	0.79	0.97	0.86	0.88

5 Results

5.1 Evaluation Methodology

Our evaluation framework was designed to provide rigorous, comprehensive assessment across diverse document types and writing systems. We constructed a carefully balanced test set comprising 500 images per language, strategically distributed across different document categories to ensure broad coverage of real-world scenarios. The dataset draws 40% of its content from academic papers sourced from arXiv, another 40% from medical literature in PubMed, and the remaining 20% split equally between newspaper content and advertising materials. This distribution reflects the varying complexity and specialized requirements of different document processing applications.

To ensure methodological rigor and fair cross-linguistic comparison, we developed parallel versions of each document across all ten languages while maintaining identical visual layouts and content structures. This parallel corpus approach enables precise isolation of script-specific challenges while controlling for variations in document complexity and formatting. Such controlled comparison proves essential for understanding the true impact of script differences on model performance.

5.2 Comparative Analysis

Our comprehensive evaluation framework encompasses three distinct categories of document processing systems, each representing different approaches to multilingual document understanding. We first examined traditional OCR systems, including industry standards like Tesseract Smith (2007) and PaddleOCR (Du et al. (2020)), which have established strong baselines in multilingual text recognition. These systems, while specialized for OCR tasks, provide important reference points for performance evaluation.

The second category comprises recent vision-language models, including cutting-edge systems like Phi-3.5 Vision (Abdin et al. (2024)) and Llama-3.2 (Dubey et al. (2024)). These models, despite their impressive capabilities in general vision-language tasks, demonstrate the ongoing challenges in specialized document processing. Our analysis of their performance reveals important insights about the limitations of general-purpose architectures when applied to script-specific document understanding tasks.

Our Nayana-OCR variants, built upon the GOT OCR (Wei et al. (2024b)) architecture, represent the third category. Through extensive training on approximately 850,000 synthetic images spanning 10 Indic languages, these models demonstrate significant advantages in multilingual document processing. The results reveal substantial improvements across key metrics, most notably a 76% reduction in Character Error Rate compared to the base GOT OCR model. This improvement is particularly significant given that it maintains consistency across all evaluated languages.

The performance gains extend beyond simple

Table 5: Average performance metrics across all evaluated languages. Results show mean values for each model across the ten tested languages. Lower values (↓) are better for CER and WER, while higher values (↑) are better for other metrics. Best results in each category are highlighted in **bold**.

Model	CER↓	WER↓	BLEU↑	ANLS↑	METEOR↑
Tesseract	**0.206**	0.583	0.318	**0.797**	0.540
PaddleOCR	0.621	0.880	0.020	0.287	0.069
Llama-3.2 11B	3.858	3.900	0.007	0.091	0.055
Phi-3.5 Vision	2.420	2.461	0.007	0.086	0.044
Qwen2-VL 2B	1.776	1.793	0.025	0.129	0.086
GOT-OCR	0.945	1.041	0.016	0.071	0.052
Nayana-OCR	0.227	**0.463**	**0.395**	**0.796**	**0.630**

character recognition. Our models show markedly improved BLEU scores, indicating enhanced capability in handling complex linguistic structures and maintaining semantic coherence. The reduced standard deviations across performance metrics suggest robust cross-language stability, a crucial factor for practical deployment in multilingual environments. These improvements stem from our innovative approach to model adaptation and the sophisticated synthetic data generation pipeline described in previous sections.

5.3 Detailed Performance Analysis

Examining Table 6, several patterns emerge that illustrate the strengths and limitations of different approaches. Traditional OCR systems like Tesseract (Smith (2007)) show strong performance in character-level accuracy (CER: 0.206) but struggle with higher-level semantic understanding, as evidenced by lower BLEU scores (0.318). In contrast, Nayana-OCR achieves competitive character-level accuracy (CER: 0.227) while substantially outperforming all baselines in semantic metrics (BLEU: 0.395).

The performance gap between general-purpose vision-language models and specialized OCR systems is particularly noteworthy. Despite their larger parameter counts, models like Llama-3.2 11B (Dubey et al. (2024)) and Phi-3.5 Vision (Abdin et al. (2024)) show significantly higher error rates across all metrics. This disparity underscores the importance of architectural choices specifically optimized for document understanding tasks.

5.4 Limitations and Future Work

While our approach demonstrates significant progress, several limitations should be noted. When compared to traditional OCR systems, our models show higher inference latency, reflecting the complexity of vision-language processing. Performance variations across scripts suggest room for improvement in handling certain complex writing systems. Additionally, our synthetic data generation, while efficient, may not capture all real-world variations in document layouts and styles.

Future work will focus on expanding the diversity of seed datasets, incorporating more complex document structures, and developing specialized architectures that better balance performance and computational efficiency. We also plan to explore how our synthetic data approach can benefit other vision-language tasks and create open-source tools to facilitate broader adoption of multilingual vision-language technologies.

6 Conclusion

This work establishes that vision-language models can be effectively adapted to new languages using purely synthetic data, reducing dependency on costly manual annotation. Our results demonstrate that Nayana provides a practical, scalable solution for extending AI capabilities to low-resource languages. By achieving strong performance across diverse scripts while maintaining computational efficiency, our framework opens new possibilities for democratizing AI technologies across linguistic boundaries. The success of our approach not only validates the effectiveness of synthetic data generation and efficient adaptation techniques but also establishes a promising direction for developing more inclusive AI systems that can serve diverse linguistic communities worldwide.

References

Marah Abdin, Jyoti Aneja, Hany Awadalla, Ahmed Awadallah, Ammar Ahmad Awan, Nguyen Bach, Amit Bahree, Arash Bakhtiari, Jianmin Bao, Harkirat Behl, et al. 2024. Phi-3 technical report: A highly capable language model locally on your phone. *arXiv preprint arXiv:2404.14219*.

Stanislaw Antol, Aishwarya Agrawal, Jiasen Lu, Margaret Mitchell, Dhruv Batra, C Lawrence Zitnick, and Devi Parikh. 2015. Vqa: Visual question answering. In *Proceedings of the IEEE international conference on computer vision*, pages 2425–2433.

Lukas Blecher, Guillem Cucurull, Thomas Scialom, and Robert Stojnic. 2023. Nougat: Neural optical understanding for academic documents. *arXiv preprint arXiv:2308.13418*.

Musa Dildar Ahmed Cheema, Mohammad Daniyal Shaiq, Farhaan Mirza, Ali Kamal, and M Asif Naeem. 2024. Adapting multilingual vision language transformers for low-resource urdu optical character recognition (ocr). *PeerJ Computer Science*, 10:e1964.

Zhe Chen, Jiannan Wu, Wenhai Wang, Weijie Su, Guo Chen, Sen Xing, Muyan Zhong, Qinglong Zhang, Xizhou Zhu, Lewei Lu, et al. 2024. Internvl: Scaling up vision foundation models and aligning for generic visual-linguistic tasks. In *Proceedings of the IEEE/CVF Conference on Computer Vision and Pattern Recognition*, pages 24185–24198.

Yuning Du, Chenxia Li, Ruoyu Guo, Xiaoting Yin, Weiwei Liu, Jun Zhou, Yifan Bai, Zilin Yu, Yehua Yang, Qingqing Dang, et al. 2020. Pp-ocr: A practical ultra lightweight ocr system. *arXiv preprint arXiv:2009.09941*.

Abhimanyu Dubey, Abhinav Jauhri, Abhinav Pandey, Abhishek Kadian, Ahmad Al-Dahle, Aiesha Letman, Akhil Mathur, Alan Schelten, Amy Yang, Angela Fan, et al. 2024. The llama 3 herd of models. *arXiv preprint arXiv:2407.21783*.

Manuel Faysse, Hugues Sibille, Tony Wu, Bilel Omrani, Gautier Viaud, Céline Hudelot, and Pierre Colombo. 2025. Colpali: Efficient document retrieval with vision language models. *Preprint*, arXiv:2407.01449.

Hao Feng, Qi Liu, Hao Liu, Jingqun Tang, Wengang Zhou, Houqiang Li, and Can Huang. 2024. Docpedia: Unleashing the power of large multimodal model in the frequency domain for versatile document understanding. *Science China Information Sciences*, 67(12):1–14.

Jay Gala, Pranjal A Chitale, Raghavan AK, Varun Gumma, Sumanth Doddapaneni, Aswanth Kumar, Janki Nawale, Anupama Sujatha, Ratish Puduppully, Vivek Raghavan, et al. 2023. Indictrans2: Towards high-quality and accessible machine translation models for all 22 scheduled indian languages. *arXiv preprint arXiv:2305.16307*.

Edward J Hu, Yelong Shen, Phillip Wallis, Zeyuan Allen-Zhu, Yuanzhi Li, Shean Wang, Lu Wang, and Weizhu Chen. 2021. Lora: Low-rank adaptation of large language models. *arXiv preprint arXiv:2106.09685*.

Geewook Kim, Teakgyu Hong, Moonbin Yim, Jinyoung Park, Jinyeong Yim, Wonseok Hwang, Sangdoo Yun, Dongyoon Han, and Seunghyun Park. 2021. Donut: Document understanding transformer without ocr. *arXiv preprint arXiv:2111.15664*, 7(15):2.

Haotian Liu, Chunyuan Li, Qingyang Wu, and Yong Jae Lee. 2024a. Visual instruction tuning. *Advances in neural information processing systems*, 36.

Zheng Liu, Hao Liang, Xijie Huang, Wentao Xiong, Qinhan Yu, Linzhuang Sun, Chong Chen, Conghui He, Bin Cui, and Wentao Zhang. 2024b. Synthvlm: High-efficiency and high-quality synthetic data for vision language models. *arXiv preprint arXiv:2407.20756*.

Ray Smith. 2007. An overview of the tesseract ocr engine. In *ICDAR '07: Proceedings of the Ninth International Conference on Document Analysis and Recognition*, pages 629–633, Washington, DC, USA. IEEE Computer Society.

Peng Wang, Shuai Bai, Sinan Tan, Shijie Wang, Zhihao Fan, Jinze Bai, Keqin Chen, Xuejing Liu, Jialin Wang, Wenbin Ge, et al. 2024. Qwen2-vl: Enhancing vision-language model's perception of the world at any resolution. *arXiv preprint arXiv:2409.12191*.

Haoran Wei, Lingyu Kong, Jinyue Chen, Liang Zhao, Zheng Ge, Jinrong Yang, Jianjian Sun, Chunrui Han, and Xiangyu Zhang. 2024a. Vary: Scaling up the vision vocabulary for large vision-language model. In *European Conference on Computer Vision*, pages 408–424. Springer.

Haoran Wei, Chenglong Liu, Jinyue Chen, Jia Wang, Lingyu Kong, Yanming Xu, Zheng Ge, Liang Zhao, Jianjian Sun, Yuang Peng, et al. 2024b. General ocr theory: Towards ocr-2.0 via a unified end-to-end model. *arXiv preprint arXiv:2409.01704*.

Zhiyu Wu, Xiaokang Chen, Zizheng Pan, Xingchao Liu, Wen Liu, Damai Dai, Huazuo Gao, Yiyang Ma, Chengyue Wu, Bingxuan Wang, et al. 2024. Deepseek-vl2: Mixture-of-experts vision-language models for advanced multimodal understanding. *arXiv preprint arXiv:2412.10302*.

Ya-Qi Yu, Minghui Liao, Jiwen Zhang, and Jihao Wu. 2024. Texthawk2: A large vision-language model excels in bilingual ocr and grounding with 16x fewer tokens. *arXiv preprint arXiv:2410.05261*.

Zhiyuan Zhao, Hengrui Kang, Bin Wang, and Conghui He. 2024. Doclayout-yolo: Enhancing document layout analysis through diverse synthetic data and global-to-local adaptive perception. *arXiv preprint arXiv:2410.12628*.

A Appendix

A.1 Language-wise Performance Analysis

Table 6: Detailed Performance Analysis Across Languages. The table compares various OCR models across multiple languages using metrics such as CER, WER, BLEU, ANLS and METEOR.

Model	CER↓	WER↓	BLEU↑	ANLS↑	METEOR↑
			Hindi		
Tesseract	**0.090**	**0.287**	**0.636**	**0.908**	**0.791**
PaddleOCR	0.414	0.864	0.023	0.575	0.117
Phi-3.5 Vision	2.878	2.500	0.023	0.126	0.069
Llama-3.2 11B	4.654	3.455	0.020	0.116	0.070
Qwen2-VL 2B	2.360	2.022	0.066	0.172	0.153
GOT OCR base	1.013	1.190	0.004	0.052	0.043
Nayana-OCR	0.160	0.297	0.532	0.850	0.756
			Kannada		
Tesseract	**0.155**	**0.609**	0.259	**0.847**	0.541
PaddleOCR	0.814	0.918	0.020	0.110	0.048
Phi-3.5 Vision	2.655	2.877	0.006	0.084	0.046
Llama-3.2 11B	4.670	4.991	0.004	0.075	0.047
Qwen2-VL 2B	1.394	1.599	0.013	0.075	0.063
GOT OCR base	0.936	1.008	0.019	0.067	0.063
Nayana-OCR	0.361	0.648	**0.341**	0.740	**0.554**
			Tamil		
Tesseract	0.265	0.811	0.109	0.750	0.324
PaddleOCR	0.545	1.076	0.003	0.450	0.051
Phi-3.5 Vision	1.531	2.033	0.000	0.082	0.035
Llama-3.2 11B	3.009	4.229	0.002	0.086	0.052
Qwen2-VL 2B	1.260	1.515	0.007	0.125	0.053
GOT OCR base	0.956	1.020	0.013	0.056	0.051
Nayana-OCR	**0.181**	**0.551**	**0.377**	**0.829**	**0.592**
			Telugu		
Tesseract	**0.158**	0.589	**0.296**	**0.821**	**0.551**
PaddleOCR	0.435	0.934	0.014	0.550	0.088
Phi-3.5 Vision	2.442	2.464	0.001	0.067	0.036
Llama-3.2 11B	2.736	3.586	0.015	0.090	0.068
Qwen2-VL 2B	1.580	1.696	0.010	0.115	0.065
GOT OCR base	0.925	1.007	0.022	0.075	0.066
Nayana-OCR	0.282	**0.065**	0.241	0.733	0.522
			Odia		
Tesseract	**0.290**	0.681	0.155	0.703	0.403
PaddleOCR	0.639	**0.742**	0.020	0.111	0.030
Phi-3.5 Vision	2.311	2.168	0.000	0.090	0.018
Llama-3.2 11B	2.880	2.908	0.005	0.088	0.042
Qwen2-VL 2B	1.247	1.345	0.012	0.092	0.060
GOT OCR base	0.926	1.000	0.020	0.078	0.042
Nayana-OCR	0.311	0.566	**0.305**	**0.738**	**0.551**

Model	CER↓	WER↓	BLEU↑	ANLS↑	METEOR↑
			Punjabi		
Tesseract	0.203	0.532	0.356	0.803	0.568
PaddleOCR	0.717	0.811	0.010	0.095	0.029
Phi-3.5 Vision	3.431	2.896	0.001	0.083	0.034
Llama-3.2 11B	5.801	4.535	0.000	0.065	0.029
Qwen2-VL 2B	1.260	1.515	0.007	0.125	0.053
GOT OCR base	0.954	0.994	0.010	0.066	0.046
Nayana-OCR	**0.159**	**0.440**	**0.435**	**0.853**	**0.693**
			Malayalam		
Tesseract	0.355	0.828	0.065	0.663	0.258
PaddleOCR	0.788	**0.895**	0.036	0.125	0.073
Phi-3.5 Vision	1.993	2.489	0.000	0.070	0.039
Llama-3.2 11B	2.988	3.807	0.001	0.081	0.051
Qwen2-VL 2B	1.394	1.599	0.013	0.075	0.063
GOT OCR base	0.956	1.174	0.011	0.064	0.047
Nayana-OCR	**0.270**	0.694	**0.248**	**0.740**	**0.516**
			Marathi		
Tesseract	0.157	0.460	0.513	0.862	0.738
PaddleOCR	0.355	0.849	0.035	0.630	0.154
Phi-3.5 Vision	1.592	2.063	0.023	0.150	0.073
Llama-3.2 11B	2.421	2.724	0.007	0.108	0.074
Qwen2-VL 2B	1.251	1.269	0.069	0.248	0.181
GOT OCR base	0.915	0.988	0.021	0.095	0.060
Nayana-OCR	**0.143**	**0.457**	**0.540**	**0.866**	**0.753**
			Gujarati		
Tesseract	**0.148**	0.446	**0.534**	**0.871**	**0.733**
PaddleOCR	0.800	0.914	0.026	0.124	0.068
Phi-3.5 Vision	3.329	3.008	0.006	0.091	0.047
Llama-3.2 11B	2.401	2.724	0.007	0.108	0.074
Qwen2-VL 2B	5.050	4.312	0.006	0.092	0.042
GOT OCR base	0.940	1.047	0.020	0.081	0.057
Nayana-OCR	0.172	**0.451**	0.476	0.839	0.707
			Bengali		
Tesseract	0.241	0.590	0.259	0.738	0.492
PaddleOCR	0.704	0.798	0.014	0.096	0.029
Phi-3.5 Vision	2.041	2.110	0.008	0.014	0.042
Llama-3.2 11B	7.021	6.039	0.009	0.093	0.044
Qwen2-VL 2B	0.967	1.054	0.048	0.174	0.127
GOT OCR base	0.926	0.983	0.019	0.080	0.048
Nayana-OCR	**0.235**	**0.460**	**0.452**	**0.776**	**0.656**

A.2 Model Output Analysis

To evaluate the practical effectiveness of our model, we present a visual comparison between input documents and their corresponding Document Level OCR outputs. Figures 3 and 4 demonstrate the model's performance on Hindi and Bengali documents respectively.

The results demonstrate the model's robust performance across different Indic scripts. Note the preservation of both textual content and document structure in the generated outputs, highlighting the effectiveness of our approach in handling diverse document layouts and writing systems.

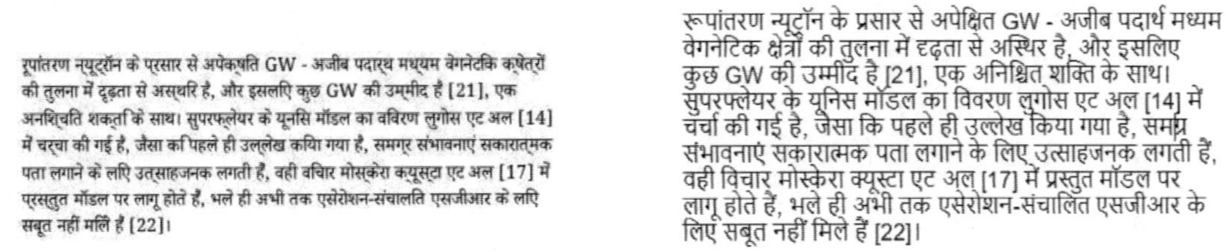
रूपांतरण न्यूट्रॉन के प्रसार से अपेक्षति GW - अजीब पदार्थ मध्यम वेगनेटकि क्षेत्रों की तुलना में दृढ़ता से अस्थरि है, और इसलिए कुछ GW की उम्मीद है [21], एक अनश्चिति शक्तकि साथ। सुपरफ्लेयर के यूनसि मॉडल का ववरिण लुगोस एट अल [14] में चर्चा की गई है, जैसा कि पहले ही उल्लेख कयिा गया है, समग्र संभावनाएं सकारात्मक पता लगाने के लिए उत्साहजनक लगती हैं, वही वचिार मोस्केरा क्यूस्टा एट अल [17] में प्रस्तुत मॉडल पर लागू होते हैं, भले ही अभी तक एसेरोशन-संचालति एसजीआर के लिए सबूत नहीं मलिे हैं [22]।

रूपांतरण न्यूट्रॉन के प्रसार से अपेक्षित GW - अजीब पदार्थ मध्यम वेगनेटिक क्षेत्रों की तुलना में दृढ़ता से अस्थिर है, और इसलिए कुछ GW की उम्मीद है [21], एक अनिश्चित शक्ति के साथ। सुपरफ्लेयर के यूनिस मॉडल का विवरण लुगोस एट अल [14] में चर्चा की गई है, जैसा कि पहले ही उल्लेख किया गया है, समग्र संभावनाएं सकारात्मक पता लगाने के लिए उत्साहजनक लगती हैं, वही विचार मोस्केरा क्यूस्टा एट अल [17] में प्रस्तुत मॉडल पर लागू होते हैं, भले ही अभी तक एसेरोशन-संचालित एसजीआर के लिए सबूत नहीं मिले हैं [22]।

Figure 3: Hindi Document Processing: Comparison between the original document (left) and the model's OCR output (right), demonstrating accurate text recognition and formatting preservation.

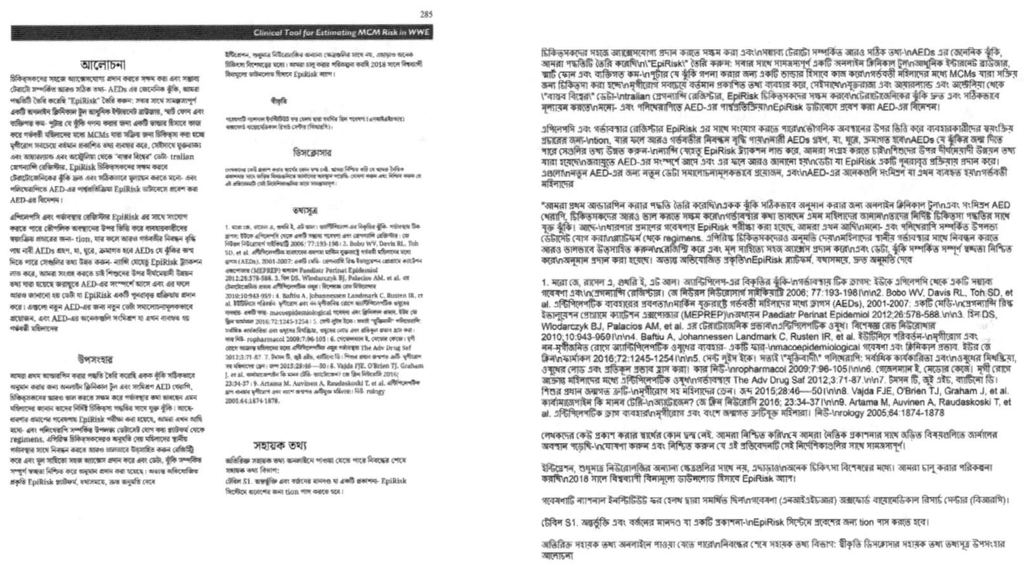

Figure 4: Bengali Document Processing: Visual comparison showing the model's capability to accurately process Bengali script while maintaining structural fidelity.

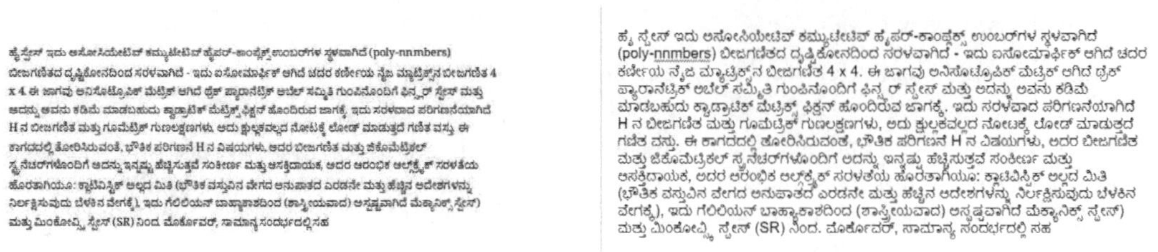

ಹೈ ಸ್ಪೇಸ್ ಇದು ಅಸೋಸಿಯೇಟಿವ್ ಕಮ್ಯುಟೇಟಿವ್ ಹೈಪರ್-ಕಾಂಪ್ಲೆಕ್ಸ್ ಉಂಬರ್‌ಗಳ ಸ್ಥಳವಾಗಿದೆ (poly-nnmbers) ಬೀಜಗಣಿತದ ದೃಷ್ಟಿಕೋನದಿಂದ ಸರಳವಾಗಿದೆ - ಇದು ಐಸೋಮಾರ್ಫಿಕ್ ಆಗಿದೆ ಚದರ ಕರ್ಣೀಯ ನೈಜ ಮ್ಯಾಟ್ರಿಕ್ಸ್‌ನ ಬೀಜಗಣಿತ 4 x 4. ಈ ಜಾಗವು ಅನಿಸೊಟ್ರೊಪಿಕ್ ಮೆಟ್ರಿಕ್ ಆಗಿದೆ ಥ್ರೆಕ್ ವ್ಯಾರಾನೆಟ್ರಿಕ್ ಅಬೆಲ್ ಸಮ್ಮಿತಿ ಗುಂಪಿನೊಂದಿಗೆ ಫಿನ್ಸ ರ್ ಸ್ಪೇಸ್ ಮತ್ತು ಅದನ್ನು ಅವನು ಕಡಿಮೆ ಮಾಡಬಹುದು ಕ್ಯಾಡ್ರಾಟಿಕ್ ಮೆಟ್ರಿಕ್ಸ್ ಫಿಕ್ಷನ್ ಹೊಂದಿರುವ ಜಾಗಕ್ಕೆ. ಇದು ಸರಳವಾದ ಪರಿಗಣನೆಯಾಗಿದೆ H ನ ಬೀಜಗಣಿತ ಮತ್ತು ಗೂಮೆಟ್ರಿಕ್ ಗುಣಲಕ್ಷಣಗಳು, ಅದು ಕ್ಷುಲ್ಲಕವಲ್ಲದ ನೋಟಕ್ಕೆ ಲೋಡ್ ಮಾಡುತ್ತದೆ ಗಣಿತ ವಸ್ತು. ಈ ಕಾಗದದಲ್ಲಿ ತೋರಿಸಿರುವಂತೆ, ಭೌತಿಕ ಪರಿಗಣನೆ H ನ ವಿಷಯಗಳು, ಅದರ ಬೀಜಗಣಿತ ಮತ್ತು ಜಿಕೊಮೆಟ್ರಿಕಲ್ ಸ್ಮನೆಚರ್‌ಗಳೊಂದಿಗೆ ಅದನ್ನು ಇನ್ನಷ್ಟು ಹೆಚ್ಚಿಸುತ್ತವೆ ಸಂಕೀರ್ಣ ಮತ್ತು ಆಸಕ್ತಿದಾಯಕ, ಅದರ ಆರಂಭಿಕ ಆಲ್ಗಕ್ಟ್ರಕ್ ಸರಳತೆಯ ಹೊರತಾಗಿಯೂ: ಕ್ಲಾಟಿವಿಸ್ಟಿಕ್ ಅಲ್ಲದ ಮಿತಿ (ಭೌತಿಕ ವಸ್ತುವಿನ ವೇಗದ ಅನುಪಾತದ ಎರಡನೇ ಮತ್ತು ಹೆಚ್ಚಿನ ಆದೇಶಗಳನ್ನು ನಿರ್ಲಕ್ಷಿಸುವುದು ಬೆಳಕಿನ ವೇಗಕ್ಕೆ), ಇದು ಗೆಲಿಲಿಯನ್ ಬಾಹ್ಯಾಕಾಶದಿಂದ (ಶಾಸ್ತ್ರೀಯವಾದ) ಅಸ್ಪಷ್ಟವಾಗಿದೆ ಮೆಕ್ಯಾನಿಕ್ಸ್ ಸ್ಪೇಸ್) ಮತ್ತು ಮಿಂಕೋವ್ಸ್ಕಿ ಸ್ಪೇಸ್ (SR) ನಿಂದ. ಮೊರ್ಕೋವರ್, ಸಾಮಾನ್ಯ ಸಂದರ್ಭದಲ್ಲಿ ಸಹ

Figure 5: Kannada Document Processing: Comparison between the original document (left) and the model's OCR output (right)

A.3 Training Dynamics Analysis

A.3.1 Single Language LoRA Adaptation

We first analyze the training dynamics for individual languages using LoRA with rank=64 and α=128. Figure 6 shows the training curves for Hindi and Kannada.

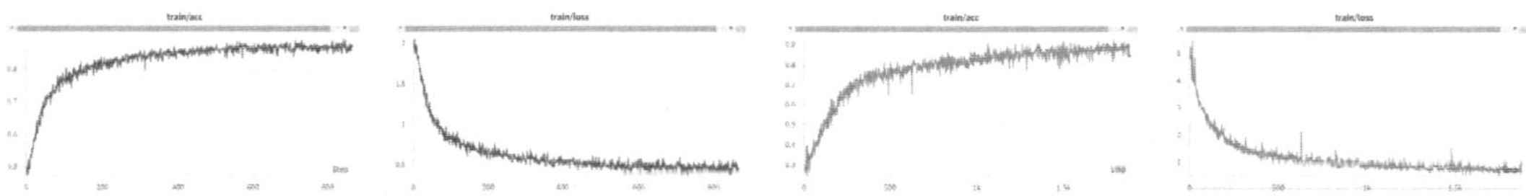

Figure 6: Single Language LoRA Training Dynamics: Training and loss curves for Hindi (purple) and Kannada (orange) using LoRA (r=64, α=128). Both languages show stable convergence patterns with Hindi achieving slightly faster convergence.

A.3.2 Multi-Language Joint Training

Building on the single language results, we investigate joint training on Hindi and Kannada. Figure 7 demonstrates the effectiveness of our multi-language approach.

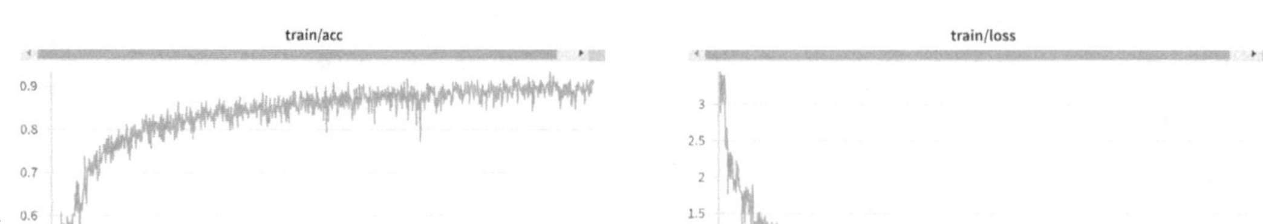

Figure 7: Joint Hindi-Kannada Training: The model maintains strong performance while learning both languages simultaneously, suggesting effective parameter sharing between related scripts.

A.3.3 Comparative Analysis of Joint vs Individual Training

To validate our multi-language approach, we compare joint training performance against individual language models. Figure 8 presents this critical comparison, where the orange line represents Kannada with rank 64 LoRA, the neon line shows the joint Hindi-Kannada LoRA (rank 64), and the green line indicates Hindi with rank 64 LoRA adaptation.

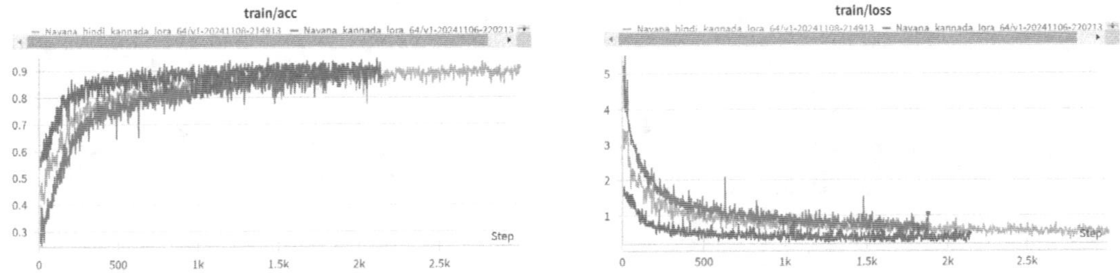

Figure 8: Comparative Analysis: Joint Hindi-Kannada training (r=64, α=128) versus individual language models. The joint model (neon) achieves comparable performance to individual Hindi (green) and Kannada (orange) models while using fewer parameters, demonstrating efficient cross-lingual transfer.

A.3.4 Vocabulary Expansion Experiments

Our initial experiments explored vocabulary expansion as a potential approach for handling multiple scripts. Figure 9 illustrates these challenges, comparing standard LoRA adaptation (purple lines) against vocabulary expansion attempts (grey lines).

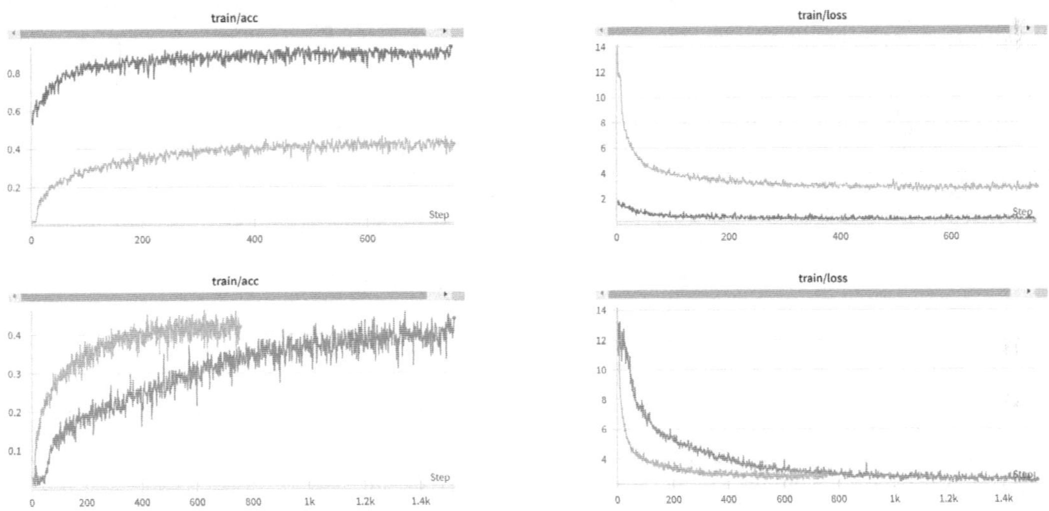

Figure 9: Vocabulary Expansion Analysis: Attempts to expand model vocabulary for Hindi showed poor convergence across different configurations. The standard vocabulary with LoRA adaptation (purple) proved more effective than expanded vocabulary approaches (grey), leading us to abandon the vocabulary expansion strategy.

A.4 Data Generation Examples

A.4.1 Page-Level Translation Examples

Our pipeline demonstrates robust translation capabilities while preserving document structure across all supported languages. Figures 10, 11, 12, 13 and 14 showcase these capabilities across different Indic scripts.

A.4.2 Section-Level Translation Examples

Figures 15, 16, 17 and 18 showcase section level translation capabilities across different Indic scripts.

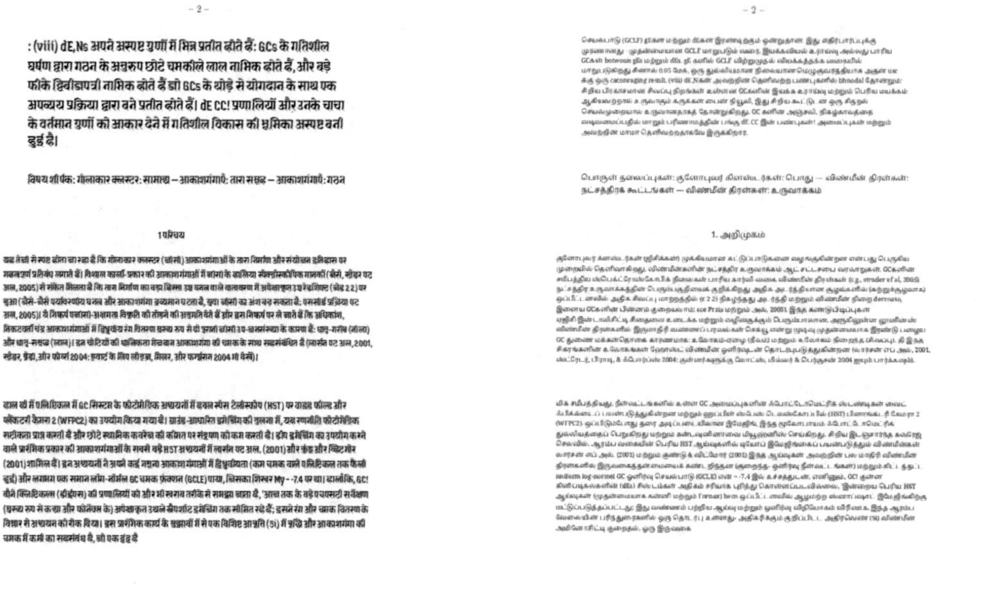

Figure 10: Page-level translation examples showing Hindi (left) and Tamil (right) translations with preserved document layout.

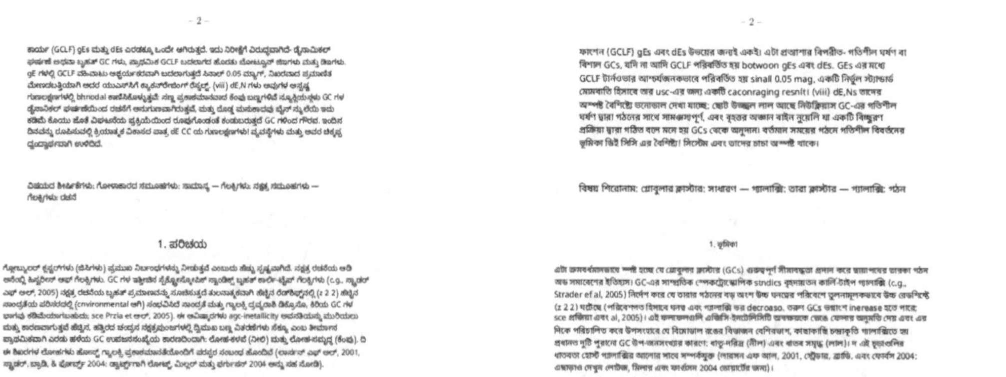

Figure 11: Page-level translation examples demonstrating Kannada (left) and Bengali (right) translations.

Figure 12: Page-level translation examples showing Malayalam (left) and Gujarati (right) translations.

Figure 13: Page-level translation examples demonstrating Marathi (left) and Telugu (right) translations.

Figure 14: Page-level translation examples showing Odia (left) and Punjabi (right) translations.

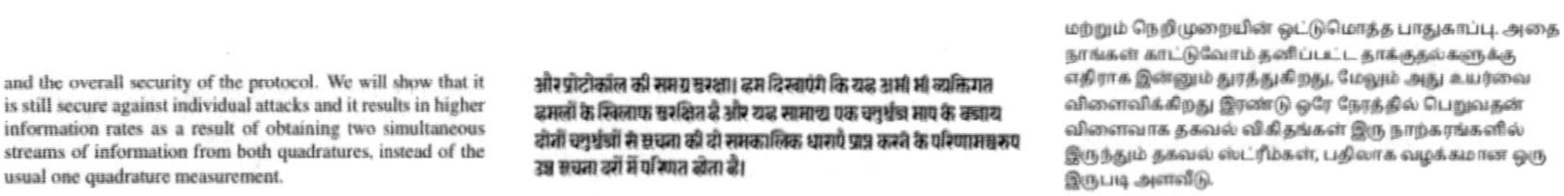

Figure 15: Section-level translation examples showing English (original), Hindi, and Tamil translations.

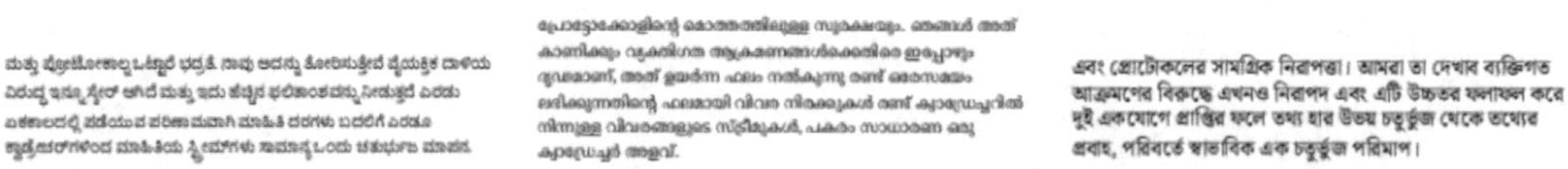

Figure 16: Section-level translation examples showing Kannada, Malayalam, and Bengali translations.

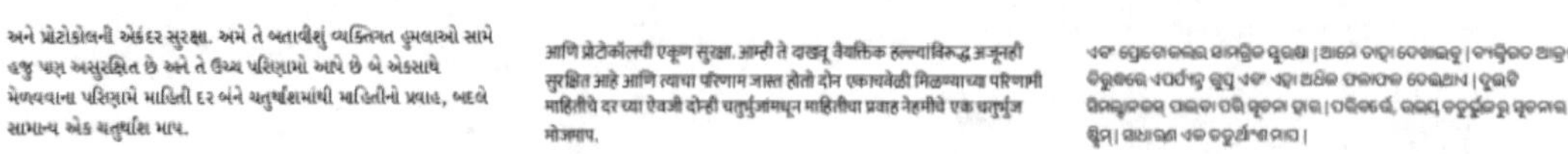

Figure 17: Section-level translation examples showing Gujarati, Marathi, and Odia translations.

Figure 18: Section-level translation examples showing Punjabi and Telugu translations.

A.5 Data Augmentation Examples

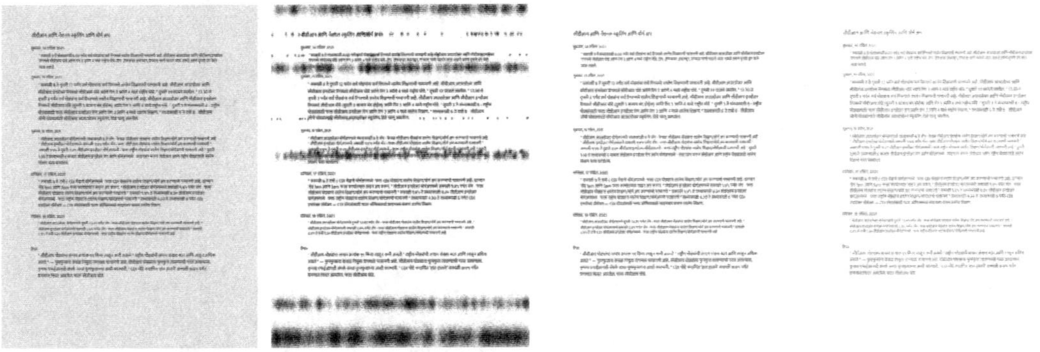

Figure 19: Document degradation examples showing (from left to right): background texturization, printer drum defects, ink mottling effect, and letterpress impression.

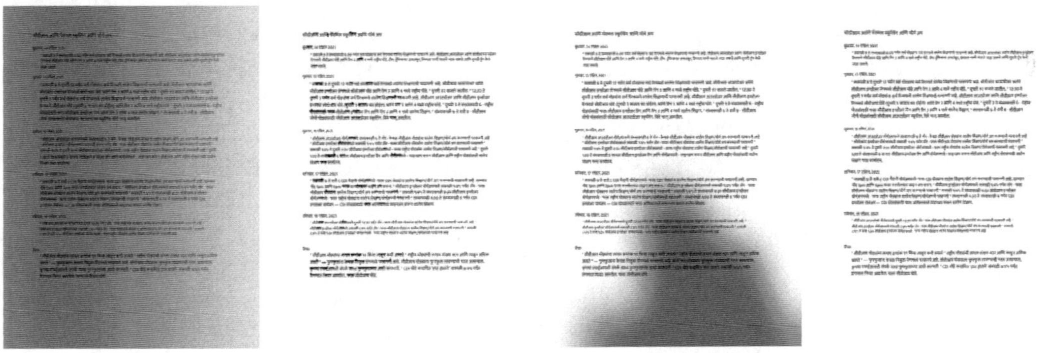

Figure 20: Document degradation examples showing (from left to right): lighting gradient, line degradation, shadow effects, and ink bleeding.

On Tables with Numbers, with Numbers

Konstantinos Kogkalidis
Aalto University
Department of Computer Science
kokos.kogkalidis@aalto.fi

Stergios Chatzikyriakidis
University of Crete
Department of Philology
stergios.chatzikyriakidis@uoc.gr

Abstract

This paper is a critical reflection on the epistemic culture of contemporary computational linguistics, framed in the context of its growing obsession with tables with numbers. We argue against tables with numbers on the basis of their epistemic irrelevance, their environmental impact, their role in enabling and exacerbating social inequalities, and their deep ties to commercial applications and profit-driven research. We substantiate our arguments with empirical evidence drawn from a meta-analysis of computational linguistics research over the last decade.

1 Introduction

Throughout its evolution, computational linguistics has undergone multiple identity crises. In its present from, and despite its logical origins and linguistic ambitions, it is almost entirely aligned with positivist principles and ideals (Church and Liberman, 2021). The imprint of this alignment is an idealization of experimental quantification, most commonly manifesting in the form of *tables with numbers*. Tables with numbers can certainly be useful. That said, their centrality in contemporary computational linguistics research is indicative of both scientific reductionism and technological obsession. Beneath the numbers lie signs of a field in disarray: a waning reliance on theory (linguistic or otherwise), nowadays substituted by model scale; a disproportionate representation of big industry and big academia, in turn associated with a lack of transparency, accessibility and inclusion; an experimental paradigm dominated by stagnant "task-and-benchmark" practices, detached from technical rigor as well as scientific insight; and a progressive estrangement from societal, humanistic and environmental context. And while the community seems to be both alert to and uneasy with the current state of affairs (Michael et al., 2023; Gururaja et al., 2023), a holistic analysis of these issues has been long missing from the literature.

In this paper, we brave a look under the number rock. We conduct a critical assessment of the epistemic culture of computational linguistics, focusing specifically on its relation to tables with numbers. We narrow down on four axes of interest:

- The epistemological preconditions that granted tables with numbers the status of scientific currency, and the mechanisms that affect their actual value (§2).
- Their environmental footprint and the normative discourse around it (§3).
- Their cause-and-effect relation to the perpetuation and exacerbation of inequality and harmful power structures (§4).
- Their intrinsic ties with corporate interest, profit, and the accumulation of technoscientific capital (§5).

2 The Multiple Facets of Number

The field's dominant scientific approach embodies a wildly exaggerated version of positivism. This is evident both in the themes prevalent in the mainstream discourse, and in those notably absent from it. In this context, two critical perspectives arise. First, how faithfully does computational linguistics *actually* adhere to its positivist posture? And second, what are the *implications* of computational linguistics as a singularly positivist discipline? We begin by addressing the former, setting off with a simplified introduction to the positivist worldview and its tenets.

2.1 Number as Virtue

As a scientific meta-theory, positivism asserts that knowledge is the yield of systematic, unbiased and reproducible observation. A prospective theory is evaluated based on how well it can predict and interpret observations. An impartial and irrefutable

Proceedings of the 1st Workshop on Language Models for Underserved Communities (LM4UC 2025), pages 104–115
May 4, 2025 ©2025 Association for Computational Linguistics

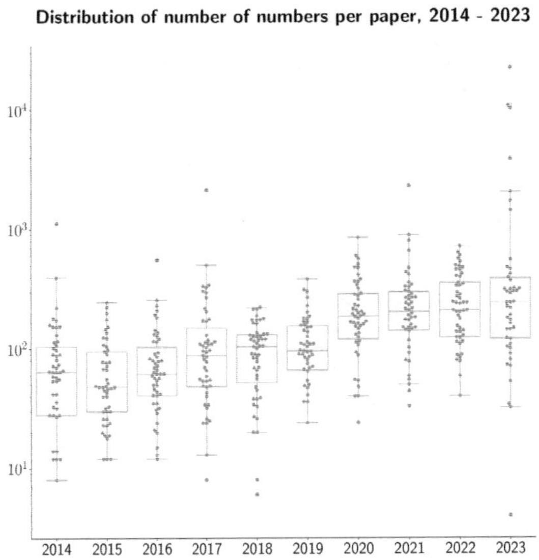

Figure 1: Box- and swarm-plots of the distribution of the number of experimental results per paper, grouped by year. We manually count the number of numbers within tables from the 50 most cited papers per year. We do not include numbers that pertain to descriptive dataset statistics, nor numbers reporting dispersion statistics (*e.g.*, confidence intervals, standard deviations *etc.*). The pattern indicates a marked upwards trend over time. Most (75%) contemporary papers contain 100 to 300 numbers, while some (25%) contain up to 1 000.

evaluation is what ensures theories can be refuted and reliably compared. Ultimately, the essence of scientific progress lies in the iterative process of theory testing, rejection, and refinement. This worldview holds truth as objective and unique, asserted as such by reproducibility, generalization, neutrality, and universality (Ayer, 1959). Tables with numbers attain epistemic significance in bearing witness to this (idealization of) truth.

2.2 Number as Number

Alas, linguistic theories have fallen short of historical expectations. To date, there is no hint of a consensus on what a concretely implementable mechanization of human language should (or even could) look like. In lieu of theories, computational linguistics had to turn to the next best thing: models.[1,2] Models promise less but do more, prioritizing tangible solutions over abstract notions of inquisitive deduction. Apart from this deviation, the positivist methodological narrative is easy to recognize in the field's experimental pipeline. Large datasets are heralded as authoritative collections of empirical observations, systematically condensing linguistic truth. Datasets enact "benchmarks", standardized and fair test suites through which we can "track progress", *i.e.*, decide whether a model advances science, and if so, by *how much*. Congruent with the literature's makeup over the last decade, this suggests that contributions may come in one of two primary forms: models and benchmarks, dual facets of one and the same thing – tables with numbers.

Nonetheless, in having discarded theory, the model-and-benchmark pipeline fails to uphold the scientific promise upon which it was built. A first problem lies in the fact that the models developed and adopted nowadays are almost exclusively generic and theory-neutral (Sutton, 2019). In making no assumptions and yielding no hypotheses over their domain, they are infallible in all aspects except for their performance (Schlangen, 2021). The side effect is that the field's progress translates to technical know-how rather than an advance in the sum total of "pure" knowledge (Krenn et al., 2022; Messeri and Crockett, 2024). Other than modeling insights, nothing gets in and nothing gets out, confining a traditionally interdisciplinary endeavour to a technocratic and opinionless monoculture.

A second, perhaps bigger, problem lies in the reductionist view of language faculty as something that can be broken apart into high-level "tasks", at the intersection of which one can find, and therefore *quantify*, "understanding" (Raji et al., 2021). The verity of this assumption is not immediately obvious; modern models breeze through benchmarks, yet we remain as far as ever from attaining a holistic and comprehensive computational account of language. The picture is sufficiently clear: sidetracked by models and benchmarks, computational linguistics has given way to natural language processing: a domain-specific engineering discipline that is happy to answer more questions than it asks.

2.3 Number as Nothing

Ironically, the remarkable ease of model iteration (as compared to the painstakingly slow process of theory iteration) is an inflationary factor for the epistemic value of numbers. When experimental superiority becomes a prerequisite to publi-

[1] This is one reading. Another reading is that when machine learning "solved" vision, it moved over to NLP, setting aside linguistic expertise to make room for all the luggage it brought with it.

[2] The modern tendency to look for a theory *within* the model (see Baroni (2022); Piantadosi (2023), *inter alia*) is further evidencing the poverty of historical theories.

cation (Rogers, 2020), all publications invariably achieve it, rendering both the message (experimental superiority) and the messenger (publications) meaningless. Immediate, short-sighted gains dominate the research agenda, and difficult questions become eschewed for the sake of incremental tweaks and micro-improvements (Bhattacharya and Packalen, 2020). Short-sighted goals are echoed in short-term memory, leading to plentiful instances of knowledge recycling, paper duplication and citation amnesia (Singh et al., 2023). The over-standardization of form gradually turns into an equilibrium of intent – contributions are pushed towards structural and semantic uniformity, ending up virtually indistinguishable from one another. The frantic pace of "progress" turns scientific enterprise into a competition for experimental superiority, eroding integrity and transparency. The most successful models are too time- and resource-consuming to replicate and cross-validate, leading to statistically insignificant tables filled with under-sampled and noisy numbers of dubious quality and utility (Dodge et al., 2019; Ethayarajh and Jurafsky, 2020; Belz et al., 2021). Scientific communication espouses sales pitch aesthetics, exaggerating merit, obscuring weakness and purposefully avoiding critical self-reflection and honest self-assessment (Smaldino and McElreath, 2016; Lipton and Steinhardt, 2019). After a bountiful decade of benchmarking frenzy, there is now growing consensus that annotation is subjective (Geva et al., 2019; Plank, 2022), datasets are statistically biased, and models are sensitive to heuristics and label noise (McCoy et al., 2019; Geirhos et al., 2020) – the numbers *have been lying all along* (Recht et al., 2019; Liao et al., 2021)![3] Put simply, the more tables with numbers there are, the less a table with numbers means, and the less it can be trusted.

2.4 Number as Vice

Its failure to really adhere to the positivist ethos does not absolve computational linguistics from having adopted it in the first place. The idealization of science as an entity far and above subjective human reference provides the grounds for its disconnect from social context; there's no reflection on its production and consumption, the people involved in it and the people affected by it, or its effect on broader society and the world at large. This detachment is reinforced by a techno-determinist narrative of a "progress" moving of its own accord, which the scientist neither can influence, nor is responsible for (Wyatt, 2008). Tables with numbers are the embodiment of techno-determinism. The quest for experimental superiority (*i.e.*, "progress") is perceived as a self-efficient treadmill that continues on, regardless of who walks it – there's no challenging the pace.

Setting off from a different axiomatization of scientific truth allows for different inference paths. By reflecting on the philosophy of contemporary computational linguistics, we are afforded the opportunity to challenge this particular interpretation of progress – not just for its lack of scientific merit, but more importantly for its active role in perpetuating and amplifying social and environmental harm. We build on this perspective in the following sections.

3 Resource Exhaustion

As the field is witnessing a constant influx of progressively larger models, each vying for supremacy over increasingly more challenging benchmarks, tables are growing in both size and count; see Fig. 1. Meanwhile, the numbers within are getting more resource-intensive by the day (Sharir et al., 2020). As a result, the environmental footprint of contemporary research is expanding at an alarming rate (Strubell et al., 2019; Li et al., 2023).

3.1 No NLP to Be Done on a Dead Planet

The point has resonated with the ecological sensibilities of the community, prompting a number of responses to the issue. By now, these have come to coalesce into a niche of their own, united under the common banner of a so-called "green AI" (Schwartz et al., 2020). So far, most of this green literature has gravitated around two thematic pillars (Verdecchia et al., 2023). The first involves matters of high-level policy: promoting greener models, raising awareness, stamping algorithms and models with eco-labels, *etc.* The second involves matters of low-level practice: truncating or quantizing models, optimizing resource utilization, improving performance-to-emission ratios, *etc.* While both are valuable research avenues, neither really addresses the essence of the problem: the benchmarking practice itself. Indeed, ecologically rooted condemnations of the current *modus*

[3] The fact that benchmarking is being made obsolete by a handful of closed source models far beyond the community's reach is clearly just a coincidence to the timing of this realization.

operandi are rare and far between (with Brevini (2020, 2021, 2022, *inter alia*) and Heilinger et al. (2024) being among the few notable exceptions).

In this case, failing to note the obvious is not (just) a problem of deductive inadequacy; the omission is actually a take in disguise. An ideological child of techno-determinism, on the one hand, and eco-modernism, on the other, it implicitly proclaims that there is no standing in the way of progress – yet *good* progress *can* save the world! The incompatibility of these two positions is glaring. There is little point debating the inherent benevolence of a progress that we cannot contest or control. That said, there is no need to shy away from connecting the dots either. Experimental obsession negatively contributes to a rapidly deteriorating environment, and computational linguistics can never truly be "green" as long as it remains attached to it. The ecologically responsible course of action is not to alleviate the effects – it is to dismantle the cause.

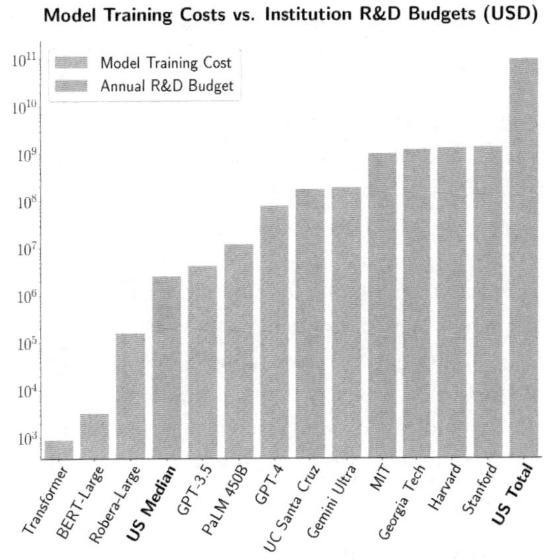

Figure 2: Contemporary model training costs compared to the total annual R&D budgets of select U.S. institutions in 2022. The cost of training a large model is comparable to the budget of a university in the top 15th percentile, which is two orders of magnitude larger than the median budget. Budget data sourced from the 2022 report by the US National Center for Science and Engineering Statistics[a]. Model cost estimates from Epoch AI (2023). The U.S. was the globe's highest spender for the year, in terms of R&D expenditures.

[a] https://ncsesdata.nsf.gov/profiles/

4 Institutional Bias & Privilege

Besides environmental concerns, keeping up with contemporary research trends comes at a (literal) heavy price. As the cost of the *"state of the art"* explodes at a super-exponential rate (Sharir et al., 2020; Epoch AI, 2023; Perrault and Clark, 2024, *inter alia*), the severe budget inequalities in higher education become further pronounced (O'Sullivan, 2016; Goyes and Skilbrei, 2023), and the minimum requirements for scientific relevance becoming prohibitively high for smaller and lesser-funded institutions to acquire and maintain (Ahmed and Wahed, 2020); see also Fig. 2. Consequently, a few dominant institutions get to consolidate their competitive advantage by effectively gatekeeping the means necessary to conduct exactly the kind of research that is perceived as groundbreaking and impactful (Münch, 2014). This is problematic on multiple levels.

4.1 Science of the Few

To begin with, the insurmountable entry barrier perpetuates and exacerbates a cycle of entrenched privilege, where only a few voices retain access to the platforms of expression. This disparity translates the lack of diversity in *what* research is done to a lack of diversity in *who* gets to do it (Ahmed and Wahed, 2020; Perrault and Clark, 2024). For those favored, the cycle is no easier to break. The current status quo presents a very alluring prospect: a research recipe that is universally recognized as superior, and that only few have the ingredients necessary to implement. Opting out is not just a matter of critical reflection – it is actually harmful to one's own interests (as measured in publications, citation counts, employment opportunities, *etc.*). Beyond the individual, the same dynamics appear at the institutional scale. Steering a unit away from the competition for experimental superiority and towards niche research means condemning it into academic obscurity and irrelevance; both too easy to mistake for incompetence. This further disincentives scientific plurality, placing the field on a convergent path toward a strict hierarchy of methodologies and ideas, mirrored in a dual hierarchy of institutions and individuals (Rungta et al., 2022).

Effect being all too easy to mistake for cause, a few institutions have by now come to be lauded as hubs of research pioneers, their output singled out and preemptively lauded on the basis of origin alone (Rigney, 2010; Brennen et al., 2019). Privileged individuals are granted undue influence over the field's trajectory, effectively getting to dictate both *what questions to ask* (*e.g.*, which datasets to tackle), and *where to look for the answers* (*e.g.*, which models to adopt). This concentration of technical and scientific authority creates clearly delineated points of vulnerability for the field. Alternative viewpoints and methodologies are at an increased risk of being left unnoticed or becoming squelched, suppressing innovation and inducing inertia. Worse yet, it allows for the biases, norms and opinions of a few dominant actors to be perpetuated unhindered, except now disguised as universal and irrefutable truths characterizing the entire discipline.

4.2 Science for the Few

This last issue is exacerbated exactly by the inherent narrowness of these biases, norms and opinions. Prestigious (read: *wealthy*) institutions are neither evenly distributed across geographic regions, nor equally accessible across social, cultural, ethnic and economic backgrounds. As such, the perspectives and priorities they represent are inevitably skewed towards certain demographics, fostering homogenization at the expense of further marginalizing under-represented groups and identities (Amsler and Bolsmann, 2012; Shamash, 2018; Field et al., 2021; Talat et al., 2022; Hershcovich et al., 2022; Bender and Grissom II, 2024; Perrault and Clark, 2024, *inter alia*). On the premise that cultural diversity is indeed worth nurturing and preserving (Harmon, 2001), the absence of plurality caused by this delegation of scientific and technological authority is bad – for any scientific field. For a field like computational linguistics in particular, it is *catastrophic*. Allowing research agendas to be shaped by a handful of actors endorses hegemonialism: not just technological and scientific, but importantly also cultural and linguistic.

This is particularly evident in the stark geographic disparity between citation-producing networks and centers of linguistic diversity (Rungta et al., 2022). Trending terms like "natural language understanding" carefully conceal the assumptions made on *which* languages are actually worth understanding – or what *understanding* means, for that matter (Bender et al., 2021). The perspective that chasing after benchmarks and competing for the top spots in scoreboards carries some inherent value to the study of language becomes immediately exposed as biased and flawed upon noticing that the majority of benchmarks and scoreboards pertain only to a minuscule fragment of the globe's peoples (Joshi et al., 2020; Ruder, 2022).

Finally, a disproportionate allocation of resources creates the necessary preconditions for scientific tokenism. Technological abundance for the few is indistinguishable from technological sparsity for the many. The surging pressure for inclusivity is temptingly easy to relieve, either by reducing the bar when it comes to work in under-represented languages and cultures, or by "allowing" it to coexist along the mainstream as a secondary, self-referential niche. And while this might indeed expedite its progress or increase its visibility, it carries the risk of negatively impacting its (perceived) quality, further cementing the gap between center and periphery worlds – in terms of language, culture and research alike.

4.3 From Inequality to Alienation

Along the same lines, in monopolizing the resources essential for "frontier" research, "world-class" institutions gain a competitive edge in attracting highly sought-after global talent. Predictably, transnational academic mobility flows along research capacity gradients shaped by global wealth inequalities (Bilecen and van Mol, 2017). The exclusivity of "frontier" research turns academic mobility into a violent dilemma: move, or (academically) perish. Built on this premise, "frontier" research cannot but carry a commodified and socially charged undertone (Stein, 2017).

Two orthogonal aspects of this perspective share a single common effect. First, the same process that accelerates well-funded and globally competitive research decelerates regional institutions and projects by starving them of (yet) another precious resource: talent (Auriol et al., 2013; van der Wende, 2015, *inter alia*). Second, the inherently globalized nature of benchmarking and its constructed significance means that researchers employed abroad are predominantly engaged with work far detached from their own cultural and linguistic heritage. The mirror image of an international researcher pushing the boundaries of "cutting-edge" research is an expatriated researcher not getting their own mother tongue up to speed with that very same research. This reveals benchmarking as a driver for scientific assimilation, which turns linguistic coverage into a matter of institutionalized charity – left to the discretion of exactly those fueling (and benefiting from) its absence.

5 Science & Profit

Albeit alarming, institutional bias is to some extent mitigated by a common (if subjective and vague) promise of scientific integrity, a culture of transparency and openness, a shared strive for intellectual inquiry, and the self-regulatory effect of the (occasionally functional[4]) peer-reviewing system. However, as the race for experimental superiority intensifies, turning increasingly exclusive, each new milestone gains greater appeal. Beyond signaling intellectual achievement or academic accomplishment, this appeal extends to the material plane. There, leading the benchmark race translates to a tangible competitive edge in commercial (and/or state) applications. The allure of such an edge has been persistently attracting profit-driven entities into the computational linguistics ecosystem. Over the span of a decade, these entities have evolved from circumstantial players to dominant figureheads. For such entities, *none* of the safeguards above hold. This reality poses an existential threat for the field; a threat which nonetheless remains largely unaddressed.

5.1 Stand on the Shoulders of (Tech) Giants

The current state of affairs can be traced to a historical affinity between computational linguistics and machine learning (Manning, 2015). Such an affinity is hardly surprising. Language poses challenges at a variety of modalities and difficulty scales, enacting a boundless source of benchmarks for machine learning models. Conversely, models and techniques developed for language-related tasks have frequently demonstrated their versatility as general-purpose machine learning tools, making their way to distant or even unrelated disciplines. Until recently, this reciprocal relationship has been beneficial to both fields. In the last few years, however, and as the pace of progress in machine learning has been consistently exceeding expectations, computational linguistics has lost its primacy, becoming increasingly dependent on imported expertise. This trend is reflected in the silent but perfectly evident shift of the field's main inquiries, which have gradually moved from the computational study of language to an evaluation arena for application-oriented machine learning. And even though this transition might disappoint or alienate some, there is not much inherently wrong about it; after all, it is not uncommon for a research field to retroactively change direction, or even be altogether absorbed or subsumed by another. What *is* problematic in the present context is the nature of the subsumer.

The main pathology of machine learning, having become synonymous with AI, is none other than its public and commercial appeal. The commercialization of science demands tangible advantages against competitors: the product is easier to sell when it's visibly and quantitatively better than alternatives. The success of this commercialization depends largely on "*wow!*" factors: publicity stunts, catchy claims, and a degree of speculative futurism (Funk, 2019). For the global actors invested in the AI race, the concept of performance is thus of prime interest (Bourne, 2024). Current technology dictates one base ingredient as the necessary and sufficient condition for performance: scale (Epoch AI, 2023). And so, we get once more caught up in a vicious cycle. As profit requires performance, performance requires scale, and scale requires budget, a positive feedback loop ensures the growth of a handful of tech giants – at a rate far exceeding that of even the wealthiest research institution. And as performance just so happens to be our currency of choice when quantifying scientific advancement (Birhane et al., 2022), machine learning research becomes *de facto* dominated by exactly these giants (Perrault and Clark, 2024; de Sousa, 2024). This elevates the resource allotment problems discussed earlier to an altogether different scale: what's at stake now is not just equal and fair access to an equal and fair science, but rather the very idea of independent scientific inquiry (Abdalla and Abdalla, 2021; Jurowetzki et al., 2021).

5.2 Research (and Development)

In practice, as long as computational linguistics research remains results-oriented, reliance on technology and infrastructure provisioned by tech giants is a nonchoice – there is, after all, *no one else* to provision them from (Whittaker, 2021; Abdalla et al., 2023; Ferrari, 2023). One might argue that such an arrangement is not without merits. The narrative would usually be that putting corporate technology into the scientific spotlight facilitates the assessment of its risks and potentials, promoting accountability through transparency. Conversely, integrating corporate resources into academia accelerates the actualization of research and increases its impact: rough prototypes turn into concrete tools, ensuring that scientific advancements reach the pub-

[4]See Rogers (2020) and Rogers and Augenstein (2020).

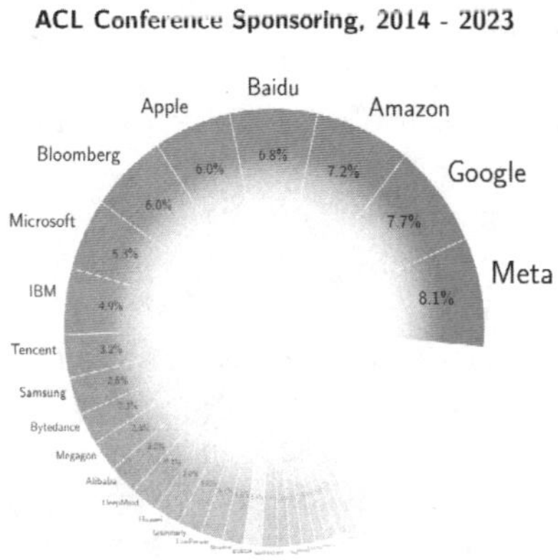

Figure 3: Major sponsors of the main ACL conferences over the last 10 years. To convert tiered participation counts to contributions, we assign a weight of 1 to the year's top tier, and divide the weight of each consecutive sponsorship tier by 2. The treasurer of the ACL did not respond to our request for accurate donation figures.

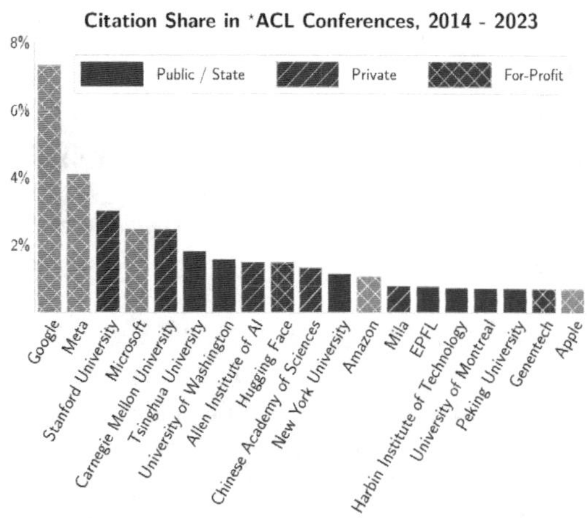

Figure 4: Citation share by organization in *ACL conferences over the last 10 years. Colors are inherited from Fig. 3, when applicable. The 19 organizations listed amount for approximately one third of the total citations during this period. We associate (i) papers to authors, by parsing the ACL bibliography file, (ii) authors to affiliations, by crawling `google scholar` with `scholarly`, and (iii) papers to publication counts, using `Zotero` and the `ZoteroCitationCountsManager` plugin. We collapse affiliations to organizations (*i.e.*, remove job titles and departments) by instructing `mistral-7B` (Jiang et al., 2023). We compose and aggregate over the above to produce a map from organizations to citation counts, disregarding organizations with less than 5 citations as likely parsing errors. The result is imperfect: there are multiple sources of error, and affiliations at retrieval time are likely to differ from those at publication time. Nonetheless, it paints a sufficiently clear picture of which organizations are exerting the most influence in the field, and what the extent of this influence is.

lic domain faster. But such a narrative depends on, and in fact presupposes, an alignment between scientific and commercial agendas. The implication is that the pursuit of knowledge becomes conditional on its compatibility with the interests and capabilities of big tech, *i.e.*, the very same actors academia was supposed to scrutinize in the first place.

The conflict of interest is immediately apparent. The overwhelming power asymmetry between big tech and academia (be it big or otherwise) erodes any potential merits that could ever be argued for. Under the present conditions, the scientific spotlight can no longer be critical or investigative. Conferencing devolves to a campaigning stage, a ticketed tech show, and a marketplace where for the colossi to display their latest wares and recruit new talent; see Fig. 3, and juxtapose with Fig. 4. Corporate resources do not "spill over", nor do they "trickle down" – they are rationed; a means of scientific coercion (Noble, 1979; Moore et al., 2011; Phan et al., 2022). Corporate interests do not actualize knowledge – they predate, appropriate and monetize it (Rikap and Lundvall, 2022). Ideas that survive the ecosystem's selection process do not turn into socially relevant tools – they turn into economically viable products (Dale, 2019; Klinger et al., 2020; Luitse and Denkena, 2021). Scientific involvement itself degrades into a "networking filter": an inconvenient but unavoidable stepping stone towards a high-stakes career in tech (Ahmed et al., 2023; Gofman and Jin, 2024). The researcher becomes a glorified spokesperson for big tech, a consumer of their infrastructure, a public advocate of their science, a safety net between them and the public – an eager and dispensable part of their production pipeline.

The extent and degree of the infiltration have become impossible to ignore. We are on the verge of a corporate takeover, legitimized by an acquired taste for big datasets, big models and big numbers. Put simply, we have been voluntarily handing the field over to an industry we are realistically incapable of challenging, let alone regulating.

5.3 (The Irrelevance of) Corporate Ethics

As of late, the community's growing awareness (Michael et al., 2023) of these developments and their public ramifications has spurred numerous works on so-called "AI ethics". The conversation is heavily skewed by well-documented lobbying efforts and a broader ethics-washing campaign aimed at soothing public concern and deterring regulatory oversight. The "debate" often revolves around virtue signaling gestures, assertions of corporate responsibility (or accusations of its absence), suggestions for self-regulatory accountability guidelines, techno-positive musings of an all-inclusive tomorrow, "critical" perspectives from within, vague calls for a misconstrued "democratization", and the like. In their majority, these works range from malicious manipulation at worst, to harmful diversions at best (Ochigame, 2019; Benkler, 2019; Slee, 2020; Hagendorff, 2020; Whittaker, 2021; Phan et al., 2022; Seele and Schultz, 2022; Himmelreich, 2023, *inter alia*).

This premeditated and narrow notion of ethics subtly chooses to ignore the possibility of us reappropriating the scientific discourse. Besides negotiating matters of representation and inclusion, bias aversion, model explainability, linguistic diversity, open-sourcing, carbon impact, *etc.* as they arise within the *current* environment, we have a far more fundamental series of questions to be confronted with. Are we assuming that big tech, running rampant on the field's collective advancements, will (or even can) ever align their agenda with the public's interests? Do we trust them with upholding the values of scientific integrity and technological accountability? Are we at peace with the prospect of a privatized and application-centric future for computational linguistics, removed from the world, its people and their needs? If the answer to the above is no, how can we justify our implicit yet unwavering support and commitment to big tech's cause throughout the last decade? Why are we so susceptible to their influence, so eager to adopt their values and principles, so tolerant of their technologically exclusionary practices? Ultimately, what benefits do *we* get to derive from contributing to *their* endeavors – and at what cost?

6 Ways Ahead

The paradigm shift advocated for might seem radical or untenable. In reality, it is neither. The epistemic rewiring it calls for can be set in motion with as little as individual adjustments in research consumption and production attitudes.

As *readers*, we need to stop allowing ourselves to be dazzled by big numbers. We must ask what their utility and cost are, who benefits from them, and who bears their expense. We should not only grow resilient to hollow benchmarking hypes, but also openly refute and disarm them.

As *authors*, *colleagues* and *advisors*, we have to be conscious of our (and each other's) research goals and practices. We ought to look beyond numbers and benchmarks and focus on what questions our research really answers. We must challenge the notion of science as a competition or enterprise, and scorn endeavors that depend solely on experimental superiority to be deemed successful. We must be mindful and explicit of the resources we use and their accessibility, but also of the artifacts we produce and their inclusivity. Above all, it is our responsibility to be vocal and assertive about the issues in our field; despite –or rather *in spite of*– normative resistance and calls for conformity and "moderation".

As *reviewers*, we should each recognize our respective academic privileges, and be cautious in our technical demands; not everyone has access to the same number of GPUs. Conversely, we should not be intimidated by big tables and bold face fonts; we need to be critical of the research we are exposed to, and call out opaque methodologies, exclusionary practices and useless flourishes. Finally, our exclusive access to the reviewing process means it is our own duty to monitor it; each one of us has a role in identifying and confronting poor practices.

7 Conclusion

We discussed tables with numbers, and related them to several issues that affect contemporary computational linguistics research. We argued that the focus on experimental superiority has shifted research priorities towards technical optimization, at the expense of theoretical depth and societal context. This has led to an inflationary effect on the epistemic value of experimental results, rendering them (and, by extension, the field itself), increasingly meaningless. We explained how the pressure for experimental superiority, while advancing technology, has fostered environmental degradation, institutional biases, and the commodification of research. To address these issues, we urge the field to critically reassess its methodologies, and prioritize a more holistic and socially responsible approach to scientific inquiry, balancing technical achievements with ethical and environmental considerations. Such a shift is essential for ensuring that advancements in computational linguistics positively contribute to scientific knowledge, societal well-being, cultural diversity, and environmental sustainability.

Limitations

We tried to substantiate our claims with (references to) empirical evidence and contemporary critical perspectives. Nonetheless, this paper is first and foremost an opinion piece; the ideas presented are the product of subjective and ideologically signed mental processes. For a reader that ascribes to the epistemic foundations of positivism, this is an argumentative weakness. For us, it is a strength. We acknowledge our biases and limitations, and welcome critiques from all angles; a broader discussion on the field's epistemic culture is exactly what our work hopes to instigate.

Our analysis is by no means exhaustive, especially considering the complexity and volatility of the subject matter. The most critical omission, due to the temporal gap between writing this piece (August 2024) and getting it published (March 2025), is a reflection on how recent political developments have further validated the transient and opportunistic nature of big tech's so-called ethics. Following the change in power after the USA 2024 elections, tech companies have been increasing their stakes in transnational military and surveillance applications, while simultaneously backpedaling on their own commitments on ecological sustainability and social diversity, equity and inclusion. We defer a discussion on the military-industrial complex emerging from key players in the language technology industry for another occasion.

Finally, there are several experiments we would have hoped to carry out to quantify some of our claims, but we failed to bring to fruition. We explicitly mention them here for the sake of clarity and transparency, and to bring them to the attention of other interested parties:

- A paper-wise computational cost estimation would allow a quantification of the financial entry barrier to modern research. Overlaid with citation counts, this would allow answering whether the most impactful papers are really just the most expensive ones.
- A longitudinal topic modeling analysis could provide evidence for the narrowing of research topics and methodologies over the last decade. Combined with an evolutionary analysis of writing norms (e.g., paper structure), this would allow us to correlate homogenization of tone with the loss of content diversity.

Acknowledgments

erc The second author is partially funded by the European Union (ERC ADG, PhylProGramm, 101096554).

The second author is also partially funded by the Special Account for Research Funding of the Technical University of Crete (grant number: 11218).

References

Mohamed Abdalla and Moustafa Abdalla. 2021. The grey hoodie project: Big tobacco, big tech, and the threat on academic integrity. In *Proceedings of the 2021 AAAI/ACM Conference on AI, Ethics, and Society*, pages 287–297.

Mohamed Abdalla, Jan Philip Wahle, Terry Ruas, Aurelie Neveol, Fanny Ducel, Saif Mohammad, and Karën Fort. 2023. The elephant in the room: Analyzing the presence of big tech in natural language processing research. In *Proceedings of the 61st Annual Meeting of the Association for Computational Linguistics (Volume 1: Long Papers)*, pages 13141–13160.

Nur Ahmed and Muntasir Wahed. 2020. The dedemocratization of AI: Deep learning and the compute divide in artificial intelligence research. *arXiv preprint arXiv:2010.15581*.

Nur Ahmed, Muntasir Wahed, and Neil Thompson. 2023. The growing influence of industry in AI research. *Science*, 379(6635):884–886.

Sarah Amsler and Chris Bolsmann. 2012. University ranking as social exclusion. *British journal of sociology of education*, 33(2):283–301.

Laudeline Auriol, Max Misu, and Rebecca Ann Freeman. 2013. Careers of doctorate holders: Analysis of labour market and mobility indicators. *OECD Science, Technology and Industry Working Papers*.

Alfred Jules Ayer. 1959. *Logical positivism*, volume 2. Simon and Schuster.

Marco Baroni. 2022. On the proper role of linguistically oriented deep net analysis in linguistic theorising. In *Algebraic structures in natural language*, pages 1–16. CRC Press.

Anya Belz, Shubham Agarwal, Anastasia Shimorina, and Ehud Reiter. 2021. A systematic review of reproducibility research in natural language processing. In *Proceedings of the 16th Conference of the European Chapter of the Association for Computational Linguistics: Main Volume*, pages 381–393, Online. Association for Computational Linguistics.

Emily Bender, Timnit Gebru, Angelina McMillan-Major, and Shmargaret Shmitchell. 2021. On the dangers of stochastic parrots: Can language models be too big? In *Proceedings of the 2021 ACM conference on fairness, accountability, and transparency*, pages 610–623.

Emily Bender and Alvin Grissom II. 2024. Power shift: Toward inclusive natural language processing. *Inclusion in Linguistics*, page 199.

Yochai Benkler. 2019. Don't let industry write the rules for AI. *Nature*, 569(7754):161–162.

Jay Bhattacharya and Mikko Packalen. 2020. Stagnation and scientific incentives. Technical report, National Bureau of Economic Research.

Başak Bilecen and Christof van Mol. 2017. Introduction: International academic mobility and inequalities.

Abeba Birhane, Pratyusha Kalluri, Dallas Card, William Agnew, Ravit Dotan, and Michelle Bao. 2022. The values encoded in machine learning research. In *Proceedings of the 2022 ACM Conference on Fairness, Accountability, and Transparency*, pages 173–184.

Clea Bourne. 2024. AI hype, promotional culture, and affective capitalism. *AI and Ethics*, pages 1–13.

Scott Brennen, Anne Schulz, Philip Howard, and Rasmus Kleis Nielsen. 2019. Industry, experts, or industry experts? Academic sourcing in news coverage of AI. *Reuters Institute for the Study of Journalism*.

Benedetta Brevini. 2020. Black boxes, not green: Mythologizing artificial intelligence and omitting the environment. *Big Data & Society*, 7(2):2053951720935141.

Benedetta Brevini. 2021. *Is AI good for the planet?* John Wiley & Sons.

Benedetta Brevini. 2022. Dispelling the 'green' AI myth: The true environmental cost of producing and supplying digital technologies. Accessed: 26-06-2024.

Kenneth Church and Mark Liberman. 2021. The future of computational linguistics: On beyond alchemy. *Frontiers in Artificial Intelligence*, 4:625341.

Robert Dale. 2019. NLP commercialisation in the last 25 years. *Natural Language Engineering*, 25(3):419–426.

Miguel Angelo de Abreu de Sousa. 2024. The shift of artificial intelligence research from academia to industry: Implications and possible future directions. *AI & SOCIETY*, pages 1–10.

Jesse Dodge, Suchin Gururangan, Dallas Card, Roy Schwartz, and Noah A. Smith. 2019. Show your work: Improved reporting of experimental results. In *Proceedings of the 2019 Conference on Empirical Methods in Natural Language Processing and the 9th International Joint Conference on Natural Language Processing (EMNLP-IJCNLP)*, pages 2185–2194, Hong Kong, China. Association for Computational Linguistics.

Epoch AI. 2023. Key trends and figures in machine learning. Accessed: 2024-05-29.

Kawin Ethayarajh and Dan Jurafsky. 2020. Utility is in the eye of the user: A critique of NLP leaderboards. In *Proceedings of the 2020 Conference on Empirical Methods in Natural Language Processing (EMNLP)*, pages 4846–4853.

Fabian Ferrari. 2023. Neural production networks: AI's infrastructural geographies. *Environment and Planning F*, 2(4):459–476.

Anjalie Field, Su Lin Blodgett, Zeerak Waseem, and Yulia Tsvetkov. 2021. A survey of race, racism, and anti-racism in NLP. In *Proceedings of the 59th Annual Meeting of the Association for Computational Linguistics and the 11th International Joint Conference on Natural Language Processing (Volume 1: Long Papers)*, pages 1905–1925.

Jeffrey Funk. 2019. What's behind technological hype? *Issues in Science and Technology*, 36(1):36–42.

Robert Geirhos, Jörn-Henrik Jacobsen, Claudio Michaelis, Richard Zemel, Wieland Brendel, Matthias Bethge, and Felix Wichmann. 2020. Shortcut learning in deep neural networks. *Nature Machine Intelligence*, 2(11):665–673.

Mor Geva, Yoav Goldberg, and Jonathan Berant. 2019. Are we modeling the task or the annotator? an investigation of annotator bias in natural language understanding datasets. In *Proceedings of the 2019 Conference on Empirical Methods in Natural Language Processing and the 9th International Joint Conference on Natural Language Processing (EMNLP-IJCNLP)*, pages 1161–1166, Hong Kong, China. Association for Computational Linguistics.

Michael Gofman and Zhao Jin. 2024. Artificial intelligence, education, and entrepreneurship. *The Journal of Finance*, 79(1):631–667.

David Rodriguez Goyes and May-Len Skilbrei. 2023. Rich scholar, poor scholar: Inequalities in research capacity, "knowledge" abysses, and the value of unconventional approaches to research. *Crime, Law and Social Change*, pages 1–20.

Sireesh Gururaja, Amanda Bertsch, Clara Na, David Widder, and Emma Strubell. 2023. To build our future, we must know our past: Contextualizing paradigm shifts in natural language processing. In *Proceedings of the 2023 Conference on Empirical Methods in Natural Language Processing*, pages 13310–13325, Singapore. Association for Computational Linguistics.

Thilo Hagendorff. 2020. The ethics of AI ethics: An evaluation of guidelines. *Minds and machines*, 30(1):99–120.

David Harmon. 2001. On the meaning and moral imperative of diversity. In Luisa Maffi, editor, *On Biocultural Diversity: Linking Language, Knowledge, and the Environment*, pages 53–70. Smithsonian Institution Press.

Jan-Christoph Heilinger, Hendrik Kempt, and Saskia Nagel. 2024. Beware of sustainable AI! Uses and abuses of a worthy goal. *AI and Ethics*, 4(2):201–212.

Daniel Hershcovich, Stella Frank, Heather Lent, Miryam de Lhoneux, Mostafa Abdou, Stephanie Brandl, Emanuele Bugliarello, Laura Cabello Piqueras, Ilias Chalkidis, Ruixiang Cui, et al. 2022. Challenges and strategies in cross-cultural NLP. In *Proceedings of the 60th Annual Meeting of the Association for Computational Linguistics (Volume 1: Long Papers)*, pages 6997–7013.

Johannes Himmelreich. 2023. Against "democratizing AI". *AI & SOCIETY*, 38(4):1333–1346.

Albert Jiang, Alexandre Sablayrolles, Arthur Mensch, Chris Bamford, Devendra Singh Chaplot, Diego de las Casas, Florian Bressand, Gianna Lengyel, Guillaume Lample, Lucile Saulnier, et al. 2023. Mistral 7b. *arXiv preprint arXiv:2310.06825*.

Pratik Joshi, Sebastin Santy, Amar Budhiraja, Kalika Bali, and Monojit Choudhury. 2020. The state and fate of linguistic diversity and inclusion in the NLP world. In *Proceedings of the 58th Annual Meeting of the Association for Computational Linguistics*, pages 6282–6293.

Roman Jurowetzki, Daniel Hain, Juan Mateos-Garcia, and Konstantinos Stathoulopoulos. 2021. The privatization of AI research(-ers): Causes and potential consequences. *arXiv preprint arXiv:2102.01648*.

Joel Klinger, Juan Mateos-Garcia, and Konstantinos Stathoulopoulos. 2020. A narrowing of AI research? *arXiv preprint arXiv:2009.10385*.

Mario Krenn, Robert Pollice, Si Yue Guo, Matteo Aldeghi, Alba Cervera-Lierta, Pascal Friederich, Gabriel dos Passos Gomes, Florian Häse, Adrian Jinich, AkshatKumar Nigam, et al. 2022. On scientific understanding with artificial intelligence. *Nature Reviews Physics*, 4(12):761–769.

Pengfei Li, Jianyi Yang, Mohammad A Islam, and Shaolei Ren. 2023. Making AI less" thirsty": Uncovering and addressing the secret water footprint of AI models. *arXiv preprint arXiv:2304.03271*.

Thomas Liao, Rohan Taori, Inioluwa Deborah Raji, and Ludwig Schmidt. 2021. Are we learning yet? A meta review of evaluation failures across machine learning. In *Thirty-fifth Conference on Neural Information Processing Systems Datasets and Benchmarks Track (Round 2)*.

Zachary Lipton and Jacob Steinhardt. 2019. Troubling trends in machine learning scholarship: Some ML papers suffer from flaws that could mislead the public and stymie future research. *Queue*, 17(1):45–77.

Dieuwertje Luitse and Wiebke Denkena. 2021. The great transformer: Examining the role of large language models in the political economy of AI. *Big Data & Society*, 8(2):20539517211047734.

Christopher Manning. 2015. Computational linguistics and deep learning. *Computational Linguistics*, 41(4):701–707.

Tom McCoy, Ellie Pavlick, and Tal Linzen. 2019. Right for the wrong reasons: Diagnosing syntactic heuristics in natural language inference. In *Proceedings of the 57th Annual Meeting of the Association for Computational Linguistics*. Association for Computational Linguistics.

Lisa Messeri and M.J. Crockett. 2024. Artificial intelligence and illusions of understanding in scientific research. *Nature*, 627(8002):49–58.

Julian Michael, Ari Holtzman, Alicia Parrish, Aaron Mueller, Alex Wang, Angelica Chen, Divyam Madaan, Nikita Nangia, Richard Yuanzhe Pang, Jason Phang, et al. 2023. What do NLP researchers believe? Results of the NLP community metasurvey. In *Proceedings of the 61st Annual Meeting of the Association for Computational Linguistics (Volume 1: Long Papers)*, pages 16334–16368.

Kelly Moore, Daniel Lee Kleinman, David Hess, and Scott Frickel. 2011. Science and neoliberal globalization: A political sociological approach. *Theory and Society*, 40:505–532.

Richard Münch. 2014. *Academic capitalism: Universities in the global struggle for excellence*. Routledge.

David Noble. 1979. *America by design: Science, technology, and the rise of corporate capitalism*. 588. Oxford University Press, USA.

Rodrigo Ochigame. 2019. The invention of 'ethical AI': How big tech manipulates academia to avoid regulation. *Economies of virtue*, 49.

Michael O'Sullivan. 2016. *Academic barbarism, universities, and inequality*. Springer.

Ray Perrault and Jack Clark. 2024. Artificial intelligence index report 2024. *Human-Centered Artificial Intelligence*.

Thao Phan, Jake Goldenfein, Monique Mann, and Declan Kuch. 2022. Economies of virtue: The circulation of 'ethics' in big tech. *Science as culture*, 31(1):121–135.

Steven Piantadosi. 2023. Modern language models refute Chomsky's approach to language. *Lingbuzz Preprint, lingbuzz*, 7180.

Barbara Plank. 2022. The "problem" of human label variation: On ground truth in data, modeling and evaluation. In *Proceedings of the 2022 Conference on Empirical Methods in Natural Language Processing*, pages 10671–10682.

Inioluwa Deborah Raji, Emily Denton, Emily M Bender, Alex Hanna, and Amandalynne Paullada. 2021. AI and the everything in the whole wide world benchmark. In *Thirty-fifth Conference on Neural Information Processing Systems Datasets and Benchmarks Track (Round 2)*.

Benjamin Recht, Rebecca Roelofs, Ludwig Schmidt, and Vaishaal Shankar. 2019. Do imagenet classifiers generalize to imagenet? In *International conference on machine learning*, pages 5389–5400. PMLR.

Daniel Rigney. 2010. *The Matthew effect: How advantage begets further advantage*. Columbia University Press.

Cecilia Rikap and Bengt-Åke Lundvall. 2022. Big tech, knowledge predation and the implications for development. *Innovation and Development*, 12(3):389–416.

Anna Rogers. 2020. Peer review in NLP: reject-if-not-SOTA.

Anna Rogers and Isabelle Augenstein. 2020. What can we do to improve peer review in NLP? In *Findings of the Association for Computational Linguistics: EMNLP 2020*, pages 1256–1262.

Sebastian Ruder. 2022. The State of Multilingual AI. `http://ruder.io/state-of-multilingual-ai/`.

Mukund Rungta, Janvijay Singh, Saif M. Mohammad, and Diyi Yang. 2022. Geographic citation gaps in NLP research. In *Proceedings of the 2022 Conference on Empirical Methods in Natural Language Processing*, pages 1371–1383, Abu Dhabi, United Arab Emirates. Association for Computational Linguistics.

David Schlangen. 2021. Targeting the benchmark: On methodology in current natural language processing research. In *Proceedings of the 59th Annual Meeting of the Association for Computational Linguistics and the 11th International Joint Conference on Natural Language Processing (Volume 2: Short Papers)*, pages 670–674, Online. Association for Computational Linguistics.

Roy Schwartz, Jesse Dodge, Noah Smith, and Oren Etzioni. 2020. Green AI. *Communications of the ACM*, 63(12):54–63.

Peter Seele and Mario Schultz. 2022. From greenwashing to machinewashing: A model and future directions derived from reasoning by analogy. *Journal of Business Ethics*, 178(4):1063–1089.

Rebecca Shamash. 2018. (Re)production of the contemporary elite through higher education: A review of critical scholarship. *Berkeley Review of Education*, 8(1).

Or Sharir, Barak Peleg, and Yoav Shoham. 2020. The cost of training NLP models: A concise overview. *arXiv preprint arXiv:2004.08900*.

Janvijay Singh, Mukund Rungta, Diyi Yang, and Saif Mohammad. 2023. Forgotten knowledge: Examining the citational amnesia in NLP. In *Proceedings of the 61st Annual Meeting of the Association for Computational Linguistics (Volume 1: Long Papers)*, pages 6192–6208, Toronto, Canada. Association for Computational Linguistics.

Tom Slee. 2020. The incompatible incentives of private-sector AI. *The Oxford Handbook of Ethics of AI*, pages 106–123.

Paul Smaldino and Richard McElreath. 2016. The natural selection of bad science. *Royal Society open science*, 3(9):160384.

Sharon Stein. 2017. Internationalization for an uncertain future: Tensions, paradoxes, and possibilities. *The Review of Higher Education*, 41(1):3–32.

Emma Strubell, Ananya Ganesh, and Andrew Mccallum. 2019. Energy and policy considerations for deep learning in NLP. In *Proceedings of the 57th Annual Meeting of the Association for Computational Linguistics*, pages 3645–3650.

Richard Sutton. 2019. The bitter lesson. *Incomplete Ideas (blog)*, 13(1):38.

Zeerak Talat, Aurélie Névéol, Stella Biderman, Miruna Clinciu, Manan Dey, Shayne Longpre, Sasha Luccioni, Maraim Masoud, Margaret Mitchell, Dragomir Radev, Shanya Sharma, Arjun Subramonian, Jaesung Tae, Samson Tan, Deepak Tunuguntla, and Oskar Van Der Wal. 2022. You reap what you sow: On the challenges of bias evaluation under multilingual settings. In *Proceedings of BigScience Episode #5 – Workshop on Challenges & Perspectives in Creating Large Language Models*, pages 26–41, virtual+Dublin. Association for Computational Linguistics.

Marijk van der Wende. 2015. International academic mobility: Towards a concentration of the minds in Europe. *European review*, 23(S1):S70–S88.

Roberto Verdecchia, June Sallou, and Luís Cruz. 2023. A systematic review of green AI. *Wiley Interdisciplinary Reviews: Data Mining and Knowledge Discovery*, 13(4):e1507.

Meredith Whittaker. 2021. The steep cost of capture. *Interactions*, 28(6):50–55.

Sally Wyatt. 2008. Technological determinism is dead; long live technological determinism. *The handbook of science and technology studies*, 3:165–180.

Author Index